Jojo Pedro

It's another quality book from CGP...

Grade 9-1 GCSE Religious Studies is no picnic, but help is at hand —
this fantastic CGP book has everything you need for success in the exams!

It's packed with crystal-clear study notes covering Christianity, Catholic Christianity, Islam
and Judaism, plus plenty of exam-style questions to make sure you're ready for the real thing.

How to access your free Online Edition

This book includes a free Online Edition to read on your PC, Mac or tablet.
To access it, just go to **cgpbooks.co.uk/extras** and enter this code...

2487 1226 0948 5528

By the way, this code only works for one person. If somebody else has used
this book before you, they might have already claimed the Online Edition.

CGP — still the best! ☺

Our sole aim here at CGP is to produce the highest quality books —
carefully written, immaculately presented and dangerously close to being funny.

Then we work our socks off to get them out to you
— at the cheapest possible prices.

Contents

For some topics, your course might require you to learn about the views of different religions, or about a single religion.

The green religion tags on the pages of each section tell you whether the page covers:

| Christianity | ...information about a specific religion... | All religions | ...information about all religions... | General | ...or general information. |

Sometimes more than one religion is covered on a page — if so, the yellow section headings will tell you which bits of the page are relevant to each religion. If a heading doesn't mention a religion, that section is relevant for all religions.

Some pages have exam-style questions at the bottom — if you're studying that topic from the point of view of only one religion, answer the question in the context of that religion. If not, you should include views from different religions.

Published by CGP

Editors: Chloe Anderson, Cathy Lear, Ruth Wilbourne

Contributors: Jill Hudson, Duncan Raynor, Paul Smith, Philip West

Proofreading: Stephen Darlington, Glenn Rogers

ISBN: 978 1 78294 644 1

With thanks to Ana Pungartnik for the copyright research.

Sacred Text References

References from the Bible always go in the order: Book Chapter:Verse(s). So whenever you
see something like: Genesis 1:14, it means it's from the book of Genesis, Chapter 1, verse 14.

Similarly, references from the Qur'an are shown with the Surah (Chapter) followed by the Ayah (Verse).

For all collections of hadith, we've used the English referencing system.
This gives the book number followed by the hadith number, e.g. Sahih al-Bukhari 1:3.

Some exam-style questions are based on the style of Edexcel.

Some exam-style questions are based on the style of OCR from the GCSE Religious Studies - J625 2016 sample assessment materials

Scripture quotations [marked NIV] taken from the Holy Bible,
New International Version Anglicised
Copyright © 1979, 1984, 2011 Biblica, Used by permission of Hodder & Stoughton Ltd, an Hachette UK company
All rights reserved
'NIV' is a registered trademark of Biblica
UK trademark number 1448790.

Holy Qur'an quotations taken from the Holy Qur'an, Sahih International Version. https://quran.com/

Quotations from the Catechism of the Catholic Church © Libreria Editrice Vaticana
Quotations from Lumen gentium on page 10, Gaudium et spes on page 13, Evangelii Gaudium on pages 13 and 14,
Humanae Vitae on pages 38 and 51, Familiaris Consortio on pages 42, 43 and 45, and a speech by Pope Francis on page 47
© Libreria Editrice Vaticana

Quotes on pages 2, 4, 6, 9, 39, 47 and 81 from The Church of England, https://www.churchofengland.org.
© The Archbishops' Council.

Image on page 24 © REUTERS / Alamy Stock Photo

Quotes on pages 26 and 70 from Chabad.org

Image on page 51 © Isabelle Plasschaert / Alamy Stock Photo

Sahih Muslim 16:4152 quote on page 62 from https://muflihun.com

Image on page 71 © iStock.com / sadikgulec

Source of statistic on belief in evolution on page 73: Theos

Quote on page 74 from The Guide of the Perplexed, Volume 1 by Moses Maimonides, translated by Shlomo Pines.
Published by The University of Chicago Press, 1963.

Quote on page 83 from Islam and the West: A Rational Perspective by Mohammed Jabar,
published by Mereo Books, an imprint of Memoirs Publishing, 2014.

Quotation on page 84 © www.cbcew.org.uk

Data about wealth inequality on page 87 contains public sector information licensed under the Open Government Licence v3.0.
http://www.nationalarchives.gov.uk/doc/open-government-licence/version/3/

Every effort has been made to locate copyright holders and obtain permission to reproduce sources. For those sources where it has
been difficult to trace the originator of the work, we would be grateful for information. If any copyright holder would like us to
make an amendment to the acknowledgements, please notify us and we will gladly update the book at the next reprint. Thank you.

Printed by Elanders Ltd, Newcastle upon Tyne
Clipart from Corel®

Based on the classic CGP style created by Richard Parsons.

Introduction to Christianity

Christianity is based on the belief in <u>Jesus Christ</u> being the <u>Son of God</u>. It is the <u>main</u> religion in Britain.

The Bible is the Christian Sacred Text

The Bible is divided into two main parts — the <u>Old</u> and <u>New Testaments</u>:

1) Depending on the version, the <u>Old Testament</u> has at least 39 books, which include the <u>Creation</u> story (see p.3) and the <u>Ten Commandments</u>. These 39 books are the <u>Jewish scriptures</u> — they are also considered <u>sacred</u> by Jews.

2) The <u>New Testament</u> is the <u>specifically Christian</u> part of the Bible. Its 27 books include the <u>4 Gospels</u> (Matthew, Mark, Luke and John), which are accounts of <u>Jesus's life</u>. The <u>Acts of the Apostles</u> and the <u>letters of St Paul</u> describe the <u>early years</u> of Christianity.

Christianity is Divided into Different Traditions

The different branches of Christianity are called <u>denominations</u>. They share key beliefs, but interpret some points of the faith differently and worship in different ways (see p.8).

1) <u>Roman Catholics</u> respect the authority of the <u>Bible</u> and <u>Church tradition</u>, plus the authority of the <u>Pope</u> and his teachings. The <u>seven sacraments</u> (which include the Eucharist — see p.10) are an important part of their faith.

2) <u>Protestants</u> base their beliefs and practices on the <u>Bible</u>, rather than Church tradition or the teachings of the Pope. In England and Wales, Protestant denominations that are not part of the 'Anglican Communion' are often called '<u>Nonconformists</u>'. These include Methodists, Baptists, Pentecostals, The Society of Friends (Quakers) and the Salvation Army.

> The <u>Church of England</u> has both Roman Catholic and Protestant features. Its beliefs are set out in the <u>39 Articles</u>. <u>Anglicanism</u> is the worldwide 'communion' of Churches in fellowship with the parent Church of England.

3) <u>Orthodox Christians</u> are found mainly in Eastern Europe, Russia and Greece. They also have <u>7 sacraments</u>, and honour (but don't worship) <u>icons</u> — pictures of Saints.

There are Many Beliefs About the Nature of God

Christianity is a <u>monotheistic</u> (one god) religion. The Ten Commandments say "you shall have no other gods" (Exodus 20:3 NIV). Christians believe God has the following <u>characteristics</u>, though they <u>differ</u> in the <u>emphasis</u> placed on each, e.g. some focus more on God's loving nature than his role as judge.

1) **OMNIPOTENT** — God is <u>all-powerful</u>, although he still allows each person <u>free will</u>.

2) **BENEVOLENT** — God is <u>loving</u> and <u>caring</u>: "For God so loved the world that he gave his one and only Son" (John 3:16 NIV). Christians try to <u>follow</u> his example in their actions.

3) **JUST JUDGE** — God <u>judges</u> people's actions fairly. Those who reject him and live sinful lives will be <u>punished</u>, as shown in the story of the sheep and goats in Matthew 25:31-46 (see p.14). But God <u>forgives</u> people who are sorry for what they've done and become faithful to him — the story of the <u>prodigal son</u> (Luke 15:11-32) shows God will forgive anyone who returns to his ways.

4) **OMNISCIENT** — God <u>knows</u> everything — in the past, present and future.

5) **ETERNAL** — God has always existed, and he will continue to exist forever.

6) **TRANSCENDENT** — God is <u>beyond</u> this world — he doesn't depend on it to exist.

7) **IMMANENT** — But God is <u>present</u> in the human world, and takes an <u>active role</u> in humanity.

8) **PERSONAL** — God is a '<u>person</u>', albeit an almighty and <u>divine person</u>. If God is personal, then a relationship is possible through <u>prayer</u> — which can be a '<u>conversation</u>' with God.

Omnipotent or omniscient? Get them the right way round...

Cover this page and see how many characteristics of God you can write down. No peeking now...

Christianity & Catholic Christianity	# The Trinity

Although Christians believe in one God, they also believe that God has three parts.

Christians Believe in God as the Trinity

The Trinity is the idea that God exists in three 'persons' — the Father, the Son (Jesus) and the Holy Spirit. The importance of all three is shown in the Bible:

> Matthew 3:16-17 describes how at Jesus's baptism, Jesus "...saw the Spirit of God descending like a dove and alighting on him. And a voice from heaven said, 'This is my Son, whom I love; with him I am well pleased.' " (NIV)

> In Philippians 2:6, St Paul described Jesus as having "equality with God" (NIV).

The Trinity is Explained in the Nicene Creed

1) In 325 AD, Church leaders from around the world gathered at the Council of Nicaea. They produced a creed — a statement of beliefs. This was further developed at the Council of Constantinople in 381 AD, and is known as the Nicene Creed. It describes how Christians see God:

> "We believe in one God, the Father, the Almighty, maker of heaven and earth... We believe in one Lord, Jesus Christ, the only Son of God... of one Being with the Father... was made man... he suffered death and... he rose again... We believe in the Holy Spirit... the giver of life, who proceeds from the Father and the Son... who has spoken through the prophets."

2) Before this, not everyone had agreed that the Son of God (Jesus) was one with God, rather than having been made by God. Now they agreed that he was equally important.

3) The importance the early Church placed on the Trinity in the Nicene Creed means it is a key belief for most Christians — it is usually recited during the Eucharist service (see p.8). But some groups, such as Christadelphians, don't believe in the Trinity.

4) Christians see the three parts of the Trinity as having different characteristics and roles:

The Father

- For many Christians, God the Father is the God of the Old Testament. He created Heaven and Earth and sustains them. God the Father might be described as the transcendent part of God.
- The title 'Father' is a mark of respect for God, e.g. the Lord's Prayer starts with 'Our Father' (see p.11).

The Son

- Christians believe Jesus (see p.4-5) is the incarnation of God in human form. He is seen as both divine and human — the immanent and personal part of God, who understands human suffering.
- Christians believe that Jesus provides a model for Christian behaviour in obedience to God the Father. The Gospels contain a record of his life and teachings, and are an important source of guidance for Christians on how they should live their lives.

The Holy Spirit

- Christians believe that the Holy Spirit is the presence of God in the world. Before his death, Jesus promised his disciples: "I will ask the Father, and he will give you another advocate to help you and be with you for ever — the Spirit of truth" (John 14:16-17 NIV).
- The Holy Spirit is seen as the immanent yet impersonal part of God — it continues to guide the Church.
- Some Christians feel that the Holy Spirit also guides them personally in being good Christians. The Catechism of the Catholic Church 736 says "By this power of the Spirit, God's children can bear much fruit."

Three into one doesn't go in maths — but this is RS...

For some exam questions you'll have to refer to sacred texts or religious teachings to get full marks. You can write quotes or describe what is said — you'll need to say where the information comes from.

Creation

The story of creation can be understood in different ways. Some take it <u>literally</u>, for others it's a <u>metaphor</u>.

The Bible Describes how God Created the Universe

1) <u>Genesis</u> chapter 1 says that <u>God</u> created everything. The process took <u>six days</u>, and on the seventh day God <u>rested</u>.

2) On day one, <u>light</u> and <u>darkness</u> were made, and on day two the <u>sky</u>. On the third day <u>oceans</u>, <u>land</u> and <u>plants</u> on the land were created, and on the fourth day the <u>sun</u>, <u>moon</u> and <u>stars</u>. On the fifth day it was the creatures of the water and sky (e.g. <u>fish</u> and <u>birds</u>) and on the sixth day, <u>land animals</u> and <u>people</u>.

3) Christians see God the Father as the <u>creator</u>, but the Bible also describes how the other <u>beings</u> of the Trinity were involved. God created the world by acting <u>through</u> the Holy Spirit.

> "...the Spirit of God was hovering over the waters. And God said, 'Let there be light,' and there was light." Genesis 1:2-3 NIV

4) The role of the <u>Son of God</u> is described in the Gospel of John. He uses the phrase '<u>the Word</u>', but it is clear he is referring to <u>Jesus</u> as he later says "The Word became flesh and made his dwelling among us" (John 1:14 NIV). John makes it clear that Jesus was <u>vital for creation</u>.

> "In the beginning was the Word, and the Word was with God, and the Word was God. He was with God in the beginning. Through him all things were made; without him nothing was made that has been made." John 1:1-3 NIV

It Explains how Human Beings were Created

1) The creation of human beings is described in <u>Genesis</u> chapters <u>1</u> and <u>2</u>. The first two humans were <u>Adam and Eve</u>, and they lived in the <u>Garden of Eden</u>.

2) <u>Genesis</u> chapter 1 says "So God created mankind in his own image, in the image of God he created them; male and female he created them" (Genesis 1:27 NIV).

3) Genesis chapter 2 says "the Lord God formed a man from the dust of the ground" (Genesis 2:7 NIV) and "made a woman from the rib he had taken out of the man" (Genesis 2:22 NIV).

4) The fact that God created humans in <u>his image</u> is important. Because of this, Christians believe that humans are <u>special</u>. They think humans should <u>behave</u> like God by being <u>loving</u> and <u>fair</u> (see p.1). It also shows that humans are <u>important to God</u>, and so <u>everyone</u> should be treated with <u>respect</u>.

5) In Genesis 1:28, God told Adam and Eve to "Rule over the fish in the sea and the birds in the sky and over every living creature that moves on the ground" (NIV). Some Christians believe God gave humans '<u>dominion</u>' (power) over his creation and they can <u>use</u> it as they like. However, Genesis 2:15 says "The Lord God took the man and put him in the Garden of Eden to work it and take care of it" (NIV). Many Christians interpret this as humans having '<u>stewardship</u>' of the Earth — God expects them to <u>care</u> for it.

There are Different Ways to Interpret the Creation Story

1) Some Christians take the creation story <u>literally</u> — they are known as <u>creationists</u>. They believe that the process took six days, and humans are descended from Adam and Eve.

2) Other Christians are more <u>liberal</u> in their understanding of the Bible's events. They view Genesis as more of a <u>parable</u>, or a <u>symbolic</u> description — they acknowledge God as the creator, but are open to <u>other theories</u>, such as the <u>Big Bang theory</u> and <u>evolution</u>. These theories can offer more <u>information</u> to Christians about how <u>God</u> made the universe. The Roman Catholic Church has <u>accepted</u> both theories.

3) The creation story can help Christians further understand <u>God's nature</u>. God is <u>eternal</u> as he made time, and was present 'prior' to it. He is <u>omnipotent</u> as he created the universe through words. God's <u>benevolence</u> can be seen through creation too as he brought humankind to life and gave them the world.

And you thought revision was tiring...

Grab a pen and paper and see if you can quickly summarise what Genesis chapters 1 and 2 say about the story of creation. Once you've done that, try jotting down some different interpretations of creation.

Jesus Christ and Salvation

Christians believe that Jesus Christ, the second Person of the Trinity, is the <u>Son of God</u>.

God Became Human at the Incarnation

1) The <u>incarnation</u> was the act by which <u>God</u> became a <u>human being</u> as Jesus Christ. John's Gospel describes Jesus as the <u>Word of God</u>, made human.

2) An <u>angel</u> told a woman called <u>Mary</u> in Nazareth that she would have a <u>son</u> — and that "the holy one to be born will be called the Son of God" (Luke 1:35 NIV).

3) This belief is stated in the <u>Nicene Creed</u>: "he... was incarnate from the Holy Spirit and the Virgin Mary and was made man".

4) Christians don't believe that Jesus was 'half God and half man' — he was <u>fully both</u>. The Bible describes how God "appeared in the flesh" (1 Timothy 3:16 NIV).

5) Jesus is referred to as '<u>Christ</u>' or '<u>Messiah</u>' — the '<u>Anointed One of God</u>'.

6) Christians see Jesus's time on Earth as God's way of showing how much he <u>loves</u> the world. They study the <u>Gospels</u> to find out about <u>Jesus's life</u>, and to see how they should live their own.

> "The Word became flesh and made his dwelling among us. We have seen his glory, the glory of the one and only Son, who came from the Father, full of grace and truth." John 1:14 NIV

> After being baptised by John the Baptist, Jesus began <u>teaching</u>. He had many followers, including <u>12 chosen disciples</u>. Some of his key teachings are in the <u>Sermon on the Mount</u> (Matthew 5-7) — he taught how the poor and meek are <u>highly valued</u> by God, and how <u>peacemakers</u> are blessed. He also taught the importance of <u>kindness</u>, such as in the story of the <u>Good Samaritan</u> (Luke 10:30-37). He performed miracles such as <u>healing</u> the sick, showing that he was the <u>Son of God</u> and demonstrating God's <u>love</u>.

Jesus was Crucified and Resurrected

The Last Supper, Jesus's Arrest and Trial

1) Shortly before his death, Jesus and his disciples ate their <u>Passover</u> meal in Jerusalem. It was their <u>final meal</u> together and became known as the <u>Last Supper</u>.

2) At the meal, Jesus gave the disciples <u>bread</u> saying "this is my body" and <u>wine</u> saying "this is my blood" (Mark 14:22-24 NIV). Luke's Gospel tells us he said "do this in remembrance of me" (Luke 22:19 NIV). These words are important to many Christians today who remember Jesus with bread and wine through the <u>Eucharist</u> (see p.9).

3) At the Last Supper, Jesus also <u>washed</u> his disciples' <u>feet</u>, which teaches Christians about how important it is to <u>serve</u> others.

4) Next, Jesus went to pray in the <u>Garden of Gethsemane</u>, where he was <u>arrested</u> after Judas <u>betrayed</u> him. The authorities felt <u>threatened</u> by Jesus — earlier that week, crowds had called him the '<u>King of Israel</u>'.

5) He was put on <u>trial</u> before the Jewish <u>high priest</u> and found guilty of <u>blasphemy</u>. Then Jesus was tried before the Roman governor, <u>Pilate</u> — he offered to release Jesus, but the crowd said "<u>Crucify him!</u>" (Mark 15:13 NIV). He was <u>flogged</u>, before being sent to die.

Crucifixion

1) Jesus was <u>crucified</u> at a place called <u>Golgotha</u>, next to two robbers. A sign was fixed to Jesus's cross that read 'The King of the Jews', to record the <u>charge</u> against him. Passers-by threw <u>insults</u> at Jesus, saying that he could <u>save others</u>, but couldn't <u>save himself</u>.

2) In his suffering, Jesus cried out, "My God, my God, why have you forsaken me?" (Mark 15:34 NIV). This shows that Jesus understands how people can feel abandoned in their <u>suffering</u>.

3) Christians also believe the crucifixion helped to <u>repair</u> the <u>relationship</u> between God and mankind — the <u>atonement</u> (see next page).

Resurrection

1) After the crucifixion, Jesus's body was put in a tomb. But he was <u>resurrected</u> (brought back to life), and his tomb was found <u>empty</u>.

2) Jesus talked to two women and told them "Go and tell my brothers to go to Galilee; there they will see me" (Matthew 28:10 NIV).

3) The resurrection is important to Christians as it shows them that there is <u>life after death</u> — <u>death</u> becomes <u>less frightening</u>.

4) It shows them just how <u>powerful</u> God is. This power that raised Jesus from the dead gives people the <u>strength</u> to live Christian lives.

5) Christians also see the resurrection as further <u>proof</u> that Jesus is the <u>Son of God</u> as he was "...appointed the Son of God in power by his resurrection from the dead..." (Romans 1:4 NIV). This strengthens people's <u>faith</u>.

> "...Why do you look for the living among the dead? He is not here; he has risen!" Luke 24:5-6 NIV

> Roman Catholics refer to the crucifixion, resurrection and ascension of Jesus as 'The Paschal Mystery'.

Jesus Christ and Salvation

<u>Salvation</u> is needed before Christians can go to Heaven, and <u>Jesus's actions</u> made it possible.

Jesus Going to Heaven is Called the Ascension

1) Over the <u>40 days</u> after the resurrection, many of Jesus's disciples said they had met him <u>alive</u> in various places around <u>Jerusalem</u>.

2) Then, Jesus '<u>ascended into Heaven</u>' to be with God the Father once again. He had <u>done</u> what he was sent to <u>Earth</u> to do, and it was time for him to <u>go back</u> to God.

"While he was blessing them, he left them and was taken up into heaven." Luke 24:51 NIV

3) In John 14:2, Jesus tells his disciples he will "prepare a place" (NIV) for them in heaven. 1 John 2:1 says that, in Jesus, Christians have an 'advocate' with God (someone who will look out for them).

4) <u>Pope Benedict XVI</u> said that since <u>Jesus</u> was <u>human</u> and went to be with God, the <u>ascension</u> shows there's a <u>place</u> for all human beings <u>with God</u>.

5) The ascension shows <u>Jesus's power</u> — he is now "at the right hand of the mighty God" (Luke 22:69 NIV).

Jesus Died to Save Humanity

1) '<u>Original sin</u>' (see p.7) means that <u>everyone</u> is born capable of sin. Many Christians believe that Jesus's <u>suffering</u> and <u>death</u> won <u>forgiveness</u> for everyone and ensured their <u>redemption</u> (freeing them from sin).

2) They believe that Jesus was <u>perfect</u> (without sin), but God placed <u>all the sins of the world</u> on him at his crucifixion. Romans 3:21-26 teaches that his sacrifice <u>paid</u> for their sins, so long as they have <u>faith</u> in him.

3) Jesus's actions brought about the <u>reconciliation</u> between God and humanity — known as the <u>atonement</u>.

"For God so loved the world that he gave his one and only Son, that whoever believes in him shall not perish but have eternal life. For God did not send his Son into the world to condemn the world, but to save the world through him." John 3:16-17 NIV

4) His power and goodness were so <u>great</u> that after he was crucified, death couldn't keep hold of him.

5) However, <u>not</u> all Christians believe that Jesus <u>had to die</u> to pay for people's sins:

- 1 Corinthians 13:5 says that love "keeps no record of wrongs" (NIV). Many Christians think that Jesus's death <u>wasn't required</u> for a loving and merciful God to be able to <u>forgive</u> people's sins.
- Some people argue that it was Jesus's <u>ministry</u> that showed people how to be free from sin — he showed them how to live their lives in a <u>Godly</u> way.
- Some say Jesus's death shows <u>God's love</u> for humankind through his <u>willingness</u> to <u>suffer</u> and die as humans do. His resurrection showed how God could <u>triumph</u> over <u>sin</u> and <u>death</u>, so people don't have to fear <u>evil</u>.

Christians Must Seek Salvation to Get to Heaven

1) Salvation means the <u>soul</u> being <u>saved</u> from <u>death</u> and <u>sin</u>, allowing it to reach <u>heaven</u>. For this to happen, Christians believe they must have faith in Jesus: "Salvation is found in no one else..." (Acts 4:12 NIV).

2) Salvation is only possible through <u>God's grace</u> — God showing <u>favour</u> to those who <u>haven't</u> earned it: "For it is by grace you have been saved, through faith... it is the gift of God" (Ephesians 2:8 NIV).

3) But people can't just <u>say</u> they believe — if they're a true believer they'll try to <u>live</u> a Christian life. The Bible contains many <u>laws</u>, such as the <u>Ten Commandments</u> (see p.28), which provide Christians with <u>guidance</u> on how they should behave. Everyone will <u>sin</u>, but the laws mean they'll "become conscious of ... sin" (Romans 3:20 NIV) and "turn to God in repentance" (Acts 20:21 NIV).

4) The <u>Holy Spirit</u> helps Christians to <u>follow</u> the teachings of God and his laws and keep their <u>faith</u>, helping them to find salvation.

Revision can save you from exam failure...

Explain two Christian teachings about salvation.
Your answer should include an example from a sacred text.   [5]

Christianity & Catholic Christianity	# The Afterlife

What people believe will happen to them after <u>death</u> can influence the way they <u>live</u> their lives.

Christians Believe in Heaven and Hell

1) <u>Life after death</u> is the idea that, although your <u>body</u> may die and decay, your <u>soul</u> can live on.

2) Christianity teaches that the <u>soul</u> lives on after death (<u>immortality</u> of the soul), and that the body will be <u>resurrected</u> (brought back to life) for Judgement Day, just as Jesus was resurrected after his crucifixion.

3) Christians believe that God will judge you, and you'll go to either <u>heaven</u> or <u>hell</u>:

> Heaven is often portrayed as a place of great beauty and serenity, a <u>paradise</u> where you'll spend eternity with God — as long as you believe in <u>Jesus</u> and have followed his <u>teachings</u>, you can be saved by <u>God's grace</u> (see p.5). The <u>soul</u> can go to heaven even though the body ('earthly tent') is gone.

> "I am the resurrection and the life. The one who believes in me will live, even though they die..." John 11:25 NIV

> "For we know that if the earthly tent we live in is destroyed, we have a building from God, an eternal house in heaven, not built by human hands." 2 Corinthians 5:1 NIV

Freshly-washed bedding was Arnie's idea of heaven.

> Hell, on the other hand, is often portrayed as a place of <u>torment</u> and <u>pain</u> — the final destination of <u>nonbelievers</u> and those who have led <u>bad</u> lives.

> "Then they will go away to eternal punishment, but the righteous to eternal life." Matthew 25:46 NIV

4) However, not all Christians believe that heaven and hell are <u>real</u> places — many Christians see heaven and hell as <u>states of mind</u>. In heaven you'll be <u>happy</u>, and know God — in hell you'll be <u>unable</u> to know God's love. Pope John Paul II said that hell was a <u>metaphor</u> for how people who've <u>rejected</u> God will <u>feel</u>.

5) Some Christians, for example Roman Catholics, believe that going to hell means that any <u>connection</u> they have to God will be <u>severed</u> forever: "This state of definitive self-exclusion from communion with God... is called 'hell' " (Catechism of the Catholic Church 1033).

6) Some believe God <u>wouldn't</u> punish people for <u>eternity</u>. A few believe that those who God finds <u>unacceptable</u> will be <u>annihilated</u>. In a report called 'The Mystery of Salvation', senior members of the <u>Church of England</u> said that for those people "the only end is <u>total non-being</u>".

Purgatory

Roman Catholics believe in a place, or state of existence, called <u>Purgatory</u>. Here <u>sins</u> are punished and the person must "undergo purification" (Catechism of the Catholic Church, 1030) before the soul can move on to heaven. Protestants believe this isn't in the Bible, so they <u>reject</u> it.

7) Some believe that a loving God <u>wouldn't</u> allow anyone to go to hell.

Christians Believe Resurrection Happens at the Last Judgement

1) Many Christians believe that Jesus will return to Earth in the <u>Second Coming</u> (<u>Parousia</u>), and everyone who has died will be <u>resurrected</u>: "in Christ all will be made alive" (1 Corinthians 15:22 NIV).

> "Christ... ascended into Heaven, and there sitteth, until he return to judge all Men at the last day." 39 Articles IV

2) Some believe that all of humanity will then be judged at the <u>Last Judgement</u>. Those that God finds <u>acceptable</u> will enter <u>heaven</u> — the rest will go to hell, as in the story of the sheep and the goats (Matthew 25:31-46).

> "For we must all appear before the judgment seat of Christ, so that each of us may receive what is due to us for the things done while in the body, whether good or bad." 2 Corinthians 5:10 NIV

3) Some Christians, e.g. <u>Roman Catholics</u>, believe in a <u>personal</u> day of <u>judgement</u> straight after a person <u>dies</u> — their actions will be judged and they'll go to heaven or hell <u>straight away</u>. Some think they'll be <u>judged again</u> at the Last Judgement, and will <u>re-enter</u> heaven or hell in their <u>resurrected forms</u>.

4) Others don't believe in a personal judgement — the soul must <u>wait</u> to be judged at the <u>Last Judgement</u>.

The examiners will be judging your answers...

Outline three Christian beliefs about judgement.   [3]

Evil and Suffering

Evil comes in <u>different forms</u>, and can have an <u>impact</u> on a person's relationship with their faith.

Free Will Led to Evil Entering the World

1) <u>Christianity</u> teaches that evil <u>entered</u> the world as a result of <u>Adam and Eve</u> giving in to <u>temptation</u> in the Garden of Eden — they <u>disobeyed</u> God by eating the <u>fruit</u> of the tree of knowledge. This switch from a perfect world to one containing evil is known as '<u>The Fall</u>'.

2) After the Fall, every human being was born with a <u>flawed</u> nature, capable of causing suffering — this is the idea of <u>original sin</u>.

3) Christians believe God created humans with <u>free will</u> — it's up to them to <u>choose</u> whether they perform evil deeds or not, just as it was up to <u>Adam and Eve</u> whether to give in to temptation or not. <u>Good</u> is the opposite of <u>evil</u>, and since God is good, Christians try to follow his <u>example</u>.

"When the woman saw... the fruit of the tree... she took some and ate it. She also gave some to her husband... and he ate it." Genesis 3:6 NIV

Suffering can be Human-Made or Natural

Suffering can be divided into <u>two types</u>:

Moral (human-made) Suffering	Natural Suffering
1) This is when suffering is brought about by the <u>cruel</u> actions of <u>people</u>. 2) This includes things like murder, war, rape and torture. 3) The person causing the suffering is able to make a <u>choice</u> about what is morally <u>right or wrong</u>.	1) This kind of suffering is <u>caused by the world</u> in which we live, and is <u>no one's 'fault'</u>. 2) This includes things like disease, floods, earthquakes and hurricanes. 3) However, many <u>recent natural disasters</u> may have been caused by <u>human interference</u> in the natural world, raising the question of whether that makes those events human-made.

Evil can Lead People to Question their Faith

1) <u>Evil</u> and <u>suffering</u> may lead some people to <u>question</u> their belief in God — or even to <u>reject</u> their faith.

2) Some might say that since suffering exists, God <u>can't</u> be <u>both</u> benevolent and omnipotent — a loving and all-powerful God wouldn't <u>allow</u> it to happen. They might argue that he <u>doesn't exist</u>, or that he can't have the <u>characteristics</u> that believers say he has.

"the Lord is compassionate and gracious, slow to anger, abounding in love... he does not treat us as our sins deserve..." Psalm 103:8-10 NIV

3) But others would say that although God has these characteristics, he gave people <u>free will</u> and so doesn't <u>interfere</u>. Or some may say that he <u>wants</u> to <u>help</u>, but isn't <u>powerful</u> enough.

4) Christians <u>react</u> to evil and suffering in various ways. <u>Suffering</u> is often seen as a <u>test of faith</u> — <u>God</u> has his <u>reasons</u> (even if we <u>don't know</u> what they are). Many believe that God is <u>with</u> people in their suffering, and that it can bring people <u>closer</u> to him.

"I know, Lord, that your laws are righteous, and that in faithfulness you have afflicted me. May your unfailing love be my comfort..." Psalm 119:75-76 NIV

5) Others say life on Earth <u>isn't</u> meant to be perfect — the focus should be on reaching <u>heaven</u>.

6) Some believe in the '<u>vale of soul-making</u>' — responding to suffering in both themselves and others <u>develops</u> the human <u>soul</u>, improving people's character so they live as God wants them to.

7) The <u>Book of Job</u> tells of the <u>suffering</u> Job endures and how he <u>questions</u> God. He concludes that God is <u>all-powerful</u> and knows what he's doing, and that suffering must be <u>accepted</u> because people can't really <u>understand</u> the world or <u>God's plan</u>: "Though he slay me, yet will I hope in him..." (Job 13:15 NIV).

8) Christians try to <u>help</u> people who are suffering — <u>practically</u> (charity) and by <u>praying</u>. Jesus said: "whatever you did for one of... these brothers and sisters of mine, you did for me" (Matthew 25:40 NIV).

Not the cheeriest of topics...

Christians explain and respond to evil and suffering in a variety of different ways.
Cover this page, see how many you can think of and write them all down.

Christianity &
Catholic Christianity

Different Forms of Worship

Christian Denominations have Different Forms of Worship

For Christians, Sunday is the 'Lord's Day', when they celebrate the Sabbath (the holy day of rest). Most churches have their main service on a Sunday morning. Worship often includes prayers, readings from the Bible, a sermon and the Eucharist (see p.9) — the different denominations place varying amounts of importance on each, creating differences in worship.

Some Worship is Liturgical...

'Liturgical' means that services follow a set pattern written out by the Church.

1) Anglican Sunday morning services usually include the Eucharist, and Catholic Sunday morning services always do (Catholics call the Eucharist 'Mass'). For Catholics, the 'Roman Missal' sets out the contents of the service. Anglican worship is guided by the 'Common Worship' book, based on the Book of Common Prayer from 1662. The main Orthodox Sunday service is the 'Divine Liturgy', which centres on the Eucharist — it's usually based on the liturgy of St John Chrysostom.

> Anglican and Catholic Eucharist services share many similarities:
> * A confession of sin and a request for God's mercy is said by everyone (called the 'penitential rite' by Catholics).
> * There are readings (including one gospel reading) and a sermon — this part is known as the 'liturgy of the Word'. The Nicene or Apostle's Creed is then recited.
> * The priest says prayers over bread and wine — this is called the 'liturgy of the Eucharist'.
> * Then the congregation says the Lord's Prayer (see p.11) and 'shares the peace' by shaking hands. They receive the bread and wine. Catholics call this the 'rite of Communion'.

> * Orthodox services contain similar elements to Anglican and Catholic ones: a sermon, Bible readings, the Nicene Creed and blessing of bread and wine.
> * They include the 'Litany', where the priest says prayers and the congregation responds with 'Lord have mercy'. Worshippers sing or chant for most of the service.
> * Services are often longer than most Anglican and Catholic services, and people stand for the majority of the time.

2) For many, public worship helps them to feel involved in a wider Christian community. It can also help them feel closer to Jesus as they believe he is there in the church with them: "For where two or three gather in my name, there am I with them" (Matthew 18:20 NIV). Following traditions also helps Christians to feel connected to other worshippers throughout history.

...and Other Worship is Non-Liturgical

> The worship of the Society of Friends (Quakers) is non-liturgical, and it is usually unstructured. Worshippers sit together in silence, but they are free to pray or speak out loud.

> Methodist services don't have to follow a set structure, but there is a 'Methodist Worship Book' with suggested liturgy for parts of worship, e.g. the Eucharist. Services feature hymns, readings, a sermon and prayers. The Eucharist also takes place, but not every week.

> Worship in Evangelical Churches (e.g. Pentecostals) is often spontaneous. Worshippers believe they're inspired by the Spirit — this is called 'charismatic worship'. It might inspire them to pray, clap, dance or shout. Sometimes they 'speak in tongues' — praying in an unrecognisable language.

Some Christians prefer the freedom of worshipping God in a less-structured way. Others view non-liturgical worship as unsuitable for the level of respect that religious services require.

Some Christians also Engage in Private Worship

1) Many Christians worship informally at home (not just on Sundays). This can be anything from saying grace before a meal to singing worship songs with family, to reading the Bible or praying (see p.11).

2) Lots of Christians worship both publicly and privately — private worship can help them keep God in mind throughout their everyday lives. Some also find greater freedom in private worship — they decide how they worship God and so feel a better connection with God.

Who's singing out of tune? Hymn...

Make sure you learn the differences between how Christian denominations worship.
Also learn why each type of worship is important, and why Christians might have a preference.

The Sacraments

Sacraments play a key role in worship and belief for many Christians.

Different Denominations Believe in Different Sacraments

1) A sacrament is a ceremony (usually carried out by a minister or priest) through which Christians believe they receive God's grace. It's a sign of God's grace working within them.

2) Roman Catholic and Orthodox Churches believe in seven sacraments (see p.10), but most Protestants accept only baptism and the Eucharist as sacraments — they believe only these two were prescribed by Jesus in the Gospels. Many believe that the sacraments bring people closer to God.

3) Baptists use the word 'ordinance' instead of 'sacrament' — they see them more as symbols. Quakers and the Salvation Army don't have any sacraments — they think they're unnecessary.

Baptism is an Important Sacrament for Many Christians

1) Baptism is seen as a sacrament because Jesus was baptised. After his resurrection, he told his disciples to go out and baptise people: "...go and make disciples of all nations, baptising them in the name of the Father and of the Son and of the Holy Spirit" (Matthew 28:19 NIV).

2) Jesus also said "no one can enter the kingdom of God unless they are born of water and the Spirit" (John 3:5 NIV).

3) Baptism makes someone a member of God's family and welcomes them to the Church. Some Christians believe that baptising cleanses people from the original sin that everyone is born with.

4) Babies are baptised in many denominations, e.g. Anglican, Catholic and Methodist. (They will also baptise adults if they weren't baptised as children and want to join the Church.)

5) A sign of the cross is made on the baby, and in many Churches holy water is poured three times over the forehead (in the name of the Father, Son and Holy Spirit). Orthodox Christians baptise babies by total immersion.

6) Denominations that baptise babies also usually have confirmation — a person 'confirms' their faith when they reach an age that they can declare it themselves.

7) But some denominations — for example Baptists and Pentecostals — believe you shouldn't be baptised until you're old enough to accept Christianity for yourself. They hold believers' baptisms, when adults who wish to join the Church are baptised by total immersion.

There are Many Different Understandings of the Eucharist

The Eucharist is where Christians remember the Last Supper (see p.4) with bread and wine. Many denominations see it as a sacrament, but have different beliefs about the bread and wine:

- Roman Catholics believe in transubstantiation (i.e. the bread and wine used at Mass become the flesh and blood of Christ), and every Mass is a re-enactment of Christ's sacrifice (see p.4). They believe that they receive the saving power of Jesus into themselves through the bread and wine.

- Lutherans, Methodists and most Anglicans believe Holy Communion is more than just an 'intellectual' commemoration of the Last Supper — it's a re-enactment. They believe that there is a 'real presence' of Christ in the bread and wine, but they don't believe that transubstantiation occurs.

> "Transubstantiation... in the Supper of the Lord, cannot be proved by holy Writ..." 39 Articles XXVIII

- Baptists view the bread and wine as symbols, but believe that God is present through the act of Christians coming together to share Communion. The bread and non-alcoholic wine are set out on a simple table. The bread is later offered from person to person, and the wine drunk from small individual cups.

- Denominations which place more meaning on the bread and wine (e.g. Catholicism and Orthodox) hold Eucharists more often — they believe it's essential for sustaining their relationship with God. They tend to use a more ornate table (an altar), and have more ritual surrounding the Eucharist (e.g. using incense). Catholics will be given bread by the priest and drink wine from a shared cup. Orthodox Christians are given the bread and wine together on a special spoon.

Immerse yourself and learn all about baptism...

Close the book and jot down the beliefs of the different denominations about baptism and the Eucharist.

REVISION TASK

The Sacraments

Catholics believe there are <u>seven</u> specific sacraments through which God can communicate his <u>grace</u> directly. Some see the <u>whole world</u> as <u>sacramental</u> — they can experience <u>God's grace</u> through his creation.

The Seven Sacraments — God Shows His Grace

> "The seven sacraments touch all the stages and all the important moments of Christian life..." Catechism of the Catholic Church, 1210

① Baptism This marks a person's official <u>entry</u> into the Church (see p.9).

② Confirmation In this ceremony, a Christian (often a teenager) <u>renews</u> the vows made on their behalf at baptism. <u>Confirmation</u> is believed to <u>strengthen the ties</u> of the confirmed to the Church and to God. In Catholic confirmations, the bishop anoints the believer's forehead with holy oil called <u>chrism</u>.

③ Reconciliation This involves <u>confession</u> of a sin, following by <u>contrition</u>, <u>penance</u> and <u>absolution</u>. This is how Catholics seek to obtain <u>forgiveness</u> for the sins they commit. They must <u>tell</u> a priest about any <u>sinful</u> things that they've done. The priest will give a <u>penance</u> (a certain number of prayers to be said, or an action to be done) and will then pronounce <u>absolution</u> (God's forgiveness).

④ Anointing the sick A priest or bishop anoints a <u>seriously unwell person</u> with the <u>oil of the sick</u>. Catholics believe that, through this, the <u>Holy Spirit</u> renews the person's <u>faith</u> and <u>strength</u> to <u>cope</u> with their illness and <u>accept</u> their suffering. The anointing is also believed to <u>link</u> the person's suffering to <u>Christ's</u> suffering, allow their <u>sins</u> to be forgiven and to <u>heal</u> them, if that is <u>God's will</u>.

⑤ Matrimony Catholics believe Jesus performed his <u>first miracle</u> at a <u>wedding</u>. They believe that God is <u>present</u> at the ceremony and <u>promises</u> are made before him — couples joined in <u>Holy Matrimony</u> should be together for <u>life</u>. As it's a sacrament, the union is a way that God <u>blesses</u> the couple, and he also blesses them <u>through</u> one another.

⑥ Holy orders This is the process by which men are ordained as <u>deacons</u>, <u>priests</u> or <u>bishops</u>. Like matrimony, it is a <u>commitment</u> for life.

⑦ Eucharist The Eucharist (Mass) is seen as "the source and summit of the Christian life" (Catechism of the Catholic Church 1324). Receiving the <u>body</u> and <u>blood</u> of Christ (see p.9) <u>joins</u> people together in their faith and gives them the <u>strength</u> to live Christian lives and face any <u>problems</u> they may encounter.

Some of the bread and wine that is <u>blessed</u> but <u>not consumed</u> is kept in the church — people believe <u>Jesus</u> is still <u>present</u> in it, and <u>focus</u> on it as they pray and express their love for Jesus. This is known as '<u>eucharistic adoration</u>'.

> "...in the breaking of the Eucharistic bread, we are taken up into communion with Him and with one another." Lumen gentium Chapter 1 Paragraph 7:53

Catholic Funerals have Three Parts

The funeral rite isn't a sacrament, but it's important.

1) The <u>Vigil of Prayer</u> takes place the day before the funeral and is sometimes held at home. Readings and prayers form the service, which aims to <u>help</u> family and friends prepare to say <u>goodbye</u>.

2) Attending a funeral allows Catholics to join together in <u>praying</u> to God to <u>take care</u> of the person. Funerals remind people of the hope of <u>eternal life</u> — one day the bereaved will be <u>reunited</u> with the <u>deceased</u>.

3) The <u>Funeral Liturgy</u> often includes Holy Communion (the '<u>Requiem Mass</u>'). Its purpose is to pray for the soul of the dead person. The coffin is sprinkled with <u>holy water</u> and the priest says, "In the waters of baptism [name] died with Christ, and rose with him to new life. May s/he now share with him in eternal glory." The coffin is later sprinkled again and perfumed with <u>incense</u>. The <u>Paschal candle</u> sits beside it.

4) The <u>Committal</u> is a short ceremony that happens at the <u>cemetery</u> (or the <u>crematorium</u> if the person wished to be cremated). The priest says "ashes to ashes, dust to dust" as the body goes back to the <u>earth</u>.

Big Cats Rarely Ask Me 'Ham Or Egg?'...

EXAM QUESTION

...is a handy way to remember the first letters of the sacraments. Now try out this exam question:
Explain two ways that the sacraments communicate God's grace. [4]

Prayer and Pilgrimage

Prayer and pilgrimage are both ways in which Christians might strengthen their relationship with God.

Prayer Puts People In Touch with their God

1) Prayer is when believers mentally or vocally communicate with God — it should be part of daily life. The Catechism of the Catholic Church (2559) says that "Prayer is the raising of one's mind and heart to God". During prayer people might thank God (thanksgiving), worship God (adoration) or admit sins (confession). They might ask God for something (supplication) or to help other people (intercession).

2) Believers draw comfort from the fact that God is listening to them. They also listen for what he is saying to them — many believe prayer helps them to find out what God wants them to do in life.

3) Most denominations have set (formulaic) prayers that are Church tradition — they can be said during acts of worship in church, and also in private.

4) The Lord's Prayer is very important. It's based on the words Jesus used when he told his disciples how to pray. It covers key themes — e.g. the idea that God is 'Our Father' and he provides for people's physical needs.

> "This, then, is how you should pray: 'Our Father in heaven, hallowed be your name, your kingdom come, your will be done, on earth as it is in heaven. Give us today our daily bread. And forgive us our debts, as we also have forgiven our debtors. And lead us not into temptation, but deliver us from the evil one.'"
> Matthew 6:9-13 NIV

5) Informal prayers are where the individual talks to God in their own words. They're sometimes called 'extempore' prayers, and can be used in worship and privately. Informal prayers are more personal and show the individual's connection with God — many Christians prefer them to set prayers.

Catholic Forms of Popular Piety

1) Catholics use the Rosary (a string with a cross and beads) when praying. The cross is held when reciting the Apostles' Creed, and prayers are said as the beads are moved through the fingers, e.g. Ave Maria (Hail Mary). The beads represent the key events in Christianity (known as mysteries), such as the birth, death and resurrection of Jesus — the Rosary helps people think about these while praying.

2) The 'Stations of the Cross' are pictures in church of Jesus's suffering — Catholics use them as a focus for contemplation on these events. The Catechism of the Catholic Church recognises the use of different forms of piety, but says that they "...extend the liturgical life of the Church, but do not replace it" (1675).

3) Some disagree with these forms of 'popular piety'. Some Protestants think the Rosary encourages prayers to be repeated without giving thought to the words themselves. Many Protestants wouldn't say the Hail Mary prayer, as most don't believe in praying to Mary. Some people might argue that praying while focusing on the Stations of the Cross creates a danger of worshipping idols.

Pilgrimages can help Believers feel Nearer to God

1) Pilgrimages aren't compulsory in Christianity, but many see them as important. The Catechism of the Catholic Church (2691) says that "Pilgrimages evoke our earthly journey toward heaven...". Luke 2:41-43 tells the story of the pilgrimage Jesus and his parents made to Jerusalem.

2) Christians make pilgrimages to seek healing or forgiveness, to connect to God or to deepen their faith. Pilgrimages also provide the chance to escape normal life and to concentrate more on religion. Pilgrims can learn from each other. The journey reflects the path they're trying to follow towards God.

3) People may visit places that are significant in Christianity — such as Jerusalem, where they can visit key places in Jesus's life and death. Roman Catholics often visit Rome, the home of the Pope.

4) Some Christians, especially Catholics, make pilgrimages to shrines where Mary has appeared. These include Walsingham (which is popular with some Anglicans as well as Catholics) and Lourdes. The water in Lourdes is said to have healing properties which can cure ill health, and lots of people believe miracles take place there. Catholics also visit shrines to saints.

5) Protestants are more likely to visit places they can find peace to study the Bible and pray — e.g. the quiet island of Iona (which has a long history of Christianity), or Taizé where they can join worship at the monastery. Some Christians see shrines such as Lourdes as being too commercialised, with too many people. Some regard pilgrimage as unnecessary — the journey inside is what matters.

I make a daily pilgrimage to the biscuit tin...

Make sure you know why people go on pilgrimages and the differences between the most famous sites.

EXAM TIP

12

Christmas and Easter

Christmas and Easter are the two most important celebrations in the Christian calendar.

Christmas is a Celebration of Jesus's Birth

1) Christmas is celebrated by most Christians on 25th December (for Orthodox Christians it's 7th January). It celebrates how Jesus was born in Bethlehem — there he was worshipped by shepherds after an angel told them that "a Saviour has been born to you; he is the Messiah, the Lord" (Luke 2:11 NIV).

2) Christmas comes after a period called Advent, which begins four Sundays before Christmas. Advent is significant for many Christians as it's time they spend getting ready to celebrate Jesus's birth — a time for prayer and reflection. Advent candles are lit in homes and churches, and children may use Advent calendars to count off the days until Christmas.

3) Lots of Roman Catholic, Orthodox and Anglican churches have a 'Midnight Mass' to welcome Christmas Day, and most Christians go to church on Christmas morning to celebrate.

4) Many churches hold services in the days after Christmas, carrying on to Epiphany (6th January) — the day that the Magi (wise men) went to see Jesus in Bethlehem.

5) Customs vary around the world. Gifts are exchanged to symbolise the fact that Jesus was God's gift to the world, and to remember how the Magi "presented him with gifts of gold, frankincense and myrrh" (Matthew 2:11 NIV).

6) Some Christians dislike modern Christmas traditions and customs, e.g. Santa Claus (Father Christmas), giving expensive presents, and excessive eating and drinking. They believe that some of these modern traditions devalue the true meaning of Christmas. Others feel that it has retained too much pagan influence, such as Christmas trees.

Easter celebrates Jesus's Resurrection

1) Easter is the most important festival for Christians, since it celebrates Jesus's victory over death, when God raised him back to life after his crucifixion (see p.4). This reminds people that God loves them so much that he was willing to suffer death on the cross and gives them hope of eternal life.

> 1 Corinthians 15:14 outlines how important the Resurrection is for Christians and their beliefs: "And if Christ has not been raised, our preaching is useless and so is your faith" (NIV).

2) Lent is the 40 days before Easter. On Ash Wednesday (the first day of Lent), ash is put on believers' foreheads to show they're sorry for their sins. Some Christians fast (eat less and have only simple food) during Lent to mark when Jesus fasted for 40 days in the desert. They stop fasting on Easter Sunday.

3) The lead-up to Easter Day, the day of resurrection, is marked by a number of important events:

- Palm Sunday is the Sunday before Easter, when Christians remember Jesus's triumphant entry into Jerusalem. This marks the beginning of Holy Week — Jesus's final week before his crucifixion.
- Maundy Thursday commemorates the Last Supper held on the night before Jesus died.
- Good Friday recalls Jesus's crucifixion — special services are held, particularly on Friday afternoon. Some services last three hours to mark Jesus's final three hours on the cross, when the sky became dark.

4) Easter Day is a joyous occasion when Jesus's resurrection is celebrated.

- Some churches hold services on the Saturday night, and most have special services on the Sunday morning.
- The Paschal candle is lit during services in Anglican and Catholic churches. Worshippers light their own candle from its flame, which represents Jesus as the Light of the World.
- Some churches hold sunrise services to remember how Mary Magdalene discovered at daybreak that Jesus's tomb was empty. The rising of the sun is symbolic of God's Son rising from the dead.
- Eggs are associated with Easter as a symbol of new life. Some view chocolate Easter eggs as commercialisation of the festival.

Learning about Easter is an eggcellent way to gain marks...

Working from Lent to Easter Sunday, draw a timeline of Christian Easter celebrations. Next to each day, scribble down what happens and then check your answers against this page.

The Work of the Church

Churches aren't just about holding services. They're active in the local community too.

Churches are Important in the Local Community

Most communities in the UK have access to at least one church. The role of the local church is to put the Christian faith into action — this includes caring for the community, as seen in lots of Christian teaching:

In 1 Peter 5:2-3, the leaders of the church are asked to set an example for the congregation through their actions: "...be shepherds of God's flock that is under your care, watching over them... being examples to the flock" (NIV).	In Mark 12:31, Jesus said that the second most important commandment is "Love your neighbour as yourself" (NIV).	Paragraph 26 of Gaudium et spes, a key Catholic document of the Second Vatican Council, states: "Every social group must take account of the needs and legitimate aspirations of other groups, and even of the general welfare of the entire human family."

Churches put this into practice in many different ways:

1) By providing regular services and a place for quiet reflection — most churches hold a Sunday service and may also have other acts of worship throughout the week.

2) By providing rites of passage such as baptisms, confirmations, weddings and funerals (see p.9-10).

3) By running youth groups and Sunday Schools to engage young people in the local community.

4) By offering support and advice to people in need — e.g. visiting and praying for people in hospital.

5) Some churchgoers work as Street Pastors — they volunteer in towns and cities on Friday and Saturday nights to support anyone in need of help. This demonstrates Christian love.

6) Some foodbanks in the UK are run by churches. People donate food which the foodbank then distributes to those who need it the most.

Different denominations might work together, e.g. through community projects or joint services. This is called 'ecumenism'.

7) Many churches also raise money for charity.

Evangelism Tells People about Christianity

1) Evangelism means spreading the Christian message with the aim of converting people. As church attendance falls, evangelism is increasingly important.

"As the Father has sent me, I am sending you." John 20:21 NIV

2) In Mark 16:15, Jesus told his disciples to "Go into all the world and preach the gospel to all creation" (NIV). Many Christians believe that they should be prepared to do the same.

3) They believe that by evangelising they can help people discover their real purpose in life and find salvation. They feel excited to tell other people about Jesus's love — Pope Francis said "The primary reason for evangelizing is the love of Jesus which we have received..." (Evangelii Gaudium 264).

4) For some, evangelism is about telling people directly about God. This can cause problems — people may feel offended. Others try to demonstrate God's love through their actions, to bring people closer to God. Churches might ask the congregation to bring along a friend who wouldn't normally go to church.

5) Missionaries spread the Christian message abroad. In the past they went where Christianity was unknown, with the aim of converting people. Now many missionaries use their skills to help disadvantaged people, e.g. a doctor working in a poor country. These people show what Christianity is through their actions.

Other examples of evangelism

- The Church of England and Church in Wales are finding ways to interest new people in churches that don't follow the traditional model — for example worshipping in alternative venues like cafés, or creating a café atmosphere in church. Through initiatives called 'Fresh Expressions' and 'Pioneer Ministry', they offer a new approach for modern society.
- Gideons distribute copies of the Bible in places like hotels and care homes.
- The Salvation Army helps people by providing hot meals and beds for homeless people. They also attend emergencies, such as floods.

It's my mission to get you to learn this page...

Outline three ways that Christians might try to evangelise others.   [3]

The Work of the Church

Reconciliation works Towards Peace and Unity

1) Christians believe in justice — all people are equal in God's eyes, so they should be treated fairly. Christian organisations help people being treated unfairly due to war, religious persecution or poverty.

2) In Matthew 5:9 Jesus said "Blessed are the peacemakers" (NIV). Christians believe that reconciliation (coming together and making peace) is needed between people who have been in conflict with one another — just as Jesus brought God and humankind together through the atonement (p.5).

3) These are two examples of organisations that work for reconciliation:

> The Corrymeela Community in Northern Ireland was founded to help heal the country's political and religious divisions. It works with people in areas where there is tension and strives to help people understand each other and reconcile through group activities and discussions.

> Pax Christi is an international Catholic organisation working for human rights, disarmament and peace. They believe violence should be avoided, and they work to create a world where people can live in harmony.

Organisations and Churches help Persecuted Christians

1) Millions around the world suffer for being Christians — some endure prison sentences or even death.

2) Organisations give support by providing Bibles so people can continue worshipping in secret. They offer training to church members and support people who have lost their homes.

3) Churches pray for the persecuted and may send money. Christians might petition for government help.

Christian Charities help Those in Need

1) In the story of the sheep and goats (Matthew 25:31-46), Jesus explains that people who have been good (the sheep) and have helped others will be looked after by God. People who haven't (the goats) will suffer. The story tells Christians that they are helping Jesus when they help others.

2) Because of this, charity is very important to many Christians. But it's not all about giving money — it must be done with love. In 1 Corinthians 13:3, St Paul said "If I give all I possess to the poor... but do not have love, I gain nothing" (NIV).

> Christian Aid works globally to relieve poverty. They set up projects in the developing world, drawing on the skills of local people. The organisation also aims to change government policy to help reduce the suffering of the world's poor, e.g. through debt relief, and fair-trade products.

> CAFOD (Catholic Agency for Overseas Development) works to fight poverty and injustice around the world. They work through churches, helping in emergencies, but also giving people the skills to help themselves.

> Tearfund® is an evangelical organisation — it helps communities with projects run through their churches. Their work includes trying to end hunger, resolving tension in conflict zones and helping refugees. They also help areas hit by natural disasters.

Christian Aid and CAFOD believe in development — 'helping people to help themselves', whatever their faith.

There are many Catholic Charities

Evangelii Gaudium (187) says that Catholics should strive to help the poor "to be fully a part of society". CAFOD (see above) is a Roman Catholic organisation, and there are many others that help those in need:

- Trócaire, part of the Irish Catholic Church, provides aid abroad. They help people escape poverty, but also help in emergencies.
- The St Vincent de Paul Society (SVP) helps people in poverty. They provide support by visiting the isolated and ill, helping them with daily tasks, providing schemes and clubs to help the disabled, and donating food to the homeless.
- Missio is an organisation that supports churches abroad that are struggling to fund themselves, e.g. by training church leaders. It also runs projects to provide education and healthcare for children living in poverty.

Sheep — good, goats — baaaad...

You'll have quite a lot of questions to answer in the exam and not much time to do it in. Be sure to manage your time properly — the more marks a question is worth, the more time you should spend on it.

EXAM TIP

Revision Summary

That was a lot to take in there, so now see how you get on with these exam-style questions.
They should give you an idea of how much you'll be expected to write in the exam.

If there's anything you can't answer, go back through the section and have another go when you've re-read it.
For some questions — you'll be told which ones — there are extra marks for spelling, punctuation, grammar and specialist terminology, so check your writing carefully.

Let's get cracking — have a go at these 1 mark multiple choice questions.
1) Which of the following words means that God is all-powerful?
   a) just   b) omnipotent   c) immanent   d) benevolent
2) Which of the following is Jesus's return to heaven to be with God the Father?
   a) resurrection   b) Last Supper   c) ascension   d) crucifixion

You've found your feet now, so let's jump up to 2 marks.
3) Give two beliefs about the Last Judgement.
4) Give two examples of different types of evil.
5) Give two ways that Christians celebrate Easter.

Comfortable with the 2 mark questions? Try your hand at some 3 mark ones.
6) Outline three beliefs about purgatory.
7) Outline three Christian teachings about the Trinity.
8) Outline three Christian beliefs about suffering.

Jumping up to 4 marks now. You need to give two points and develop them.
9) Explain two reasons why liturgical worship is important for some Christians.
10) Explain two Christian beliefs about creation.
11) Explain two contrasting Christian views on the Eucharist.

Organise your points and write concisely in the 4, 5 and 6 mark questions — make your points crystal clear to the marker.

Up to 5 marks now. Explain your points and make sure you refer to a sacred text.
12) Explain two reasons why evangelism is important to Christians.
13) Explain two reasons why prayer is important to Christians.
14) Explain two Christian teachings on baptism.

Just for fun, have a go at this 6 mark question. You'll need to explain and analyse to get full marks.
15) Explain why Jesus's resurrection is important for Christians.

It's the one you've been looking forward to — the 12 mark question.
Many essay questions like this one will have extra marks for SPaG and specialist terminology too.
16) 'Pilgrimage is the best way for a Christian to develop their relationship with God.'
    Evaluate this statement.
    Give arguments that support the statement and arguments that disagree with the statement.
    You must include:
    • examples from Christian teachings
    • different Christian opinions
    • a conclusion.

Turn to the 'Do Well in Your Exam' section for tips on writing essays.

Islam	Introduction to Islam

Islam was founded in the 7th century. It shares some ideas with Judaism and Christianity. Muslims believe in one god, Allah. The Qur'an is the Muslim holy book — Muslims also follow the prophet Muhammad's teaching.

Islam is Divided into Two Main Traditions — Sunni and Shi'a

1) About 85-90% of Muslims are Sunni Muslims — most of the rest are Shi'a Muslims.

2) Muhammad was the founder of Islam — Allah revealed the Qur'an to him. After Muhammad died, Muslims had to choose a new leader (caliph). The next four caliphs were Abu Bakr, Umar, Uthman and Ali.

3) However, some Muslims had wanted Ali to be the first caliph, and thought the first three caliphs shouldn't have been given the role. Others said Ali shouldn't be the caliph at all.

4) After Ali died, two groups formed — the Sunnis and the Shi'as. Each group followed a different line of caliphs. The Sunnis accepted the next caliph after Ali, but the Shi'as (Shi'at Ali or Party of Ali) followed Ali's descendants. Sunnis and Shi'as have been separate groups ever since.

Sunnis and Shi'as have Many Similar Beliefs

Sunnis and Shi'as share many beliefs, but have some different ideas. Their basic beliefs — articles of faith — are slightly different, but they share beliefs in Allah, the holy books, prophets and a day of judgement. These, along with a belief in angels, are mentioned in the Qur'an (4:136) and other teachings, e.g. Sahih Muslim 1:4.

There are six articles of faith in Sunni Islam: 1) belief that Allah is the one and only god (Tawhid) 2) belief in angels (Malaikah) 3) belief in the holy books 4) belief in Allah's prophets (Nubuwwah) 5) belief in the Day of Judgement 6) belief that Allah knows and decides everything that's going to happen (predestination — al-Qadr)	There are five articles of faith in Shi'a Islam. They're known as the 'Usul ad-Din — foundations of faith: 1) belief that Allah is the one and only god (Tawhid) 2) belief in divine justice ('Adl) 3) belief in prophethood (Nubuwwah) 4) belief in the authority of imams (Imamah) 5) belief in the Day of Resurrection (Mi'ad)

Key Sunni Beliefs

1) No one after Muhammad received knowledge from Allah. Muslims should focus on Muhammad and his way of life (sunnah — see p.19) rather than paying too much attention to Ali and his sons.

2) Muslims should be guided by the consensus (majority view) of the community.

Key Shi'a Beliefs

1) Ali was the first true caliph. Allah gave him knowledge to ensure his teaching and actions were right.

2) There are many branches of Shi'a Islam. They share a common belief in a line of imams after Ali, who all had the same knowledge from Allah as Ali. Shi'a imams are leaders and figureheads of the religion. They're all descendants of Muhammad. In Sunni Islam, the word 'imam' simply means 'prayer leader'.

3) The different branches of Shi'a Islam split off from each other after disagreements about the line of imams. The Twelvers are the largest branch, but there are many others.

4) Twelver Shi'as believe in a line of 12 imams, the last of whom is in hiding and will eventually return. The Twelvers are led by religious scholars while they wait for the last imam's return.

5) Isma'ili Shi'as (often called 'Seveners') thought the seventh imam should be Isma'il, the elder brother of the one chosen by the Twelvers. The biggest group of Isma'ilis today, the Nizaris, think each imam can select the next and are still led by an imam now, known as the Aga Khan.

Seveners, Twelvers — sounds like maths, not RS...

As a quick task to keep you on your toes — shut this book, grab a piece of paper and see if you can write down the articles of faith for Sunni and Shi'a Islam.

REVISION TASK

Key Beliefs in Islam

Islam is a monotheistic religion — Muslims believe in only one god, Allah. They believe in many prophets.

Tawhid is Central to Islam

"Say, 'He is Allah, [who is] One.' " Qur'an 112:1

1) The word Allah is from the Arabic al-ilah, meaning 'the god', i.e. the only god. Several of the ninety-nine names of Allah (see below) make this clear, including al-Ahad (the one and only) and al-Wahid (the one).

2) Saying Allah is the only god is the first part of the shahadah, the Muslim declaration of faith (see p.21).

3) Shirk — believing in other gods as well as Allah, or that anyone or thing could share in Allah's oneness — is seen as the worst sin. Muslims therefore disagree with the Christian idea of the Holy Trinity (see p.2) and with polytheism (believing in multiple gods). Images of Muhammad aren't allowed, in case of shirk.

"Allah does not forgive association with Him, but He forgives what is less than that..." Qur'an 4:116. 'Association with Him' is worshipping other gods as well as Allah.

"let the first thing to which you will invite them, be the Tauhid [Tawhid] of Allah." Sahih al-Bukhari 93:469

4) According to a hadith (see p.19), Muhammad said that when telling non-Muslims about Islam, the first thing Muslims should mention is Tawhid.

Allah has Many Characteristics

"In the name of Allah, the Entirely Merciful, the Especially Merciful" (Qur'an 1:1) is the phrase known as the bismillah.

1) MERCIFUL — Muslims believe Allah shows mercy and compassion. All but one of the Qur'an's chapters begin by saying this — it's known as the bismillah. They believe Allah is kind and forgives people's sins.

2) OMNIPOTENT — Allah is all-powerful. He created the universe and is in control of everything. He has predetermined people's lives (decided what will happen), though people do have free will (see p.20).

3) BENEVOLENT — Allah is all-good — he can do no evil. He cares for his people — this is seen in his intervention in the world, e.g. his revelations to the prophets were to show people how to live a good life.

4) JUST — Muslims believe Allah will judge people's behaviour in a fair way. This concept is particularly important to Shi'a Muslims — known as 'Adl, it's one of the 'Usul ad-Din (see p.16).

5) IMMANENT — Allah is present and involved in the world. He's close to every human and knows them.

6) TRANSCENDENT — Allah's also above everything — he can't be thought of in human terms. He has no equal.

"And We have already created man and know what his soul whispers to him, and We are closer to him than [his] jugular vein." Qur'an 50:16

There are ninety-nine names for Allah listed in the Qur'an. Each refers to one of his characteristics. Points 1-4 above are each English translations of one of these names (originally in Arabic). Muslims recite them in daily prayers.

Adam and Ibrahim were Prophets...

Belief in the prophets is an article of faith for both Sunnis and Shi'as (p.16).

1) Allah's compassion means he can't leave people to sin without helping them. So he sends messages about how to live a good life. He almost always does this via angels, who pass on his words to human prophets (rasuls). Risalah is the concept of messengership — the way Allah communicates with humans.

2) Allah chose many people as prophets. 25 prophets are mentioned in the Qur'an, although some believe there have been 124 000. Some prophets were given holy books to pass on to humankind.

3) Muslims believe the prophets taught the same basic ideas, most importantly belief in one god. They see all the prophets as equal to each other — "We make no distinction between any of them" (Qur'an 2:136).

4) Muslims believe the prophets performed miracles — they did so to prove they were really prophets.

5) The first prophet was Adam, who was also the first man, created by Allah in his image. Others were Ibrahim (Abraham), Isma'il (Ishmael), Musa (Moses), Dawud (David), Isa (Jesus) and Muhammad.

6) Adam was sent to Earth after eating fruit forbidden to him by Allah. Allah forgave him his sin though. Adam is considered to have been the first Muslim. Some believe he first built the Ka'aba (p.23).

7) Ibrahim rejected the idea of many different gods. Muslims can learn from his devotion to Allah — he proved his faith by being willing to sacrifice his own son, Isma'il (see p.24). Ibrahim is thought to have rebuilt the Ka'aba and he and his family's story plays an important role in the hajj rituals (see p.23).

Key Beliefs in Islam

...Isma'il, Musa, Dawud, Isa and Muhammad were Prophets too

1) Ibrahim's son Isma'il was also a prophet and helped him build the Ka'aba. It's believed many Arabs, including Muhammad, are descended from Isma'il — he's known as Abul Arab, the father of the Arabs.

2) Musa is the only prophet that Allah spoke to directly, rather than through the angel Jibril (Gabriel). He's important as he kept trying to guide people to believing in one god, even when they worshipped others.

3) Dawud is known for killing Jalut (Goliath) during a battle between Jalut's large army and Talut's (Saul's) smaller one. Dawud later succeeded Talut as king. As well as his bravery, Muslims can learn from his wisdom and his loyalty to Allah — he would pray for a third of each night.

4) Allah sent Isa when he thought people had strayed from Musa's teachings. Muslims believe Isa wasn't crucified (Allah wouldn't let that happen) but after 3 years' teaching Allah brought him up into heaven.

5) Muslims believe all these prophets paved the way for Muhammad:

Muhammad

- Muhammad was born about 570 CE in Makkah (Mecca). One day, while Muhammad was meditating, Allah sent the angel Jibril to him with a message.
- Muhammad was scared at first, but as Jibril gradually revealed more and more of the message from Allah, Muhammad began preaching this message to others.
- The early messages said people should worship one god, Allah, and that people would be judged on their behaviour. Later on, the revelations gave more detail on how Muslims should live their lives.
- Eventually, this message from Allah was written down as the Qur'an. The Qur'an is seen by Muslims as a miracle — the final revelation from Allah.
- Muhammad is often called the 'seal of the prophets' — most Muslims believe he was the last prophet that there will be. He is believed to have been a wise leader, who settled disputes and brought different communities together. He performed several miracles.
- As Muhammad was Allah's last prophet, Muslims pay particular attention to his words and actions. They use them to work out how to live their lives (p.19), as they see him as a role model.

The Qur'an is the Word of Allah

Qur'an is sometimes spelt 'Koran' in English.

1) Muslims think the Qur'an is the most important holy book. They believe it's a complete and accurate record of Allah's exact words to Muhammad, as Qur'an 53:10-11 describes: "he revealed to His Servant what he revealed. The heart did not lie [about] what it saw." The Qur'an allows humans to know Allah.

2) In the Qur'an, Allah tells Muslims what they need to know and how to lead their lives to please him. Muslims try to live according to its guidance. This helps them be rewarded by Allah and get to Paradise.

3) Many Muslims learn the Qur'an by heart. The Qur'an was revealed in Arabic — if it's written in another language the meaning might change, so Muslims learn Arabic to ensure they're reading the true Qur'an.

4) There's often dispute over how to interpret the Qur'an though, e.g. in relation to jihad (p.23). It can be difficult to apply its teachings to modern life, because so much has changed since it was revealed.

The Qur'an is Divided into 114 Surahs

1) The Qur'an is organised into 114 surahs (chapters), each made up of ayahs (verses). The surahs are in order of length — longest first, shortest last (except surah 1, a short statement of Muslims' basic beliefs).

2) Because the Qur'an is so important, Muslims treat it with great respect. The Qur'an is often ornately decorated, inside and out. Many Muslims:

1. keep their Qur'an wrapped up to keep it clean
2. wash their hands before touching it
3. keep it on a higher shelf than all other books
4. place it on a special stand when they read it

3) The Qur'an is read during private and public prayers, so Muslims get to know it well.

Key Beliefs in Islam

Allah revealed <u>holy books</u> to <u>other prophets</u> as well. Angels were <u>messengers</u> for Allah.

There are Other Holy Books in Islam

As well as the <u>Qur'an</u>, Muslims see the <u>Sahifah</u>, the <u>Tawrat</u>, the <u>Zabur</u> and the <u>Injil</u> as <u>holy books</u>. But they believe they've been <u>changed</u> over time through <u>editing</u>, and <u>only the Qur'an</u> exists in its <u>original form</u>.

1) The first <u>holy book</u> is thought to have been given to <u>Ibrahim</u>. Known as the <u>Sahifah</u> (scrolls), it is now <u>lost</u>. The Qur'an <u>mentions</u> it several times, for example in Qur'an 87:18-19.

2) The <u>Tawrat</u> (Torah) is the book given to <u>Musa</u>. It's the main <u>Jewish</u> holy book. The Qur'an says it contains the "judgement of Allah" (Qur'an 5:43) so it's <u>valued</u> by Muslims. It includes the <u>Ten Commandments</u>, basic rules for a <u>religious life</u>.

> "We sent down the Torah, in which was guidance and light." Qur'an 5:44

3) The <u>Zabur</u> (Psalms) was given to <u>Dawud</u>. It's thought to be linked to the <u>Psalms</u> of <u>David</u> in the Christian <u>Bible</u> and the Jewish <u>Tenakh</u>, but many Muslims believe the <u>original</u> has been corrupted, perhaps beyond recognition.

> "...to David We gave the book [of Psalms]." Qur'an 4:163

4) Muslims believe Allah gave the <u>Injil</u> to <u>Isa</u> — Qur'an 57:27 says "We sent ... Our messengers and followed [them] with Jesus ... and gave him the Gospel". They think the Injil <u>prophesies</u> the coming of <u>Muhammad</u>. Many Muslims believe the Christian <u>New Testament</u> contains the <u>same ideas</u> as those given to Isa, but not his exact words. Others think the <u>Injil</u> was <u>another book</u> entirely.

5) Muslims also pay a lot of attention to the <u>guidance</u> and <u>example</u> they get from the following:

Hadith	Sunnah
The <u>hadith</u> are <u>reports</u> of <u>Muhammad's</u> words and actions, recorded by his <u>followers</u>. They're <u>not</u> in the <u>Qur'an</u> — they weren't revealed by <u>Allah</u>. <u>Each one</u>'s been assessed as to how <u>authentic</u> it is. There are different <u>collections</u> of them, e.g. Sahih al-Bukhari, Sahih Muslim and Sunan Abi Dawud.	The <u>sunnah</u> sets out <u>Muhammad's way of life</u>, as recorded in the <u>hadith</u>.

6) The <u>hadith</u> and the <u>sunnah</u> give <u>valuable advice</u> in <u>addition</u> to the Qur'an, especially on issues concerning <u>daily life</u> — but some Muslims believe it's <u>best</u> just to use the <u>Qur'an</u>, as the hadith might be <u>unreliable</u>.

7) <u>Shi'a</u> Muslims also follow the <u>hadith</u> (sayings) of the <u>imams</u>, especially those of <u>Ali</u>.

Angels are Allah's Messengers

> "They exalt [Him] night and day [and] do not slacken." Qur'an 21:20

1) The <u>purpose</u> of angels is to <u>follow</u> Allah's <u>orders</u> and <u>communicate</u> with humans, often via the <u>prophets</u>. In heaven, they <u>praise</u> him and <u>guard</u> his throne. They <u>welcome</u> humans into <u>paradise</u>.

2) They're thought to be <u>genderless</u>, made of <u>light</u> and to have <u>wings</u>. They're <u>immortal</u> and don't have <u>free will</u>, as their role is to obey Allah — they're therefore <u>incapable</u> of <u>sin</u>. Allah created them <u>before</u> humans.

3) Some angels <u>record</u> people's <u>good</u> and <u>bad deeds</u> for the <u>Day of Judgement</u> — Qur'an 43:80 says "Our messengers are with them recording". <u>Guardian</u> angels <u>protect</u> people from <u>danger</u> and <u>evil</u>. Some think they're the same thing and <u>recording</u> angels act as <u>guardians</u> too.

4) Belief in angels is an <u>article of faith</u> for <u>Sunnis</u>, so it's <u>important</u>. The thought of a guardian angel can be <u>comforting</u> for Muslims. Having an angel recording their deeds can <u>influence</u> Muslims to do <u>good things</u>.

5) <u>Jibril</u> (who you might know as <u>Gabriel</u>) is an <u>important angel</u>. He revealed Allah's words (the <u>Qur'an</u>) to <u>Muhammad</u>. He also revealed messages to <u>other prophets</u>, so he's known as the <u>angel of revelation</u>. He told <u>Maryam</u> (Mary) she was pregnant with <u>Isa</u> (Jesus) — see Qur'an 19:16-22.

> "Gabriel ... has brought the Qur'an down upon your heart, [O Muhammad], by permission of Allah." Qur'an 2:97

6) <u>Mika'il</u> (Michael) is <u>important</u> too — he's named in Qur'an 2:98. He asks <u>Allah</u> to <u>forgive</u> people's <u>sins</u>.

7) <u>Izra'il</u> (Azrael) is the <u>angel of death</u> (Qur'an 32:11). He takes <u>souls</u> from people's <u>bodies</u> when they die.

8) It's believed that <u>Israfil</u> (Raphael) will blow the trumpet on the <u>Day of Judgement</u>.

Tawrat, Zabur, Injil, Jibril, Izra'il...

...there are lots of names on this page. Without looking at the book, see if you can write down all the names of the holy books and of the angels, as well as a sentence about each one.

REVISION TASK

Islam	Life after Death

Islam teaches that people will be judged on their behaviour during their life by Allah.

Al-Qadr means Predestination

1) Al-Qadr is the idea that Allah has decided everything that will happen. This idea appears in teachings such as Sahih al-Bukhari 78:685, in which Muhammad said vowing to do something "does not bring about ... anything [Allah] has not decreed" — humans can't choose to do something Allah hasn't chosen for them.

2) This might seem to be contradicted by the idea of the Day of Judgement (see below) when Allah will judge people on the basis of their actions. That suggests people have free will and can choose how they act — there'd be no point judging them on their actions if what they did had already been decided by Allah.

3) However, many Muslims believe in a mix of these two ideas:

Sunnis tend to believe Allah knows everything that's going to happen — he's above normal laws of time, so knows what humans will choose before they've chosen it. It's believed humans choose their actions, but Allah has made it impossible that they'll choose anything other than what he's decided. Some think once someone's chosen to act, the act becomes 'theirs' so they can be judged for it.	Shi'as focus a bit more on free will. They often believe Allah has ultimate control and the power to change things in the world if he wants, but that people's lives are usually determined by their choices. Like Sunnis, they tend to believe Allah knows what's going to happen as he is outside 'human' time — but for Shi'as, what happens is what people choose for themselves.

4) To some Muslims, the idea of al-Qadr is comforting — if something bad has happened, it's reassuring to feel it's part of Allah's plan. Some people like to feel that they're guided to do Allah's will by al-Qadr.

Yawm ad-Din is the Day of Judgement

1) On Yawm ad-Din, Allah decides how people will spend the afterlife, based on their behaviour during their lives. It's then too late to beg forgiveness for any wrongdoing.

2) Allah will judge everyone — not just Muslims. On Yawm ad-Din, the dead will be resurrected to join those still living. Everyone will receive a record of their good and bad deeds, on which they'll be judged.

> "We will call forth every people with their record [of deeds]." Qur'an 17:71

3) The idea of judgement is important as it encourages Muslims to live their lives in a good way. It can be comforting to think bad people will be punished. Other Muslims think it's best to concentrate on this life — they think people should do good things anyway, not just because they're focusing on their afterlife.

4) Intentions are also important — intending to do something good counts, but intending to do something bad but not doing it doesn't count against you (Sahih Muslim 1:233).

Al-Akhirah Means the Afterlife

1) Belief in the afterlife — al-Akhirah — is a key part of Islam. The afterlife is where people go after the Day of Judgement.

It was paradise for everyone except the gardeners...

2) The reward for good people will be entry into jannah (paradise) — this is a place of peace, happiness and beauty. The Qur'an refers to Paradise as "Gardens of Pleasure" (Qur'an 31:8).

> "...for one whose scales are heavy [with good deeds], He will be in a pleasant life. ...for one whose scales are light, His refuge will be an abyss." Qur'an 101:6-9

3) For those who have done bad deeds, the punishment is jahannam (hell). The Qur'an describes jahannam as a place of scorching fire and boiling water. Here, those who have ignored Allah's teaching and failed to act righteously will be punished. Allah is merciful though, so they may eventually be sent to paradise.

4) The Qur'an sometimes mentions a 'barrier' between this world and the next called barzakh, where people's souls stay from the time they die until Yawm ad-Din. Many Muslims focus more on jannah and jahannam than barzakh.

> "...behind them is a barrier until the Day they are resurrected." Qur'an 23:100

The Day of Judgement — yeah, when is the exam exactly?

To help you when the day arrives, try out this exam-style question.

Name two concepts linked to Muslim beliefs about the afterlife.   [2]

EXAM QUESTION

Worship and Duties

To be faithful Muslims, Sunni Muslims need to follow the Five Pillars, and Shi'as the Ten Obligatory Acts.

Sunni Muslims are Required to Follow the Five Pillars of Islam

1. Shahadah — declaration of faith

"There is no god but Allah, and Muhammad is his messenger." Muslims should say this several times a day. It's said at birth and death, as well as in the call to prayer (adhan) and prayers. People can convert to Islam by saying it. The exact words aren't in the Qur'an, but come from passages such as Qur'an 3:18 — "Allah witnesses that there is no deity except Him". It's essential to Shi'a Muslims too, though it's not one of their Ten Obligatory Acts (see below). They add "Ali is the helper of Allah", as Ali is significant to their faith (see p.16).

2. Salah — prayer five times a day

The second most important duty in Islam. Muslims should pray five times a day — at sunrise, around noon, late afternoon, after sunset, and late evening. See below for more detail.

3. Zakah — charitable giving

Each person decides where to donate their money. Zakah encourages generosity and compassion. See p.22 for more detail.

4. Sawm — obligation to fast during Ramadan

Ramadan is the ninth month of the Muslim calendar. Muslims are obliged to fast during it. This teaches self-discipline, which brings Muslims closer to Allah. See p.22 for more detail.

5. Hajj — pilgrimage to Makkah

Every Muslim should do hajj at least once. It's only obligatory if you can afford it and you're healthy enough to do it. See p.23 for more.

Shi'a Muslims Follow the Ten Obligatory Acts

Four — salah, sawm, zakah and hajj — are the same as the Five Pillars. The rest are:

Sunnis may also see the acts in the blue boxes as important, but don't follow those in the purple boxes.

Khums — annual tax

Khums is a kind of tax Shi'as pay each year on any 'profit' (excess money) they earn, at a rate of 20%. It goes towards supporting Islamic education and anyone descended from Muhammad who's in need.

Jihad — 'struggle'

The word means 'struggle' or 'striving'. There are two types of jihad — the 'greater' jihad is Muslims' personal struggle to live a good life, and the 'lesser' jihad is Muslims' struggle to defend Islam against its critics. See p.23 for more.

Amr-bil-Maroof and Nahi Anil Munkar

These come as a pair. The phrase means "enjoin what is right and forbid what is wrong" (Qur'an 9:71) — it asks Muslims to encourage good deeds and avoid bad ones.

Tawalla and Tabarra

These also come as a pair. They mean 'love' and 'aloofness' — Muslims should love those who follow Allah and they shouldn't associate themselves with anyone who's an 'enemy' of Allah or Muhammad.

Twelver Shi'as follow these ten acts. Other Shi'as follow different sets of acts.

Salah is Very Important

1) Salah, the five daily prayers, should ideally take place in a mosque, but they can be done anywhere. Sunnis only combine the prayers if they have a very good reason that prevents them praying at five separate times, e.g. if they're travelling. Shi'as combine some prayers, so they tend to pray three times a day rather than five — but they still say all the same prayers.

2) Each prayer cycle (rak'ah, see p.22) includes saying 'Allahu akbar' ('God is great') multiple times, as well as reciting the first surah of the Qur'an (known as the Fatiha) and other verses from the Qur'an.

3) Most men are obliged to go to Friday prayers (Jummah) at the mosque. Requirements vary, but a certain number of people should be present. The Friday prayers are led by an imam, who also gives two sermons.

4) Salah keeps Muslims in close contact with Allah and encourages moral and spiritual discipline. This keeps them from committing shirk (see p.17) and increases taqwa (reverence for Allah). It's an expression of solidarity — doing the same as other Muslims, which is a reminder that everyone's equal.

"...prayer prohibits immorality and wrongdoing, and the remembrance of Allah is greater." Qur'an 29:45

Islam | Worship and Duties

There are Rituals to Follow with Salah

1) Wudu (washing before prayer) is important — Muslims must be pure and clean when approaching Allah, both physically and spiritually. Muslims wash their face, arms, feet and part of the hair before prayers. A prayer mat is often used when not praying in a mosque, in order to ensure cleanliness.

2) Muslims should face Makkah in Saudi Arabia when praying. The direction of Makkah is called the qiblah.

3) The rak'ah is a set prayer ritual. It may be repeated several times at each prayer session. Each rak'ah involves standing, then kneeling, then putting your forehead to the ground as a sign of submission to Allah. If several Muslims are praying in one place, then the rak'ah is done together at the same time.

4) Shi'a prayers are a bit different. Shi'as touch their foreheads to a clay or wooden tablet during the rak'ah — they believe putting their forehead on something natural is what Muhammad advised. The tablet is often made of clay from Karbala, where Husayn was killed (p.24), to remind Shi'as of his sacrifice.

5) When at the mosque, women and men pray separately — so people concentrate on Allah rather than on the opposite sex. This has changed in some mosques though, where mixed prayer is allowed.

6) Many Muslims perform salah in the home rather than at the mosque, particularly women. It's seen as an important way for children to learn about Islam. Some Muslim families may have a room just for salah.

Zakah is Charitable Giving

Some Shi'as pay khums (see p.21) in addition to zakah.

1) Zakah involves redistributing wealth. Muslims think wealth's given by Allah, so should be used to serve him.

2) The amount is usually 2.5% of a person's wealth each year. Muslims can decide how much to give and who they want to donate it to. It's often used to help Muslims who are less well off, or given to charities or mosques.

> "Zakah…[is] for bringing hearts together." Qur'an 9:60. This verse also lists who zakah is for, including the "poor and… needy".

3) Zakah is beneficial because it makes the distribution of wealth fairer and helps those in need. It encourages Muslims to think of others who may not be as well off as them. It's a sign of concern for others and encourages generosity.

Sawm is Fasting During Ramadan

> "O you who have believed, decreed upon you is fasting … that you may become righteous…" Qur'an 2:183

1) Muslims must fast between sunrise and sunset during the month of Ramadan. The Muslim calendar is lunar (determined by the moon) so Ramadan isn't always at the same time of the solar (sun) year.

2) Muslims eat just before sunrise (suhur) and just after sunset (iftar). The fast is often broken slowly with dates, before a bigger meal later. Iftar is often eaten with family or friends, or sometimes at the mosque.

> There are exceptions to the obligation to fast — the Qur'an recognises it might not be possible or healthy for everyone to fast.
> 1. Children don't have to fast until they're about 12 years old. Old people (there's no specific age) don't have to fast either.
> 2. People can be excused for medical reasons. Women who are pregnant, breastfeeding or menstruating can also be excused. It's fine to take medicine which has to be regular, e.g. antibiotics. If you're on a journey, you can be excused too.
> 3. If you've missed a few days of the fast, Qur'an 2:184 says that you should make up for it, either by fasting for the same number of days later on, or by giving food to someone who might need it.

3) Sawm doesn't just involve not eating or drinking, but also abstaining from other things such as listening to music, sex and smoking. Muslims should also try particularly hard to avoid bad thoughts or actions.

4) Ramadan is a time of both physical and moral self-discipline, and a time of obedience to Allah. It's supposed to help Muslims understand hunger, and so makes them more willing to help others.

5) It's also a time to show publicly that Allah matters more than any physical needs.

> Laylat al-Qadr (the Night of Destiny or Power) falls during Ramadan. Muslims believe Muhammad received at least part of the Qur'an during this night. So Ramadan is also a time of thanksgiving for the Qur'an — during Ramadan it's read from beginning to end at the mosque. Laylat al-Qadr is the holiest night of the year — the Qur'an says it's "better than a thousand months" (Qur'an 97:3) and many Muslims spend the whole night at the mosque to celebrate it, praying and listening to readings of the Qur'an. It's important because many Muslims believe Allah will forgive their sins on this night.

Worship and Duties

The <u>hajj</u> is an important action for a Muslim to do. Around <u>2 million</u> Muslims go each year.

The Hajj is the Pilgrimage to Makkah

"...proclaim to the people the Hajj..." Qur'an 22:27

1) Muslims must make the pilgrimage at least <u>once</u> in their lifetime, as long as they can <u>afford</u> it and they're <u>healthy</u> enough to cope with the journey. It has to happen in the Muslim month of Dhu'l-Hijja to <u>count</u>.

2) <u>Adam</u>, <u>Ibrahim</u> and <u>Isma'il</u> are all associated with <u>Makkah</u> and <u>Muhammad</u> lived there, so it's a holy place.

3) <u>All pilgrims</u> wear simple white clothing (<u>ihram</u>) so they're <u>equal</u> before Allah.

4) The <u>Ka'aba</u> is in Makkah — it's a giant <u>stone cube</u> covered with <u>black cloth</u>. Some Muslims think <u>Ibrahim</u> and <u>Isma'il</u> built it as a place of worship — Qur'an 2:127 suggests they did. Others think <u>Adam</u> built it. It's the <u>holiest place</u> in Islam. Muslims must do <u>seven circuits</u> anticlockwise of the Ka'aba, touching the stone if possible — this ritual is called the <u>tawaf</u>.

5) Next, a pilgrim must make <u>seven journeys</u> between the hills of <u>Safa</u> and <u>Marwa</u> (where Hajar, Ibrahim's wife and servant, searched for water for their son <u>Isma'il</u>). This part of the pilgrimage is called the <u>sa'y</u>. Pilgrims then draw <u>water</u> from the <u>Zamzam Well</u>, which <u>Allah</u> made for Hajar.

6) Then pilgrims go to <u>Mount Arafat</u> to <u>stand</u> and <u>pray</u> for Allah's <u>forgiveness</u>. This is where Muslims believe <u>Adam</u> was <u>forgiven</u> after being <u>thrown out</u> of Eden and also where the <u>Day of Judgement</u> will take place.

7) The pilgrims spend the night at <u>Muzdalifa</u>, a valley between <u>Arafat</u> and <u>Mina</u>, where they collect <u>pebbles</u>.

8) The <u>pebbles</u> are then thrown at three <u>pillars</u> in <u>Mina</u>, to symbolise driving the <u>devil</u> away — <u>Ibrahim</u> is believed to have once thrown stones at <u>Shaytan</u> (the devil). This happens on <u>Id ul-Adha</u> (see p.24).

9) The title '<u>hajji</u>' is given to those who <u>complete</u> the hajj. Many find the <u>hajj</u> helps their <u>faith</u> and increases <u>unity</u> between Muslims. Some <u>hadith</u> say it cleanses the hajji of <u>all sins</u>, e.g. Sahih al-Bukhari 26:596: "he will return (after Hajj free from all sins) as if he were born anew".

There are Two Kinds of Jihad

<u>Jihad</u> means '<u>striving</u>' or '<u>struggle</u>' and is often <u>misunderstood</u> by non-Muslims. It's one of the <u>Ten Obligatory Acts</u> for <u>Shi'as</u> (see p.21) but it's part of <u>Sunni</u> Islam too. Most Muslims believe there are <u>two kinds</u>:

The Greater Jihad

1) This is every Muslim's struggle to <u>obey</u> Allah, <u>follow</u> his teachings and become a <u>better</u> Muslim.

2) It's the <u>greater struggle</u> because it's <u>individual</u> and <u>personal</u>. Qur'an 35:18 says "no bearer of burdens will bear the burden of another" (burdens mean sins), so you and you alone will be held <u>responsible</u> for your <u>behaviour</u>. If you're not a good Muslim, it's <u>harder</u> to help make the world better (<u>lesser jihad</u>).

The Lesser Jihad

See p.67 for the <u>requirements</u> for declaring <u>military jihad</u>.

1) This is the <u>struggle</u> to make the world a <u>better place</u>. Part of this means struggling against wrongs such as <u>poverty</u> and <u>injustice</u>.

2) Part of it is the struggle to <u>defend Islam</u> against threats. It can be in <u>peaceful</u> ways, such as helping others be good Muslims.

When Islam began, Muslims fought to survive as people of other religions persecuted them. The Qur'an reflects this struggle, which is why it refers to defending Islam against its enemies.

3) The <u>Qur'an</u> and Islamic law say that actual fighting should only be in <u>self-defence</u> and <u>not</u> against people who <u>aren't fighting</u> (<u>non-combatants</u>) — "Permission [to fight] has been given to those who are being fought" (Qur'an 22:39). Qur'an 4:75 says Muslims should fight on behalf of people being <u>oppressed</u>.

4) <u>Islamic terrorists</u> claim the Qur'an supports <u>violence</u> to <u>defend</u> Islam against <u>oppression</u>, e.g. Qur'an 2:193 says "...if they cease, then there is to be no aggression <u>except</u> against the <u>oppressors</u>". The <u>vast majority</u> of Muslims <u>condemn</u> this and think that Islamic terrorists aren't <u>true Muslims</u>.

And that's the last of the duties...

You might see some of the Arabic words spelt slightly differently, e.g. zakat rather than zakah or Eid al-Adha rather than Id ul-Adha. Make sure you always stick to one spelling in the exam.

Islam	Festivals

Id ul-Adha is Important to Sunnis and Shi'as

1) Id ul-Adha is a festival celebrating complete obedience to Allah, as it commemorates the time when Ibrahim nearly sacrificed his own son, Isma'il. It's a very important festival and it forms part of the hajj.

2) Ibrahim dreamt that Allah told him to sacrifice Isma'il. He told Isma'il about it and Isma'il agreed it had to be done. But at the last minute, Allah told Ibrahim to sacrifice a ram in place of Isma'il, so Isma'il survived. It was a test of Ibrahim's loyalty to Allah.

" '...my son, indeed I have seen in a dream that I [must] sacrifice you ...' He said, 'O my father, do as you are commanded.' " Qur'an 37:102

3) Muslims should attend mosque on Id ul-Adha — the service includes communal prayers and a sermon focused on the importance of obedience to Allah and the lessons to be learnt from Ibrahim and Isma'il.

4) Id ul-Adha is a time of communal joy and festivity lasting up to four days. Muslims dress up in their best clothes and spend time with family and friends. Presents are often exchanged. An animal is often sacrificed — the family keeps a third, a third goes to relatives or neighbours and a third to the poor.

Id ul-Fitr Marks the End of Ramadan

Id ul-Fitr is important to Sunnis and Shi'as.

1) Id ul-Fitr is at the end of Ramadan (see p.22). It's a day of thanksgiving to Allah for giving Muslims the strength to fast for a month. It's a joyful festival which also celebrates the fact that Muslims have completed the fourth pillar of Islam by observing sawm, and therefore have become closer to Allah.

2) Muslims pay a special zakah for Id ul-Fitr. About £5, it helps Muslims who are less well off to celebrate.

3) The festival involves a service at the mosque or outdoors, and a meal to break the fast. It's a time of celebration, when family and friends meet up and presents are exchanged. Thousands attend celebrations of Id ul-Adha and Id ul-Fitr in the UK — many find it important for community cohesion between Muslims and with those of other faiths.

Id ul-Ghadeer is Important for Shi'a Muslims

Sunnis don't celebrate Id ul-Ghadeer.

1) Id ul-Ghadeer commemorates a speech, recorded in hadith, which Muhammad made after his final hajj. Shi'as believe he said Ali should be the next Muslim leader after his death — he used a word for 'master'. Sunnis think Muhammad was just saying Ali should be respected, as the word also means 'trusted friend'.

2) After the speech, it's believed Qur'an 5:3 was revealed: "This day I have perfected for you your religion".

3) Shi'as venerate Ali and celebrate the festival as the day he was chosen as leader. Shi'as fast, have a ritual bath and say prayers, including the Du'a Nudba. They reaffirm their commitment to Islam with a vow.

Ashura Commemorates the Death of Husayn

1) Ashura is mostly a Shi'a festival, but it was originally a compulsory day of fasting for all Muslims. When Muhammad said Muslims should observe sawm during Ramadan, fasting on Ashura became voluntary.

2) Sunnis now tend to think of it as a day of atonement. Many Sunnis fast, but it's not compulsory. It's believed that fasting may absolve people of their minor sins in the previous year.

3) It's significant for Shi'as as the day Husayn, Ali's son and Muhammad's grandson (see p.16), was killed in a battle. The ten days up to and including Ashura (Ashura is the tenth day) are a period of mourning.

4) On Ashura, Shi'as wear black as a sign of mourning. There are often public processions and 'passion plays', in which the story of Husayn is performed. Poems or stories about Husayn are often read out.

5) Some Shi'as hurt themselves to commemorate Husayn's suffering. This is banned in some countries.

6) For Shi'as, Ashura is a reminder of the suffering the Shi'a community has experienced — Shi'as have been persecuted as a minority. The processions are sometimes used as protests against injustice.

Feeling festive? Celebrate with an exam-style question...

Explain two ways in which Muslims celebrate Id ul-Fitr. [4]

EXAM QUESTION

Revision Summary

There was a lot in that section, so now it's your chance to find out how much you remember. These are exam-style questions, so you can get an idea of how long and detailed your answers have to be.

If you're stuck on anything, go back to the relevant page in the section and then try the question again. There are extra marks for spelling, punctuation, grammar and use of specialist terminology available in some questions, so make sure you check your writing and use technical jargon where appropriate.

We'll start off with some straightforward 1 mark multiple choice questions.

1) Which of the following is the concept of messengership?
   a) Nubuwwah   b) Risalah   c) Hadith   d) Prophets

2) Which of the following describes the way of life set out by Muhammad?
   a) Qur'an   b) Hadith   c) Salah   d) Sunnah

3) Which of the following is the obligation to fast during Ramadan?
   a) Sawm   b) Salah   c) Shahadah   d) Zakah

Now for some 2 mark questions. Two brief points are all you need.

4) Give two of the 'Usul ad-Din.

5) Name two of the prophets, other than Muhammad.

6) Give two exceptions to the obligation to fast during Ramadan.

These questions are worth 3 marks. You need to make three brief points in your answer.

7) Outline three features of the rituals that are part of salah.

8) Outline three beliefs about jihad.

These are 4 mark questions. To get full marks, you need to develop the points you make.

9) Explain two ways in which belief in Muhammad might influence Muslims today.

10) Explain two Muslim beliefs about angels.

11) Explain two contrasting understandings of Ashura.

Your points need to be nice and clear in the longer answer questions. This means you need to make sure your writing is well organised.

These questions are worth 5 marks, so you need to develop and explain your answer. You also need to refer to Muslim teachings in your answer.

12) Explain two Muslim beliefs about the Qur'an.

13) Explain two Muslim teachings about judgement.

14) Explain two reasons why performing hajj is important for Muslims.

Up to 6 marks now. You'll need to analyse as well as state your knowledge for full marks.

15) Explain why Laylat al-Qadr is important for Muslims.

And the big one — this is a 12 mark question (with extra marks for SPaG and specialist terminology). Use the bullet point list below to help you plan your answer — the list gives you the things you need to include. Remember, you'll need to make sure you've covered arguments for and against the statement.

16) 'The most important thing a Muslim can do is pray five times a day.'
   Evaluate this statement. Your answer should include the following:
   • examples from Islamic teachings
   • arguments that support and disagree with the statement
   • a conclusion.

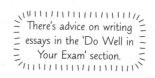

There's advice on writing essays in the 'Do Well in Your Exam' section.

Section 2 — Islam

| Judaism | **Introduction to Judaism** |

There are different branches of Judaism, but all Jews believe in one God and follow the Torah as a sacred text.

The Tenakh and the Talmud are the Jewish Sacred Texts

1) The **Tenakh** is the main sacred Jewish text. It's basically the same as the Christian Old Testament, except it's in a different order. The word 'TeNaKh' will help you remember what's in it.

T = Torah (Instructions / Law / Teachings)

The Torah is made up of Genesis, Exodus, Leviticus, Numbers and Deuteronomy.

The Torah is the first five books of the Old Testament. It's seen as the holiest part of the Tenakh — God gave it to Moses. It contains the mitzvot (commandments, see p.28) which Jews are meant to follow. 'Torah' can refer to all Jewish teachings, or to the whole Tenakh, as well as this first part of the Tenakh.

N = Nevi'im (Prophets)

The prophets are believed to have been inspired by God.

This is a collection of books, divided into two parts. The Former Prophets trace the history of the Israelites (ancestors of the Jews) after the death of Moses. The Latter Prophets contain the words of 15 prophets such as Isaiah, Jeremiah and Ezekiel. They encourage Jews to obey God and follow the Torah.

K = Ketuvim (Writings)

This part of the Tenakh is less authoritative than the others.

Among other things, this contains the 'three Ps': Psalms (hymns), Proverbs, and Philosophy.

2) The **Talmud** is a collection of teachings and a record of originally spoken discussions between Torah scholars. It's made up of two parts — the Mishnah, which explains how the mitzvot in the Torah should be applied, and the Gemara, which discusses the Mishnah. It stresses the importance of the Torah:

> "If you have learned much Torah, do not take credit ... — it is for this that you have been formed." Pirkei Avot 2:8

There are Different Branches of Judaism

Orthodox Judaism

1) Orthodox Jews believe that the Torah and Talmud are of divine origin (they come from God). They should be followed to the letter — their teachings should not be changed to adapt to life today.

2) They strictly observe Shabbat (day of rest, see p.31-32), and kashrut (dietary laws, see p.32).

Progressive Judaism

1) Progressive Jews believe the Torah and Talmud are people's interpretation of God's word. They see Judaism as a developing religion, so they apply the sacred texts to modern life in a more flexible way.

2) They tend to follow the mitzvot about morality (see p.28). However, they believe the ritual commandments, e.g. dietary laws, can be adapted or abandoned in response to changes in society.

3) There are two main movements of Progressive Jews:

Reform Judaism	Liberal Judaism
• This is a mix of new and old traditions, e.g. Reform Jews have a Shabbat service but at a different time to Orthodox Jews (p.31). • A key difference from Orthodox Judaism is that women and men are completely equal. Men and women sit together in services and there are male and female rabbis (religious leaders).	• Liberal Judaism formed from Reform Judaism — it's similar to but more radical than Reform. It has a similar emphasis on treating everyone equally. • It teaches that observing any of the mitzvot is a matter of carefully considered personal choice.

Masorti (Conservative) Jews follow Jewish law like Orthodox Jews, but with a more liberal interpretation.

Remember, the word 'Torah' can be used in different ways...

Make sure it's clear which way you're using it in the exam, so the examiner doesn't get confused.

Key Beliefs in Judaism

Jews believe they have a special relationship with God, as his chosen people.

Jews Believe God has Certain Characteristics

Some write 'G-d' to stop the word 'God' being accidentally erased or damaged. God is sometimes called 'the Almighty'.

Although there are different strands of Judaism (see p.26), nearly all Jews believe that God is...

1) ONE — Judaism is a monotheistic religion — Jews believe there's only one God. They believe God is one entity — they don't believe God has different parts, as most Christians do (p.2).

2) ETERNAL — Jews believe God has and always will exist.

3) THE CREATOR — He made everything in the universe. His role as creator is described in Genesis 1 and 2.

4) OMNIPOTENT — God is all-powerful — although he still allows each person free will.

5) OMNISCIENT — God knows everything, even people's thoughts.

6) OMNIBENEVOLENT — God is all-good — he can do no evil.

> "The Lord is good to all; he has compassion on all he has made." Psalm 145:9 NIV

7) OMNIPRESENT — God is everywhere at all times. He's beyond time and space.

8) THE LAWGIVER — Jews believe they should obey God's laws as part of the covenant (see below).

9) THE JUDGE — Jews believe their behaviour will be judged by God after they die (see p.29). However, they believe he is just and merciful. He will save his people from sin and suffering.

10) TRANSCENDENT — God is beyond this world. His existence doesn't rely on the universe.

11) IMMANENT — But God is present in the world and sustains it — see the concept of Shekhinah below.

Shekhinah is God's Presence on Earth

> "The glory of the Lord filled the temple." 2 Chronicles 7:1

1) The word Shekhinah is used to refer to God when he is present in a particular place on Earth.

2) The term is used to describe God's presence in the tabernacle (a portable place of worship used by Moses — p.28) and the Temple Jews built in Jerusalem. Many Jews pray at the remaining part of the Temple walls in Jerusalem (the Western Wall) as they believe that Shekhinah is still present there.

3) Some Jews believe that Shekhinah is present when they're praying together or discussing the Torah.

4) Shekhinah is often seen as feminine, and has 'feminine' characteristics, such as being caring.

5) The concept of Shekhinah helps Jews understand suffering, as it means God is there alongside them.

Jews Believe in a Covenant Between Them and God

A covenant is a formal agreement between two or more people. God made a covenant with the Jews which defines them as his chosen people.

1) The first covenant was between God and Abraham. Abraham was the first of the founders of Judaism. Jews call him Avraham Avinu ('our father Abraham').

2) God told Abraham to leave his home and go to Canaan (the 'Promised Land').

3) God promised to give Abraham and his wife Sarah a child, and to protect them and their descendants as his chosen people. In return, God asked Abraham and his descendants (known as the Israelites) to obey God and lead by example.

> "The whole land of Canaan ... I will give as an everlasting possession to you and your descendants ... and I will be their God." Genesis 17:8 NIV

4) He asked for all of their male descendants to be circumcised as a sign of this covenant (see p.32).

Israel, in the Middle East, is a state that was founded in 1948 in roughly the same area as Canaan had been. Many Jews see the state of Israel as the fulfilment of the promise of the Promised Land. However, some Orthodox Jews believe that Jews shouldn't have created the state themselves — they should have waited for God's action. Many Progressive Jews only became supportive of the formation of a Jewish state after the Holocaust, in which 6 million Jews were killed by the Nazis.

Make sure you learn how to spell the 'omni-' words correctly.

Shut this book and see if you can write down the characteristics of God listed above, as well as what they mean — you'll only be able to use them correctly in the exam if you understand them.

Key Beliefs in Judaism

God also made a Covenant with Moses

1) <u>Moses</u> was also a <u>founder</u> of Judaism. He led the Jews back to <u>freedom</u> in <u>Canaan</u> after they'd been <u>slaves</u> in Egypt for 400 years (they'd had to leave Canaan due to a famine). This was called the <u>Exodus</u>.

2) On the way back, God made a <u>covenant</u> with Moses at <u>Mount Sinai</u>, setting out in detail what the Israelites had to <u>do</u> in <u>return</u> for being God's <u>chosen people</u>.

> "Now if you obey me fully and keep my covenant, then out of all nations you will be my treasured possession."
> Exodus 19:5 NIV

3) God gave the <u>Torah</u> to Moses. This included the mitzvot — the <u>Ten Commandments</u> plus many other laws. The Ten Commandments (the <u>Decalogue</u>) were written separately on <u>stone tablets</u>. Moses was also given an <u>explanation</u> of the <u>Torah</u>, known as the <u>oral Torah</u>, which was eventually <u>written down</u> in the <u>Mishnah</u> (p.26).

4) The Israelites <u>promised</u> to "do everything the Lord has said" (Exodus 19:8 NIV).

5) <u>Orthodox</u> Jews believe the <u>Torah</u> came directly from God, but <u>Progressive</u> Jews believe the Torah is people's <u>interpretation</u> of God's word — they think it was written by <u>people</u> rather than <u>God</u>.

The Mitzvot are Jewish Laws

The singular form of mitzvot is <u>mitzvah</u>. It's sometimes translated as a '<u>good deed</u>'.

1) The <u>613 mitzvot</u> cover a variety of issues, including <u>food</u>, how to <u>worship God</u> and how to help the <u>poor</u>.

2) They were taken from the Torah by scholars, who made slightly different lists of them. The <u>standard</u> list was compiled by <u>Maimonides</u> in his <u>Mishneh Torah</u>. The mitzvot can be <u>divided</u> up in different ways:

- <u>248</u> of the mitzvot are <u>positive</u>, telling Jews what they should do. They're called <u>mitzvot aseh</u> in Hebrew.
- <u>365</u> mitzvot are <u>negative</u>, telling Jews what they shouldn't do. They're known as <u>mitzvot ta'aseh</u>.

- <u>Ritual</u> mitzvot list things Jews must or must not do to avoid offending God — they are between <u>a person</u> and <u>God</u>.
- <u>Moral</u> (ethical) mitzvot are about a Jew's dealings with <u>other people</u> — they are between <u>one person</u> and <u>another</u>.

3) The <u>Ten Commandments</u> are <u>important</u> mitzvot. The <u>first</u> is the central belief of Judaism (see p.31).

1. I am the Lord your God.
2. You shall have no other gods before me. You shall not make for yourself an image... [or] bow down to them or worship them.

   <u>Don't worship</u> <u>idols</u> (objects or pictures of God).

3. You shall not misuse the name of the Lord your God.
4. Remember the Sabbath day by keeping it holy.
5. Honour your father and your mother.
6. You shall not murder.
7. You shall not commit adultery.
8. You shall not steal.

   This means <u>don't lie</u> about <u>other people</u>.

9. You shall not give false testimony against your neighbour.
10. You shall not covet.

   Exodus 20:2-17 NIV

This means <u>don't be jealous</u> of what <u>other people</u> have.

4) Jews believe that humans have <u>free will</u>, so they're <u>responsible</u> for following the mitzvot. This means they can be <u>judged</u> on their actions by God. He will <u>forgive</u> someone who's <u>sorry</u> for their sins though.

5) Orthodox Jews <u>follow</u> the mitzvot <u>closely</u>. They try to go <u>further</u> than the mitzvot, so they don't <u>break</u> one by accident. Progressive Jews follow the mitzvot <u>less strictly</u> (see p.26). Some mitzvot can't be obeyed as they refer to the <u>Temple</u>, which no longer exists, but following as many as possible is a <u>key part</u> of many Jews' <u>relationship with God</u>. Doing so <u>unites</u> Jews and gives them an <u>identity</u> as <u>God's people</u>.

There are Other Important Principles

> "Every danger to human life suspends the [laws of the] Sabbath." Talmud Yoma 83a

1) <u>Pikuach nefesh</u> (saving a life) is <u>more important</u> than any mitzvot, except commandments 1, 2, 6 and 7. It follows the belief in the <u>sanctity of life</u> — life being <u>holy</u> because it's given by <u>God</u>. For example, a doctor can <u>break Shabbat</u> to <u>save</u> someone's <u>life</u>. Their life doesn't have to be in <u>immediate danger</u> — the action can be <u>preventative</u>. See p.50, 52 and 68 for more.

2) Jews believe people are the Earth's <u>custodians</u> — they have a <u>responsibility</u> to <u>look after</u> the world. This includes the idea of <u>tikkun olam</u> ('mending the world') — acting <u>morally</u> to improve life on Earth.

3) <u>Justice</u>, <u>charity</u> and <u>kindness</u> are important morals included in some <u>mitzvot</u>. <u>Gemilut hasadim</u> (acts of loving kindness) is a central principle of Judaism. The concept of <u>tzedakah</u> (charity) is also important — it should be given to make the world more <u>just</u>, so it's an <u>obligation</u> rather than a <u>choice</u>.

Key Beliefs in Judaism

Judaism focuses on this life rather than the afterlife. There are different ideas about what happens after death.

Jews have Different Beliefs about the Afterlife

1) The Torah focuses more on life on Earth than on an afterlife — Jews are encouraged to lead good lives for the sake of life on Earth, rather than the hope of what's to come.

2) The Tenakh talks about Sheol, where the souls of the dead live as shadows for eternity.

3) But ideas about the afterlife gradually developed — beliefs are now largely based on ideas in the Talmud.

   - Many Jews believe life after death is spent in Gan Eden ('Garden of Eden' or Paradise) and/or Gehinnom.
   - Some see Gan Eden as a place of banquets and sunshine. Others have a more spiritual view of it as a closeness to God. Only if you've lived a blameless life will you be sent straight to Gan Eden when you die.
   - Most souls go to Gehinnom before they reach Gan Eden. Some see it as a place of torment, where people are punished. Some see it as a place for purification, where people are shown the wrong they did in this life. The truly wicked don't move on — some think they're tormented forever, others that their souls are destroyed.

4) God judges how good or evil people have been, to decide their fate in the afterlife. Some Jews see this as a motivation for good behaviour in this life, others argue that you should do good things simply because they are good.

> "God will bring every deed into judgment ... whether it is good or evil." Ecclesiastes 12:14 NIV

5) Some Progressive Jews don't believe in the afterlife, as it's not explicitly mentioned in the Torah. Others believe we live on in how we've influenced others during our lives.

6) The term olam ha-ba (the world to come) is also used for the afterlife. It's sometimes used to refer to the Messianic Age (see below), rather than where souls go straight after death.

7) Many Jews also believe they will eventually be physically resurrected — see below. Belief in resurrection is important in Judaism. Maimonides listed it as one of his 13 principles of faith.

A Messiah will bring Peace on Earth

'Messiah' comes from the Hebrew 'mashiach' which means 'anointed one' — someone who is chosen to rule.

1) Many Jews believe that the Messiah, an inspirational leader, will bring an era of perfect peace and prosperity called the Messianic Age. He'll establish God's kingdom on Earth and everyone will acknowledge God. (Unlike Christians, Jews don't believe that Jesus was the Messiah.)

2) Jews believe that the Messiah will be human — not divine (god-like) as Jesus is for Christians (see p.2). He'll be a male descendant of the Jewish king David and will himself be "a King who will reign wisely and do what is just and right" (Jeremiah 23:5 NIV). He will spread God's laws throughout the world, reunite the Jewish people in Israel (the Promised Land) and rebuild the Temple there.

3) It is thought that the prophet Elijah will appear just before the Messiah comes.

4) It's believed that people will be judged by God and the Messiah on their actions. Some Jews believe everyone will be resurrected so they can be judged. Others think only the righteous will be resurrected to share in the Messianic Age.

> "Multitudes who sleep in the dust of the earth will awake: some to everlasting life, others to shame and everlasting contempt." Daniel 12:2 NIV

   - Orthodox Jews believe that the physical body will be resurrected, intact, in the Messianic Age. Because of this, the body shouldn't be cut after death (autopsies are frowned upon) and cremation is forbidden. A Jewish cemetery is called the 'House of Life' (Bet ha-Chaim), which reaffirms the view that the body will be resurrected.
   - Progressive Jews believe that the body is simply a vessel for the soul (which they believe carries on without the body), and reject the idea of physical resurrection. So Progressive Jews accept cremation and organ donation.

5) Not all Jews believe a Messiah will come though. Many Progressive Jews believe instead that people themselves can bring about a peaceful and prosperous age on Earth through their own good actions.

Make sure you revise this page — or I will judge you...

Have a go at this exam-style question using what you've learnt on this page.

Explain two Jewish teachings about life after death. Refer to sacred texts in your answer. [5]

Judaism	**Worship**

A Jewish place of worship is called a <u>synagogue</u>. The word means '<u>assembly</u>' or '<u>coming together</u>'. Jews sometimes call it a '<u>shul</u>' instead.

All Synagogues have the Same Four Features

There are <u>no rules</u> stating what a synagogue should look like on the <u>outside</u>.

1) The <u>layout</u> of the <u>main (prayer) hall</u> commemorates some aspects of the <u>Temple</u> in <u>Jerusalem</u>, which was the <u>centre of Jewish worship</u> before it was <u>destroyed</u> in 70 CE. All synagogues have these <u>four</u> features:

Aron Hakodesh (the Ark) a large <u>cupboard</u> or <u>alcove</u> with <u>doors</u> or a <u>screen</u>, on the <u>wall facing Jerusalem</u>. It's the <u>centrepiece</u> of the synagogue — it holds the <u>Torah</u> (see p.26) and <u>symbolises</u> the <u>ark</u> (box) that held the tablets God gave to Moses. Often, a copy of the <u>10 commandments</u> is hung above the ark.

Sefer Torah (Scroll of the Torah) a parchment <u>scroll</u> kept <u>inside</u> the <u>ark</u>. It must be <u>handwritten</u> by a <u>sofer</u> (scribe). It's usually covered with a <u>mantle</u> (cloth), or sometimes by a <u>case</u>, which is <u>ornately decorated</u>.

Ner Tamid (Perpetual Light) a <u>light</u> above the ark which <u>never</u> goes out. It represents the <u>menorah</u> (see below) which was <u>always alight</u> in the Temple.

"...keep the lamps burning before the Lord..." Exodus 27:21 NIV

Bimah or Almemar a <u>raised platform</u> with a <u>reading desk</u>. <u>Orthodox</u> synagogues usually have it in the <u>centre</u>, while <u>Progressive</u> ones often have it <u>close</u> to the <u>ark</u>. It represents the <u>altar</u> in the Temple.

2) There are <u>no pictures</u> of <u>God</u> or <u>people</u> in a synagogue. This is because the <u>second</u> of the Ten Commandments (see p.28) forbids <u>idolatry</u> (worshipping pictures or objects).

3) Some synagogues also have a <u>menorah</u> — a <u>seven-branched</u> candlestick.

4) <u>Orthodox synagogues</u> have <u>separate sections</u> for <u>women</u>. <u>Progressive</u> synagogues have <u>mixed</u> seating.

5) Synagogues are not only used for <u>worship</u> but are <u>important centres</u> for the Jewish <u>community</u> — they are used as <u>meeting places</u> for <u>study groups</u> and <u>social clubs</u>.

There are Three Daily Services

1) The <u>Tenakh</u> shows it's <u>important</u> to worship God <u>together</u> — for example, Psalm 116:14 NIV says "I will fulfil my vows to the Lord in the presence of all his people", i.e. in the presence of <u>other Jews</u>.

2) Attending <u>synagogue</u> can remind Jews of the <u>importance</u> of their <u>faith</u> and of their <u>closeness</u> to God. Some Jews believe <u>God</u> (<u>Shekhinah</u>, see p.27) is <u>present</u> when Jews worship <u>together</u>.

3) <u>Orthodox</u> synagogues hold services <u>three times a day</u> — <u>shacharit</u> (the <u>morning</u> service), <u>minchah</u> (<u>afternoon</u>) and <u>ma'ariv</u> (<u>evening</u>). <u>Minchah</u> is often just <u>before</u> sunset so that <u>ma'ariv</u> can follow <u>straight</u> afterwards (at sunset). <u>Progressive</u> synagogues tend <u>not</u> to have <u>weekday</u> services, although some <u>do</u>.

> <u>Shacharit</u> is the <u>longest</u> service (an <u>hour</u>), while <u>minchah</u> and <u>ma'ariv</u> last about <u>half an hour</u> each. They include <u>blessings</u> (<u>thanks</u> to God), <u>songs of praise</u>, <u>prayers</u> and sometimes a sermon from the rabbi. On <u>Mondays</u>, <u>Thursdays</u>, <u>Shabbat</u> and <u>festivals</u>, <u>shacharit</u> includes a <u>Torah</u> reading (<u>sidrah</u>) and a <u>Nevi'im</u> reading (<u>haftarah</u>).

4) The <u>siddur</u> (<u>prayer book</u>) is used during each service — it sets out the <u>order</u> of the <u>daily prayers</u>.

5) <u>Ten</u> people (known as a <u>minyan</u>) must be <u>present</u> for certain <u>prayers</u> to be said and the <u>Torah</u> to be read. In <u>Orthodox Judaism</u> these must all be <u>men</u>, but in <u>Progressive Judaism</u> they can be <u>women</u> too.

6) <u>Services</u> are often led by a <u>rabbi</u> — a <u>religious leader</u> responsible for <u>teaching</u> and <u>advising</u> the <u>community</u>. But any <u>adult</u> (<u>male</u> in Orthodox Judaism) with enough <u>religious knowledge</u> can do so. A <u>hazzan</u> (cantor — singer) leads the <u>prayers</u>, which are often <u>sung</u> or <u>chanted</u>. They might also lead the <u>service</u>.

7) The hazzan stands at the <u>front</u> of the hall. The <u>hazzan</u> prays in the <u>same direction</u> as everyone else in Orthodox services. If <u>Progressive</u> synagogues have a <u>hazzan</u>, they tend to <u>face</u> the congregation.

8) <u>Progressive</u> Jews pray in <u>unison</u>. <u>Orthodox</u> Jews pray at their <u>own pace</u>, often with varying <u>movements</u>.

9) <u>Orthodox</u> services are in <u>Hebrew</u>, except the sermon — <u>Progressive</u> ones are partly in the local language.

10) <u>Progressive</u> synagogues may have instruments or choirs to <u>accompany singing</u>, but <u>Orthodox</u> ones don't.

11) Jews face <u>Jerusalem</u> during prayer. There are times in prayer, e.g. during the <u>Amidah</u> (p.31), when Jews <u>bend</u> their knees and <u>bow</u> to show <u>respect to God</u>. <u>Orthodox</u> Jews often <u>sway</u> to help them <u>concentrate</u>.

Worship

The Torah is Treated with Great Respect

The Torah can't be touched, so the reader uses a yad (pointer) to keep their place in the text.

1) Members of the congregation can be called to read from the Torah, which is an honour. It's known as aliyah (going up). There's a reader to do it for them if they don't know Hebrew well enough.

2) A Torah extract is read each week, so the whole Torah is read over 1 year (or 3 in Progressive Judaism).

3) During the service, the ark (see p.30) is opened and the Torah is carried through the congregation to the bimah. As it passes them, people will bow to, kiss or touch the Torah with their tallit (see below).

Prayer is Very Important

"Evening, morning and noon I cry out in distress, and he hears my voice." Psalm 55:17 NIV

1) Prayer is a central part of Jews' relationship with God — they believe God listens to their prayers. Prayers can include giving thanks or praise, confessing to sins, or asking God for something.

2) Many Jews pray three times a day even if they don't attend synagogue — it's a mitzvah to do so. They say the same prayers as in the services, but in a reduced form. This includes the Shema and Amidah.

- The Shema is a declaration of faith in only one God. It's in three parts, taken from the Torah (Deuteronomy 6:4-9 and 11:13-21 and Numbers 15:37-41). Jews should say it morning and night. The first sentence of the Shema is said when the Torah is taken from the ark.

"Hear, O Israel: the Lord our God, the Lord is one." Deuteronomy 6:4 NIV

- Many Jews have a copy of the first two parts of the Shema on every doorpost in their house (except the bathroom). It's written on a tiny parchment scroll called a mezuzah.

The Amidah ('standing prayer') is a set of 19 blessings. It begins by praising God, then asks for things such as justice, and ends with thanksgiving and asking for peace. It's said at weekday services — a short version is used for Shabbat and other festivals.

3) Women are traditionally seen as exempt from the mitzvah concerning services and prayer, but as a minimum it's thought they should say the Amidah twice a day. They often pray at home.

4) Full concentration on prayer is vital — it's known as 'kavanah', and without it prayers don't count.

5) Jews can pray spontaneously (make up their own prayers when they want) — this should be in addition to set prayers, which provide a structure for daily prayer. Many Jews say blessings before and after meals.

6) Jewish men often wear special clothing for prayer and worship. Tefillin are two boxes containing Torah passages, worn during shacharit (except on Shabbat and festivals). One is strapped to the upper arm and one to the head, reminding them to serve God with head and heart. A tallit (prayer shawl) is also worn during shacharit — it has fringes (tzitzit) tied in a special way, to remind Jews of the mitzvot.

7) Many men wear a cap called a kippah (yarmulke) as a sign of respect to God. Orthodox men wear them all day — Progressive and Conservative Jews tend to wear them only if praying or at the synagogue.

Shabbat (Sabbath) is Celebrated in the Synagogue

Shabbat is a sign of God's covenant with Jews (Exodus 31:13).

Shabbat is a day of rest to commemorate the seventh day of creation, when God rested after creating the universe. It begins at sunset on Friday and lasts until Saturday evening. It's a time for reflection and worship, away from the stress of daily life. It's also a chance for the community to get together — Shabbat services are well-attended family occasions. The services are similar to the weekday ones, with some additions:

Friday Evening	Saturday Morning	Saturday Afternoon/Evening
Progressive synagogues tend to have this at a set time rather than at sunset. The kiddush (see p.32) is said. Shabbat is welcomed with a set of hymns, psalms and prayers called Kabbalat Shabbat (Welcoming the Sabbath).	The main service of the week. There are Torah and Nevi'im readings, and hymns and prayers about the importance of the Torah. Orthodox Jews have an additional service called musaf afterwards.	The afternoon service includes a reading from the Torah, as well as prayers. It's followed by ma'ariv, which finishes with the havdalah (see p.32) to end Shabbat.

Prayer has to be focused and sincere — like your revision...

Shut the book, and write down as much as you can about the Shema and Amidah. Just testing!

Family Life

The <u>home</u> is also an important place of <u>worship</u> and <u>ritual</u> for Jews — Judaism is a <u>family-focused</u> religion.

Shabbat is Celebrated in the Home

Challot

1) The house is <u>cleaned</u> and <u>tidied</u> before Shabbat. Any <u>food</u> to be eaten on Shabbat is cooked <u>in advance</u>, because no 'work' can be done on Shabbat. 'Work' includes things like <u>cooking</u> or <u>gardening</u>. The Torah lists what 'work' is <u>forbidden</u>, but rabbis have updated it to <u>today's world</u>, e.g. to include <u>driving</u>.

2) A <u>family member</u> (usually <u>female</u>) lights two <u>candles</u> to mark the start of Shabbat. They say a blessing while <u>covering</u> their eyes. They may pass their hands over the candles to <u>welcome</u> Shabbat to the home.

3) At the <u>start</u> of the Shabbat meal, <u>kiddush</u> is said to set the Shabbat apart as <u>holy</u>. It includes reciting Genesis 2:1-3 (in which God rests after creation) and saying a blessing over <u>wine</u> which is then drunk.

4) After kiddush, Jews <u>wash their hands</u> in a set way. <u>Challot</u> are eaten — these are <u>two plaited loaves</u> to commemorate the double portion of '<u>manna</u>' (miraculous food) provided by God the day before each Shabbat during the <u>Exodus</u> (see p.28). A blessing's said over them before they're cut and dipped in salt.

5) <u>Parents</u> (traditionally the <u>father</u>) often <u>bless</u> their <u>children</u>. Shabbat's a key way they <u>learn</u> about Judaism.

6) The <u>havdalah</u> ('division') ceremony marks the <u>end</u> of Shabbat, separating it from the six days ahead. Blessings are said over sweet-smelling <u>spices</u>, a cup of <u>wine</u> and a <u>plaited candle</u> with several wicks.

Many Jews Follow Strict Dietary Laws

You might come across '<u>treif</u>', which is <u>Yiddish</u> for '<u>treifah</u>'.

1) The set of <u>food laws</u> written in the Torah is known as <u>kashrut</u> — have a look at Leviticus 11 and Deuteronomy 14:2-21. Permitted food is called <u>kosher</u> — everything else is <u>treifah</u> ('torn').

2) To be <u>kosher</u>, a mammal must have both <u>cloven</u> (split) hooves and <u>chew cud</u>. Sea creatures with both <u>fins</u> and <u>scales</u> are kosher, but <u>no</u> other seafood is. All <u>poultry</u> is <u>kosher</u>, but some other birds aren't.

3) Animals must be killed by a specially-trained person, with <u>a cut across the throat</u> using a sharp blade. <u>Blood</u> can't be eaten, so it must be drained from meat. <u>Meat</u> and <u>dairy</u> products can't be eaten <u>together</u>.

4) Some foods <u>can't</u> be eaten if they've been cooked only by someone who isn't <u>Jewish</u>.

5) <u>Orthodox</u> Jews keep <u>kashrut</u>. <u>Progressive</u> Judaism leaves it up to the <u>individual</u> — some <u>Progressive</u> Jews only observe <u>some</u> of the laws, or keep kashrut at <u>home</u> but eat <u>non-kosher food</u> elsewhere.

6) Keeping <u>kashrut</u> shows <u>self-control</u> and <u>obedience</u> to God — it's a religious <u>ritual</u> and part of the <u>mitzvot</u>. However, because of <u>pikuach nefesh</u> (p.28), kashrut can be <u>broken</u> if necessary for <u>medical</u> reasons.

Judaism has Rituals to Mark Different Life Stages

There are <u>Jewish rituals</u> to mark different <u>life stages</u>. These tend to <u>vary</u> between different strands of Judaism. This begins from <u>birth</u>, with the <u>brit milah</u> (circumcision) for boys or <u>simchat bat</u> (naming ceremony) for girls.

Brit milah — circumcision

1. Nearly all boys are <u>circumcised</u> (have their foreskin removed), regardless of which strand of Judaism they're born into. Boys <u>don't</u> have to be circumcised to be <u>Jewish</u>, but many people worry that their son will be <u>alienated</u> if he isn't circumcised.

2. It's a sign they belong to the Jewish <u>faith</u> and it's part of the <u>covenant God</u> made with <u>Abraham</u> (p.27) — God asked that "every male among you shall be circumcised" (Genesis 17:10 NIV).

3. It's usually done at home, <u>7</u> days after the baby's born (even if it's <u>Shabbat</u>). If the boy's <u>not healthy</u> enough, it happens <u>later</u>.

4. The <u>circumcision</u> is performed by a <u>mohel</u> (a Jewish person trained to do the procedure). The mohel and the father each say a <u>blessing</u> before it starts.

5. The brit milah is followed by saying the <u>kiddush</u> and giving the boy his <u>Hebrew name</u>. Then there's a <u>celebratory meal</u>.

Simchat bat — naming ceremony

1. This can also be known as the <u>brit bat</u> or the <u>zeved habat</u> (bat means daughter).

2. This developed <u>recently</u> so that there was an equivalent ceremony in the home to <u>welcome</u> the birth of a <u>girl</u>.

3. The ceremonies <u>vary</u> a lot, but they often involve <u>songs</u> of thanks, <u>blessings</u>, a <u>ritual</u> to welcome the girl into the <u>covenant</u> (e.g. lighting candles), an explanation of the <u>choice of names</u>, and the <u>kiddush</u>.

4. <u>Orthodox</u> Jews are less likely to do this. Instead, the girl is given her <u>Hebrew</u> name during a <u>synagogue</u> service. Her father will give a <u>Torah</u> reading.

Family Life

The Bar or Bat Mitzvah is a Coming of Age Ceremony

In <u>Progressive</u> Judaism it's <u>13</u> for <u>both</u> genders.

1) At <u>13</u> a Jewish boy becomes bar mitzvah and at <u>12</u> a girl becomes bat mitzvah — a <u>son</u> or <u>daughter</u> of the <u>commandments</u>. It means they have to <u>fulfil the mitzvot</u> — they're <u>responsible</u> for living in a <u>religious way</u>.

2) They don't have to do anything to <u>become</u> bar or bat mitzvah — it's defined by their <u>age</u> — but there's often a <u>ceremony</u> to celebrate. The <u>ceremony</u> is <u>also known</u> as a <u>bar</u> or <u>bat mitzvah</u>.

3) The ceremony forms part of a <u>synagogue service</u> (often on <u>Shabbat</u>). The young person might lead some of the <u>prayers</u>, read from the <u>Tenakh</u>, give a <u>speech</u> or read some of the <u>blessings</u>. If they give a reading, they prepare for it beforehand by studying the relevant <u>portion</u> and learning to read it in <u>Hebrew</u>.

- In <u>Orthodox Judaism</u>, most <u>girls</u> don't have a bat mitzvah ceremony, as they don't have the same <u>responsibilities</u> towards <u>worship</u> as men (see p.31). There is <u>continuing debate</u> about whether this should change so they're treated <u>equally</u>.
- Instead, Orthodox girls have a <u>bat hayil</u> (daughter of valour) ceremony. It's held after one of the services, and <u>all girls</u> who have turned <u>12</u> in the previous year recite a <u>religious passage</u> or give a <u>speech</u> in front of family and friends.
- Nearly all <u>Progressive</u> Jews have a bar/bat mitzvah — as do <u>Conservative</u> Jews. They tend to be the <u>same</u> for boys and girls.

Marriage is Very Important in Judaism

1) <u>Marriage</u> is <u>important</u> in Judaism, because much of Judaism is focused on <u>family</u> and the <u>home</u>.

2) Marriage ceremonies are in <u>two parts</u>, called the <u>kiddushin</u> (the betrothal) and the <u>nisuin</u> (the wedding).

3) The wedding usually happens in a <u>synagogue</u>. It takes place under a <u>huppah</u> (canopy), which can be a simple <u>tallit</u> (p.31) or more <u>elaborate</u>. The <u>huppah</u> symbolises the <u>home</u> the couple will build together.

4) Firstly, <u>blessings</u> are said over a cup of <u>wine</u>, which the couple drinks, symbolising the <u>life</u> they will <u>share</u>.

5) The <u>groom</u> gives the <u>bride</u> a <u>ring</u> and says the <u>wedding vow</u> — this completes the <u>kiddushin</u>. At <u>Progressive Jewish</u> weddings, <u>both</u> the bride and the groom exchange rings and say the vow.

6) The <u>ketubah</u> (<u>marriage contract</u>) is read out. The <u>traditional</u> ketubah states the bride's <u>right</u> to be <u>cared for</u> by her husband and her <u>entitlements</u> in case of <u>divorce</u> or <u>death</u> (a bit like a <u>prenuptial</u> agreement). Progressive Jews have <u>rewritten</u> the ketubah to be a <u>mutual</u> statement of <u>love</u> and <u>commitment</u>.

7) The <u>nisuin</u> starts with <u>seven blessings</u> (<u>sheva b'rakhot</u>) said over wine, in which God is praised for creating the <u>universe</u> and <u>humanity</u>, and for the gift of <u>children</u>. There are also blessings for <u>Israel</u> and <u>Jerusalem</u>.

8) Finally, a <u>glass</u> is <u>broken</u> by stepping on it. There are various <u>interpretations</u> of this — it's thought to symbolise the <u>destruction of the Temple</u> (see p.30) or <u>emphasise</u> that love needs to be <u>protected</u>.

Jewish Mourning Rituals Allow People Time to Grieve

1) Mourning family members perform <u>kriah</u> — they make a <u>tear</u> in clothing or a ribbon, as a symbol of <u>grief</u>.

2) The <u>funeral service</u> often includes <u>prayers</u>, <u>psalms</u> and a <u>eulogy</u> (a <u>speech</u> praising the dead person).

3) The Kaddish, a prayer <u>praising God</u>, is said so people focus on <u>God</u> at a time they may feel <u>far</u> from him.

4) The seven days following the burial are known as <u>shiva</u>. <u>Close family</u> mourn during this time. <u>Orthodox Jews</u> (and some <u>Progressive</u>) don't leave the <u>house</u>, attend <u>synagogue</u> or <u>work</u> during shiva. Other mourners <u>visit</u> their house to <u>comfort</u> them and to form a <u>minyan</u> (see p.30) for the Kaddish.

5) The loss of a <u>parent</u> is particularly <u>significant</u> in Judaism. If someone has lost a parent they remain in mourning for a <u>whole year</u> — this is known as <u>avelut</u>. During this time, there are some <u>restrictions</u>, e.g. they won't go to parties. They also say the Kaddish <u>every day</u> for <u>11</u> months.

6) The Kaddish is also said on each <u>Yahrzeit</u> (anniversary of the death). On the eve of the Yahrzeit, many light a candle for <u>24 hours</u>. It's a day of <u>remembrance</u>, during which some people <u>fast</u>.

7) <u>Progressive Jews</u> tend to <u>choose</u> which rituals to observe. <u>Orthodox Jews</u> usually observe them <u>all</u>.

There are a fair few Hebrew words on this page...

EXAM TIP

...so make sure you learn to spell them correctly — it could get you marks for SPaG (see p.117-119).

Festivals

There are <u>many festivals</u> in the Jewish calendar. Of these, <u>Rosh Hashanah</u> and <u>Yom Kippur</u> are the most important <u>holy days</u>. They focus on <u>judgement</u> and <u>atonement</u> (making amends for wrongdoing).

The Meaning of Festivals Can Vary for Different People

1) Many members of <u>all</u> branches of Judaism tend to <u>celebrate</u> the <u>festivals</u> and do so in <u>fairly similar ways</u>.

2) They may see the festivals as being <u>important</u> for <u>different reasons</u> though. For some Jews, the <u>social aspects</u> of celebrating festivals in the <u>synagogue</u> may be just as important as the <u>religious ones</u>. Others may focus on the festivals' <u>historical importance</u> as much as their <u>religious significance</u>.

> <u>Pesach</u> (p.35) is a <u>widely celebrated</u> festival in the UK. This may be because it has <u>historical significance</u> for anyone of <u>Jewish descent</u>, regardless of how <u>religious</u> or <u>orthodox</u> they are. It's a good way of introducing <u>children</u> to Jewish <u>history</u> and <u>ritual</u>.

3) Differing beliefs may affect the <u>meaning</u> of the festival. E.g. Shavuot (p.35) celebrates the giving of the <u>Torah</u> — this makes it particularly important to <u>Orthodox</u> Jews, who think God gave it <u>directly</u> to Moses.

Rosh Hashanah is the Jewish New Year

<u>Rosh Hashanah</u> falls in September or October. It's a time for Jews to consider any wrongdoing in the <u>past year</u> and what they intend to do <u>better</u> in the <u>next</u>, in preparation for <u>Yom Kippur</u>.

> <u>Leviticus 23</u> gives <u>advice</u> on the <u>festivals</u> and how Jews should <u>observe</u> them, including <u>Rosh Hashanah</u>: "you are to have a day of sabbath rest, a sacred assembly commemorated with trumpet blasts. Do not do any of your ordinary work" Leviticus 23:24-25 NIV

1) During the <u>last month</u> of the <u>old</u> year and on the day itself, a <u>shofar</u> (ram's horn) is blown. The <u>shofar</u> is a call for <u>repentance</u> (being <u>sorry</u> for the things you've done <u>wrong</u>) and <u>spiritual reawakening</u>.

2) As on <u>Shabbat</u>, <u>no work</u> is done and Jews spend most of the day in the <u>synagogue</u>. <u>Prayers</u> describing God's <u>judgement</u> and his role as '<u>king</u>' are said, as well as ones hoping for <u>forgiveness</u>. The <u>Torah</u> is read.

3) <u>Bread</u> and <u>apples</u> dipped in <u>honey</u> are eaten, to symbolise the hope for a '<u>sweet</u>' (pleasant) year to come.

4) It's thought <u>God</u> writes <u>people's names</u> in certain <u>books</u> on Rosh Hashanah. The <u>truly good</u> go straight into the '<u>Book of Life</u>', but <u>most</u> go in the '<u>intermediate</u>' book (there's a '<u>Book of Death</u>' for the truly <u>evil</u>).

5) Those in the <u>intermediate</u> book can <u>affect</u> whether they'll end up in the Book of Life <u>during</u> the <u>days of awe</u> (the 10 days until Yom Kippur). The decision can be influenced by <u>repentance</u> — also known as <u>teshuva</u>, meaning '<u>turning</u>' back to God. <u>Prayer</u> and <u>good deeds</u> (<u>tzedakah</u>) can also help.

6) The <u>tashlich</u> ('casting away') ceremony takes place — a <u>prayer</u> is said to ask God to <u>remove</u> the <u>sins</u> of his people. The ceremony is carried out next to <u>water</u>, e.g. a river or the sea.

Yom Kippur is a Day of Atonement

Yom Kippur is the <u>holiest</u> day of the year, so <u>no work</u> is done during it. It gives Jews the chance to ask God to <u>forgive</u> the <u>sins</u> they've committed over the <u>past year</u>.

1) It involves <u>fasting</u> for <u>25</u> hours — this helps Jews focus on <u>spiritual</u> rather than <u>physical</u> matters. Washing, bathing, using cosmetics, wearing leather shoes and having sex are all <u>forbidden</u> on Yom Kippur.

2) <u>Worship</u> in the <u>synagogue</u> is <u>central</u> to Yom Kippur. It's a <u>mitzvah</u> to attend <u>all</u> the services:

> - On Yom Kippur eve, the <u>Kol Nidre</u> ('all vows') prayer is said. It <u>cancels</u> all vows between a <u>person</u> and <u>God</u> in the <u>coming year</u>. It <u>releases</u> Jews from a focus on vows they might not keep, so they can concentrate on their <u>true relationship</u> with God.
> - The <u>next day</u> is spent in the synagogue, with readings from the <u>Torah</u> and <u>prayers</u> to <u>confess any sins</u> and <u>show repentance</u>.
> - The day ends with a service called the <u>Neilah</u> ('closing of the gates'), symbolising a final chance to <u>repent</u> as the gates of heaven are about to <u>close</u> and the <u>Book of Life</u> will be <u>sealed</u>. The <u>shofar</u> is then blown to mark the <u>end</u> of Yom Kippur.

Make sure you don't need to atone for a bad mark...

...by learning this page thoroughly. Shut the book, write the headings 'Rosh Hashanah' and 'Yom Kippur', then scribble down as much as you can remember about each.

Festivals

Pesach, Shavuot and Sukkot are known as the 'Pilgrim Festivals', as Jews used to travel to the Temple in Jerusalem to celebrate them. They're also called 'harvest festivals', as they all originally had links with harvest.

Sukkot Comes Five Days After Yom Kippur

A sukkah. →
Sukkot is the plural.

1) Sukkot lasts eight or nine days (see below) and is a festival of rejoicing.

2) During Sukkot, Jews live in a tent-like structure called a sukkah. This is a reminder of how God "made the Israelites live in temporary shelters when [he] brought them out of Egypt" (Leviticus 23:43 NIV). In the UK, Jews may just eat in their sukkah, as the autumn is cold.

3) At home or in synagogue, an etrog and a lulav are waved each morning while blessings are said (Leviticus 23:40). Etrogs are like lemons, and a lulav is made of date palm, willow and myrtle.

4) On the first six days of Sukkot (except Shabbat), Jews circle the bimah (p.30) once, each holding an etrog and lulav. On the seventh day, they do so seven times with the Torah scrolls. Afterwards, they hit the willow against the floor — its falling leaves represent sins being shed.

5) Simchat Torah marks the end of the cycle of Torah readings. The Torah is carried round the bimah seven times and the last and first Torah portions are read. For non-Israeli Orthodox Jews, it's the 9th day of Sukkot. For Israelis and Progressive Jews, it's the 8th day, which is also the festival of Shemini Atzeret. On Shemini Atzeret, Jews pray for rain now harvest is over.

Pesach (Passover) Commemorates the Exodus

Pesach is in March or April.

1) Pesach commemorates the events leading up to the Israelites' escape from slavery in Egypt, as well as the Exodus itself (see p.28). Pesach means 'to spare' or 'to pass over', referring to the night when the angel of death killed the Egyptians' first-born sons, but 'passed over' the Israelites without harming them.

2) It lasts 7 or 8 days. On the first night or first 2 nights, it's celebrated with seder — a service and meal.

3) Each food symbolises a part of the Exodus story, which is retold by the head of the family during seder using a book of ritual called the Haggadah. Exodus 12:3-8 states what food to include in seder.

- Karpas — a vegetable dipped in salt water, to remind Jews of the pain and tears caused by slavery.
- Matzah (unleavened bread) — bread made from flour, water and no yeast, which Jews made for the Exodus. Anything made from grain and water that has 'risen' (fermented) is called 'chametz' and can't be eaten during Pesach.
- Maror (bitter herbs) — a bitter vegetable, usually raw horseradish, is eaten to remind Jews of the bitterness of slavery.
- Baytsah (egg) — the egg's hard-boiled and roasted. It symbolises the sacrifices once offered in the Temple.
- Z'roah (lamb bone) — this isn't eaten (neither is the egg) but it symbolises the lamb sacrificed on the night of the Exodus.

Shavuot Celebrates the Giving of the Torah at Mount Sinai

1) Shavuot takes place fifty days after Pesach and lasts two days (though only one in Israel). It celebrates two events — the start of the harvest, and the Torah being given to the Jews by God.

2) Many Jews stay up the whole of the first night of Shavuot to study and celebrate the Torah.

3) The Ten Commandments are read in the synagogue on the first day. The Ketuvim story of Ruth, a convert to Judaism, is significant to Shavuot — it shows the importance of commitment to the covenant.

4) No one can really agree why, but it's traditional to eat dairy food on Shavuot.

5) Jews decorate their homes and synagogues with flowers and plants as a symbol of the harvest. This is partly to symbolise the way Mount Sinai burst into flower after the Torah was given. It's also because Shavuot used to be the time the Jewish people would bring their wheat and fruit harvests to the Temple.

"Count fifty days ... and then present an offering of new grain to the Lord." Leviticus 23:16 NIV

Harvest the knowledge from this page and learn it...

...sorry. Anyway, moving on, have a go at this exam-style question:

Outline three aspects of Sukkot. [3]

Revision Summary

Right, we've covered an awful lot and it's now time to find out how much of that went in... These questions are similar to the ones you'll get in the exam, so should get you used to how much you're supposed to write.

If there's anything you can't answer, go back through the section and have another go when you've re-read it. For some questions — you'll be told which ones — there are extra marks for spelling, punctuation, grammar and specialist terminology, so check your writing carefully and make sure you've used technical terms.

You'll be eased in gently with 1 mark multiple choice questions.

1) Which of the following is the concept of saving a life?
   a) Gemilut hasadim   b) Ketuvim   c) Menorah   d) Pikuach nefesh

2) Which of the following is the name of the circumcision ceremony?
   a) Brit milah   b) Brit bat   c) Simchat bat   d) Bar mitzvah

2 marks for each of these questions. Two brief points should scoop the marks.

3) Give two qualities which Jews believe describe the nature of God.

4) Give two differences between Orthodox synagogue services and Progressive ones.

5) Give two examples of Jewish mourning rituals.

The clue's in the question here — they're worth 3 marks, so you need to make three brief points.

6) Outline the contents of the three parts of the Tenakh.

7) Outline three features of the Jewish marriage ceremony.

8) Outline three aspects of worship on Yom Kippur.

These are 4 mark questions. To get full marks, you need to make two points and develop them.

9) Explain two contrasting Jewish attitudes towards the Torah.

10) Explain two ways in which the covenant between God and Moses is important for Jews.

11) Explain two ways in which belief in the Messiah is important for Jews today.

5 marks available now. You need to refer to Jewish teachings in your answer.

12) Explain two Jewish teachings about the characteristics of God.

13) Explain two Jewish beliefs about God's covenant with Abraham.

14) Explain two Jewish beliefs about resurrection.

> For the longer answer questions, make sure your writing is accurate and well organised — you want the points you make to be obvious to the examiner.

6 marks up for grabs. You'll need to explain and analyse if you want full marks.

15) Explain why Shabbat is important to Jews.

This is the biggy — worth 12 marks, with extra marks for SPaG and specialist terminology. You'll often get a list of things you must include, so use it to plan your answer before you start writing. Make a list of arguments for and against so you don't miss any out in your answer — you need to include both sides.

16) 'The best way for Jews to build a relationship with God is by saying set daily prayers.'
   Evaluate this statement. Give arguments that support the statement and
   arguments that disagree with the statement. You must include:
   • examples from Jewish teachings
   • different Jewish points of view
   • a conclusion.

> Have a look at the advice on writing essays in the 'Do Well in Your Exam' section.

Sexuality and Sexual Relationships   All religions

While different faiths may have similar views about sex, there's a bigger divide among views on homosexuality.

Islam, Christianity and Judaism have Similar Attitudes to Sex

1) Traditionally, all three religions teach that the only correct context for sexual activity is within marriage — sex outside of it is seen as a sin. This means cohabitation (living together unmarried) isn't approved of.

In Judaism, Maimonides' list of mitzvot says sexual relationships shouldn't happen without a ketubah and kiddushin (p.33) — see Sefer Hamitzvot no. 355.	Qur'an 23:7 states that "whoever seeks beyond [marriage] then those are the transgressors".	The Catechism of the Catholic Church says "Sexuality is ordered to the conjugal love of man and woman" (2360). 'Conjugal' means 'within marriage'. It also says that sex is 'unitive' and 'procreative' — to bring married couples together as one and for having children.

2) Christians, Muslims and Jews are urged to keep sex within marriage for positive reasons as well — marriage is believed to make sex more special. All three religions stress the importance of enjoying sex. The Song of Solomon in the Bible and Ketuvim contains poems celebrating sexual desire and relationships.

3) 'Strict' members of all three faiths think the principle of only having sex within marriage still applies. More liberal members might see this as outdated, although they still tend to see marriage as the ideal.

4) Promiscuity (having multiple sexual partners) is often seen as wrong in all three religions. But many British people think it's acceptable, especially now contraception (see p.38) is widely available — though a large number of sexual partners is seen more negatively.

5) Atheists and humanists tend to accept sex outside of marriage. Humanists accept it as long as it causes no harm to anyone. Generally, sex outside of marriage is considered normal in British society.

Homosexuality is a Disputed Topic

> The first same-sex marriages in the UK took place in 2014 — see p.39-41 for different religions' views.

Homosexuality is attraction to members of the same sex. Heterosexuality is attraction to the opposite sex.

1) Many people in British society consider both heterosexuality and homosexuality to be natural and normal.

2) The Christian, Muslim and Jewish scriptures seem to say that homosexual sex is wrong — though the relevant bits are interpreted differently by some. They only condemn sex between men, not between women, which is hardly mentioned. (Though it's often frowned upon because male homosexuality is.)

> The story of Sodom (see Genesis 19:3-25) is used by Christianity, Islam and Judaism to argue against homosexuality. The city's destroyed after the men in Sodom demand sex with two male angels God sent, which some people use to show that homosexuality's wrong. The angels say God sent them to destroy the city because of sin, so others say he was going to destroy it anyway and it wasn't because the men wanted sex with them.

3) The texts don't condemn people who have homosexual feelings but don't act upon them. This means some people who are homosexual and religious opt for celibacy (they don't have sexual relationships).

4) Some argue that as the scriptures were written in a different cultural context from ours, we can't apply their standards today. Generally, the religions condemn homophobia and they're becoming more accepting of homosexuality, but it isn't seen as ideal and many see homosexual sex as a sin.

The Catechism of the Catholic Church says "Under no circumstances can [homosexual acts] be approved" (2357). It urges homosexual people to stay celibate but says they shouldn't face any discrimination.	The Anglican Church is split on the issue. There are some openly gay clergy in the Church of England, but conservative members don't approve of homosexuality. 1 Corinthians 6:9-10 suggests it's a sin.	Progressive Jews usually accept homosexuality. Homosexual people can become Progressive rabbis. Orthodox Jews tend to be against it — homosexual sex is forbidden in Leviticus 18:22 NIV, which calls it 'detestable'.	Many Muslims think the Qur'an bans homosexuality, due to the Sodom story (e.g. Qur'an 7:81 "you approach men with desire, instead of women ... you are a transgressing people"). Some Muslims disagree and argue that these teachings should be reinterpreted.

Within each religion there are different views...

...e.g. Orthodox and Progressive Jews differ when it comes to homosexuality. You often have to give two views in the exam and you get marks for the level of detail, so learn them well.

All religions	Contraception

Within each religion, views on contraception can vary a lot — some believers accept its use, some don't.

Contraception Prevents a Woman Becoming Pregnant

Using contraception is sometimes called 'family planning'.

1) Contraception is also known as birth control and is used to stop a woman conceiving. It can be temporary (e.g. the contraceptive pill or condoms) or permanent (sterilisation).

2) Most atheists and humanists have no objection to contraception. They think it's better if people only have children if they really want them. Contraception allows people to choose when to have sex, by limiting the risk of pregnancy. Some types also reduce the risk of STIs (sexually transmitted infections).

3) People applying situation ethics look for the most loving option — they would be likely to support contraception if it means only children who will be loved are born, and people are protected from STIs.

4) Some Christians, Muslims and Jews object to forms of contraception that might destroy a fertilised egg, such as the morning after pill — this is because they see it as being the same as abortion (see p.51).

5) Many religious people don't believe in sterilisation, which prevents people ever having children.

Christian Denominations have Different Opinions

1) The Catholic Church says anything 'deliberately contraceptive' is 'intrinsically wrong' (Humanae Vitae 14). Married couples should 'transmit human life' (Catechism of the Catholic Church 2367), i.e. have children.

2) Many individual Roman Catholics disagree with this stance, especially because of concerns about STIs.

3) The Church says contraception may lead to promiscuity (p.37) and sees some methods as abortion. It does allow natural contraception — only having sex at the less fertile times in a woman's menstrual cycle.

4) Other Christian Churches have different views. The Anglican, Methodist and Presbyterian Churches are in favour of contraception, suggesting that it lets parents plan their family in a responsible way.

Orthodox and Progressive Jews tend to have Differing Views

1) Judaism traditionally teaches that a child is a gift from God, and contraception interferes with God's plans to bless couples with children.

"A man shall not abstain from [propagating] the race unless he already has children."
Talmud Yevamot 61b

2) Most Orthodox Jews only accept contraception for compassionate reasons, e.g. if pregnancy could be physically or psychologically harmful to the mother or an existing child.

3) Some find contraception within marriage acceptable if the couple do plan to have children later on.

4) Progressive Jews find contraception more acceptable and leave the decision to each individual.

5) Sex should be as natural as possible so hormonal contraceptives like the pill are generally preferred to barrier methods like condoms. But some agree with barrier methods as a means of preventing STIs.

There are Different Attitudes to Contraception within Islam

1) Some Muslims see contraception as wrong — they might refer to the hadith Sahih al-Bukhari 34:432, which says conception is Allah's will and suggests people shouldn't try to avoid it. Other Muslims believe that another hadith, Sahih al-Bukhari 62:136, supports the use of contraception.

2) It's the right of both husband and wife to try for children, so both partners must agree to contraception.

3) Reasons for using contraception are usually focused on whether another child may cause harm to the mother, any existing children or to the potential child, e.g. if the family can't afford to feed another child.

4) Only 'reversible' methods are allowed, though — sterilisation and vasectomies are usually not accepted.

Remember that religious views focus on marital sex...

Have a go at this exam-style question using the information you've learnt on this page.

Explain two contrasting religious beliefs about contraception.   [4]

Marriage and Divorce

Marriage in the UK — Things have Changed

1) The number of marriages taking place in the UK each year has been decreasing over the last 40 years. People are also tending to get married later in life, and many people have children without being married.

2) Same-sex marriage is legal in England, Scotland and Wales. Many see this as good as it creates equality.

3) Although many non-religious people still see marriage as important, others see it as unnecessary. It's now more common (and acceptable) for people to cohabit (live together) — either before marrying or instead of getting married. Cohabiting couples don't have the same legal rights as married ones though.

4) Divorce is also far more common. Non-religious people often see it as sensible if the couple don't get on, as they'll be happier if they divorce. Some argue parents fighting can harm children more than divorce. People might apply situation ethics (looking for the most loving outcome in each situation) — even if they value marriage highly, they might see divorce as the best option in some situations. However, many religious people see marriage as very important, and try to avoid divorce if at all possible.

Christians think Marriage is Important and Holy

Pope Francis said marriage is 'indispensable' to society (Not Just Good, but Beautiful).

1) The Christian faith values marriage very highly — marriage reflects the union of Jesus with his followers.

2) Marriage is a covenant (contract) between two people to offer love, support and commitment, and to have children. Christians see marriage as sacred — they talk about the 'sanctity of marriage'.

3) Many accept cohabitation, especially as preparation for marriage. Some don't — they disagree with sex outside marriage. The Catholic Church tends to be against it, but Pope Francis has recognised it can be hard for people to marry, e.g. for financial reasons — but they should be encouraged to marry eventually.

4) Faithfulness in marriage is important — adultery is forbidden in the Ten Commandments (Exodus 20:14).

Christians are Divided Over Same-Sex Marriage

1) The decision to legalise same-sex marriage in the UK was criticised by the Catholic Church and the Church of England. Many members of the clergy are against it.

2) But some Church of England clergy hold blessings for same-sex couples after they marry in civil (non-religious) ceremonies.

> "The Church of England affirms, according to our Lord's teaching, that marriage is ... a union... of one man with one woman." Canon B30

3) It's splitting the Anglican Church. Supporters of same-sex marriage say Christians should be loving to all and should support anyone who wants to marry. Those against it say it's a sin. They also think it's wrong because one of the main purposes of marriage is having children.

4) The Catholic Church is more strongly against homosexual relationships and same-sex marriage.

Different Christian Churches have Varying Attitudes to Divorce

1) There are different views about divorce — many think it breaks the sanctity of marriage.

> The Roman Catholic Church says it's impossible to divorce (Catechism of the Catholic Church 2382). Marriage is a sacrament — God made the couple one flesh, which can't be undone. However, a marriage can be annulled (declared void) if the couple never had sex or if a partner didn't consent to or understand the marriage, or refused to have children.

> The Church of England says divorce is possible and accepts that some marriages fail. Divorcees can re-marry in church if they find a minister willing to marry them. Some Church members disagree with this.

> Nonconformist Churches (e.g. Baptists and Methodists) will usually re-marry divorcees, but an individual minister can refuse to do so if it goes against their conscience.

2) Jesus himself was anti-divorce, but in favour of forgiving people's sins.

> Matthew 19:8-9 NIV says divorce and remarriage are only allowed if someone's partner's been unfaithful.

> "A man [and] his wife ... will become one flesh. ... what God has joined together, let no one separate." Mark 10:7-9 NIV

> In John 8:2-11, Jesus forgives a woman who's committed adultery. But he tells her, "Go now and leave your life of sin" (NIV).

3) Some Christians view an unhappy marriage as a waste of two lives, and so see divorce as preferable.

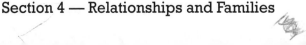

Islam	# Marriage and Divorce

Marriage is very important in Islam — Muslims are advised to marry.

Marriage is Strongly Recommended in Islam

1) Marriage provides companionship, love and stability. Muslims believe marriage is Allah's will — it says in Qur'an 24:32 "marry the unmarried among you" and 30:21 "He created for you ... mates that you may find tranquillity in them; and He placed between you affection...".

2) Islam is family-oriented, so marriage is important. It's a secure environment for having children (procreation). Cohabitation often isn't accepted as it tends to involve sex outside of marriage.

3) According to a hadith, Muhammad said that marriage was half of a Muslim's faith.

4) Qur'an 4:1-24 clearly sets out rules for who people can marry and how much different people inherit.

5) Nikah is the name for marriage under shari'ah — Islamic law. To have the marriage recognised as legal in Britain, couples must also have a civil wedding ceremony.

6) Some Muslims have arranged marriages. This is where the parents will choose a marriage partner for their child. However, both potential partners have the right to say no to marrying their parents' choice.

7) Polygamy is criticised by many Muslims, but others believe the Qur'an allows it. A man should only take multiple wives if he can treat them equally. Some criticise the fact it's only allowed for men. Polygamy is illegal in the UK, but polygamous marriages are accepted if they took place elsewhere.

8) Adultery is a sin — the Qur'an calls it "evil" (Qur'an 17:32). Some Muslim countries punish it severely.

Same-Sex Marriage is a Controversial Topic in Islam

1) Many Muslims are against same-sex marriage as they believe homosexual sex is forbidden by the Qur'an (see p.37). The Muslim Council of Britain spoke against the law legalising same-sex marriage in the UK, arguing it was unnecessary because civil partnerships gave same-sex couples equal rights anyway and that same-sex marriage undermined the definition of marriage as between a man and a woman.

2) Some Muslims see it as wrong because marriage is partly for having children. However, some Muslims do support same-sex marriage. They argue that homosexuality is normal and that it's good for same-sex couples to have the chance to be married, as marriage is important in Islam.

3) Others have argued that, since Muslims are a minority in Britain, they should help out another minority by supporting same-sex marriage, regardless of their individual views on homosexuality.

Divorce is the Last Resort, but it's Accepted

> "Of all the lawful acts the most detestable to Allah is divorce."
> (Sunan Abi Dawud 12:2173)

1) Divorce is permitted, but only as a last resort. If things aren't going well, an arbiter from each family should be appointed to try to sort things out.

2) Muslims see reconciliation as particularly important when the couple have children.

3) Qur'an 2:226-241 lays out the conditions under which divorce can happen. In both Sunni and Shi'a Islam, it's possible for a man to divorce his wife by saying 'I divorce you' three times. Some Sunni Muslims believe all three can be said at the same time, but not everyone agrees with this. In Shi'a Islam, 'I divorce you' must be said once a month for three months, and two people must witness it.

4) Both believe in having an iddah (waiting period, often of three months) to allow time for reflection. The waiting period also ensures the woman is not pregnant.

5) A woman can divorce a man in this way (divorce 'by talaq') if it was written into her marriage contract. Otherwise she has to apply to a shari'ah court for a divorce 'by khul' (if her husband agrees to divorce) or a tafreeq divorce (if the husband doesn't agree). After divorce, men and women are free to re-marry.

6) As Islamic law isn't part of British law, these kinds of divorce dissolve the nikah, but don't count as a legal divorce if the couple also had a civil marriage — they would have to get a civil divorce too.

Phew, what a lot of different opinions...

Summarise Christian or Muslim beliefs and teachings on marriage and divorce in your own words.

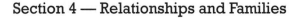

Marriage and Divorce

The family is a <u>key</u> part of the Jewish <u>faith</u>, so <u>marriage</u> is <u>important</u> within Judaism.

Marriage is Important in Judaism

1) To Jews, <u>marriage</u> is an <u>emotional</u>, <u>intellectual</u> and <u>spiritual</u> union. Many see it as the proper context for <u>sex</u> (seen as natural and God-given) and <u>having children</u> (procreation), but it is also for <u>companionship</u>.

2) Marriage is seen as a <u>sacred</u> thing — the word for the first part of the wedding ceremony, <u>kiddushin</u>, means <u>sanctification</u>. God <u>recommends</u> marriage — in Genesis 2:18 he says "It is not good for the man to be alone" (NIV) and then creates Eve to accompany Adam.

> "He who finds a wife finds what is good and receives favour from the Lord." Proverbs 18:22 NIV

3) <u>Adultery</u> is seen as <u>sinful</u>, as it goes <u>against</u> the <u>7th commandment</u> (Exodus 20:14).

4) Marriage and children <u>continue</u> the Jewish <u>faith</u>, as it's passed on through the <u>family</u>.

5) This means there's often some <u>anxiety</u> over '<u>marrying out</u>' — marrying someone who <u>isn't Jewish</u>. Jews who have '<u>intermarried</u>' are <u>less likely</u> to carry on Jewish <u>customs</u> and <u>practices</u>. '<u>Intermarriage</u>' is more <u>accepted</u> than it used to be though.

6) <u>Orthodox</u> Jews don't tend to <u>cohabit</u> because sex outside of marriage is seen as wrong. <u>Progressive</u> Jews see cohabitation in a more <u>positive</u> light, but ideally the relationship should be <u>stable</u> and <u>long-term</u>.

7) Technically, the Torah <u>allows</u> polygamy for <u>men</u> — Abraham had <u>two</u> wives, for example. But almost no Jews today are in <u>polygamous</u> marriages.

Same-Sex Marriage is a Divisive Topic in Judaism

1) <u>Liberal</u> and <u>Reform</u> Judaism both backed same-sex marriage <u>before</u> it became <u>legal</u> in the <u>UK</u>, and <u>both</u> hold same-sex weddings in their <u>synagogues</u> now that it's legal.

2) Jews who <u>support</u> same-sex marriage refer to Genesis 1:27, "God created mankind in his own image" (NIV) — they say being <u>homosexual</u> can't be wrong, as people have been <u>created</u> homosexual.

3) Many <u>Masorti</u> Jews <u>support</u> same-sex marriage. They have created a <u>shutafut</u> (<u>partnership</u>) ceremony for same-sex marriages or civil partnerships — this is different from the traditional <u>kiddushin</u>.

4) <u>Individual rabbis</u> in all <u>3</u> movements can choose <u>not</u> to hold same-sex weddings if they <u>want</u> to though.

5) <u>Orthodox</u> Jews <u>don't</u> tend to support same-sex marriage, believing it goes <u>against</u> the teachings of the <u>Torah</u> on homosexual sex. There's a <u>growing recognition</u> though among some Orthodox Jews that homosexual Jews need to be <u>welcomed</u> in synagogues and <u>supported</u>.

Divorce is Allowed, but it's the Last Resort

1) Jews <u>accept</u> that some marriages don't work out, and that it's <u>better</u> for a couple to <u>divorce</u> than to stay together and be <u>unhappy</u>. But <u>divorce</u> is a last resort after all attempts at <u>reconciliation</u> have <u>failed</u>.

2) The <u>Torah</u> teaches that a husband and wife "become one flesh" (Genesis 2:24 NIV) when they <u>marry</u>, so divorce is <u>difficult</u> and shouldn't be entered into <u>lightly</u>. However, Maimonides' <u>Mishneh Torah</u> (Ishut 24) sets out <u>conditions</u> for when divorce should happen, e.g. if a man knows his wife has committed <u>adultery</u>.

3) Traditionally, a <u>woman cannot</u> initiate divorce. This has caused an issue for <u>Orthodox</u> women who can't get their husband to agree to a divorce, as they <u>can't remarry</u> in a <u>Jewish ceremony</u> without a <u>get</u> (<u>divorce certificate</u> issued by Jewish courts). Women in this situation are known as <u>agunot</u> (<u>chained women</u>). <u>Wives</u> can also <u>refuse consent</u> for a divorce, but this happens <u>less often</u>.

4) <u>Reform</u> synagogues recognise <u>civil divorces</u>, but people may want a <u>religious divorce</u> too. A Reform Jewish court <u>can</u> issue a <u>get</u> even if the husband won't agree. Reform Jews <u>don't need</u> a <u>get</u> to remarry.

There's a lot to take in here...

...so go back over anything you're not sure about. Then test out your new knowledge by jotting down two different Jewish ideas on each of these topics: marriage, same-sex marriage, and divorce.

All religions	**Families**

As the saying goes, 'you can choose your GCSEs, but you can't choose your family'. Or something like that...

Family is Important to Christians, Jews and Muslims

1) Ideally, a stable family can give a child a sense of identity and a feeling of security. They'll learn how to behave, how to give and receive love, and about right and wrong.

2) Many Christians, Jews and Muslims think it's best for a child to have a father and a mother present (ideally the child's biological parents), so that they grow up with one role model of each sex. Ideally, the couple would be married, as it's believed this provides more stability.

3) For religious people, family life can be a way of introducing their children to their faith.

Christianity and Catholic Christianity

- Family life is important for most Christians. It's seen as a way to build a stable society.

- Many Christians believe it's important to have children and educate them in the faith — see for example Catechism of the Catholic Church 2226 and this quote.

> "family is 'the first and vital cell of society'." Pope John Paul II, Familiaris Consortio 42 (Catholic teachings on family)

> "bring [your children] up in the training and instruction of the Lord." Ephesians 6:4 NIV

- This might include activities at home such as reading the child Bible stories, or teaching them about prayer by saying grace (giving thanks) before meals.

- Children become part of the faith at baptism, and this develops as they attend church and prepare for confirmation (see p.9). Many churches provide Sunday schools, which teach Christian ideas through Bible stories. Catholic children attend catechism classes to prepare them for their first confession and communion.

- Festivals such as Christmas and Easter have a strong emphasis on celebration within the family.

- Children are asked to honour their parents — to look after and respect them (Exodus 20:12).

Judaism

- Family life is also very important to Jews, as it's through the family that the Jewish religion and customs are passed on. Children are seen as a divine gift — Psalm 127:3 NIV says "Children are a heritage from the Lord". Orthodox Jews consider anyone whose mother is Jewish to be Jewish — Progressive Jews say the father can 'pass on' Jewishness as well.

- Children should look after their parents — honouring your parents is a mitzvah (Exodus 20:12).

- Many Jewish rituals happen in the home, such as celebrating Shabbat or keeping kashrut (see p.32) so family life is important for educating children about the Jewish faith.

- Rituals like brit milah (male circumcision) and simchat bat (a girl's naming ceremony) connect the child to the faith. Their bar/bat mitzvah ceremony (p.33) requires them to learn about Judaism.

- Talmud Bava Batra 21a explains how teachers were introduced to educate children about the Torah from age 6 or 7. This ensured that knowledge about the Torah was passed from generation to generation. Now, children often attend classes at a heder (a religious school run by the synagogue) to learn Hebrew, and study the Torah and Talmud. This helps them be able to participate in prayers and services.

Islam

- Many Muslims think family life teaches people to be kind, considerate and affectionate. Strong family ties help strengthen the Muslim community — the ummah.

- The Qur'an asks people to care for their parents — "We have enjoined upon man, to his parents, good treatment" (Qur'an 46:15). Muslims place importance on the extended family too.

- Rituals such as aqiqah (a naming ritual) and the bismillah ceremony, which marks the start of the child's religious education, help connect the child to the faith.

- Following Muslim food laws by having halal food in the home helps introduce the child to Islam.

- Mosques often have schools (madrasahs) to teach children about Islam. They learn Arabic so they can read the Qur'an and say prayers. They're also taught from the hadith and sunnah (see p.19).

It's never simple, is it...

Explain why family is important for many religious people.
Include an example from a source of wisdom and authority. [6]

Families

1.8 children is the average...

Family Life in the UK has Changed

1) For a long time, the nuclear family was seen in Britain as the ideal family model. Traditionally, a nuclear family was a married man and woman and their children. Religious families are more likely than the UK average to follow this model.

2) Today, the term may include same-sex parents, unmarried couples, and reconstituted (or blended) families (where divorcees with children find new partners). Single-parent families are more common too.

3) Some people worry about children with same-sex parents, as they'll only have role models from one gender. But many believe same-sex couples can provide a stable, loving home, which is what's important.

4) An extended family includes grandparents etc. They might live together, which is more common as people live longer, house prices rise and parents work. For example, parents, children and grandparents might share a home to save money. The grandparents can be looked after but also help care for the children.

Christians Try to Welcome and Support Different Families

1) Some Christians' views on divorce and homosexuality make it difficult for them to accept certain types of family. The Catholic Church is more strongly against same-sex parenting than many other denominations. But whatever their opinions, many Christians focus on making sure blended families and single or same-sex parents feel welcome in church. They consider it important that the family remains connected to the church, particularly so that any children will still be brought up in a Christian way.

2) Churches try to support families in the local parish (area) in many ways, such as by providing counselling and offering classes to parents to help them raise their child in the Christian faith. Churches also provide support at important times in family life through rites of passage such as baptisms, weddings and funerals.

3) Jesus showed people the importance of children: "Let the little children come to me... for the kingdom of heaven belongs to such as these" (Matthew 19:14 NIV). Churches hold family worship, e.g. where children might take part in a service and the music is enjoyable for children.

4) Catholic churches support families in various ways:

- Pope John Paul II said that Catholics should take "solicitous care to make sure that [divorcees] do not consider themselves as separated from the Church" (Familiaris Consortio 84). However, divorced Catholics aren't allowed to take communion (see p.8), which could mean they feel unwelcome in church.
- Participating in church worship and the sacraments brings families together. The Catechism of the Catholic Church (2226) says that "The parish is the Eucharistic community and the heart of the liturgical life of Christian families".
- The Family Group Movement is a Catholic organisation that brings people of all ages and situations together, united by their beliefs. Members meet up regularly to do activities together and support one another.
- SVP (St Vincent de Paul Society) is a charity which offers support to whoever needs it, including families.

Jewish Views Tend to Vary, but Families are Supported

1) Single parents aren't considered the ideal but many Jews try to make them feel welcome in the community. It can be harder for single parents to have time and money to take a full part in synagogue and Jewish life.

2) It's sometimes more difficult for divorced parents in Orthodox, and especially ultra-Orthodox, communities. Family is so important that divorcees can be seen as going against the faith. Women without a get (see p.41) who have a new relationship might be seen as adulterers, and their children seen as illegitimate.

3) Progressive and Conservative Jews tend to be more accepting of divorcees, blended families and same-sex parents. They focus on each individual being happy.

4) The Jewish community believes it's important to support families:

- Some synagogues hold services with games and songs which allow children to participate. Synagogues might also hold gatherings for families to spend time together, or classes for parents.
- The Jewish community supports families during key moments in life, through rites of passage such as bar and bat mitzvahs, weddings and funerals. Organisations and rabbis offer counselling for, e.g. bereavement.

Families & Gender Equality

Muslim Views are Changing About Families

1) Some Muslims are accepting of divorced people and blended families, while others are less so.

2) Many Muslims would frown upon same-sex parents because they see homosexuality as wrong. Other Muslims believe that, whatever their personal opinion, they should be accepting of same-sex parents because no one is without sin, so they shouldn't judge. Others are in favour of same-sex parents.

3) The extended family is important in Islam, particularly for offering love and support.

4) The ummah can help to support families. The Qur'an teaches that the ummah should be united together in their faith: "And hold firmly to the rope of Allah all together and do not become divided" (Qur'an 3:103). It supports families at important times through rites of passage, such as funerals, and offers counselling.

5) Men and women worship separately. Women may pray at the mosque less often than men, so boys will often go with their fathers. During Id ul-Adha and Id ul-Fitr (p.24), often the entire family worships at the mosque. Some mosques have groups for parents and children, which exposes the children to the faith.

Men and Women Often Have Different Roles in the Family

For all religions, read the rest of this page.

1) Taking care of the family and home has often been seen as the 'woman's role', with the man's role being to earn money to support the family. Having different roles doesn't necessarily mean men and women are unequal, but these fixed ideas make it hard for either gender to do the opposite role. These traditional roles were, and often still are, supported by Christianity, Islam and Judaism (p.45).

2) These fixed roles mean many men don't get the chance to look after and spend time with their children. When a baby is born, the standard paternity leave for men is 2 weeks — many see this as too little. Shared parental leave (SPL) was introduced in the UK in 2015, giving parents the option to share the time allocated to the mother for maternity leave. But very few men have taken SPL so far.

3) Many women find it difficult to return to work after having children — many find their male colleagues have been promoted in the meantime, or they struggle to afford childcare so they can return to work.

Discrimination Based on Gender is Widespread

Religious views on gender roles have shifted over time as well — see p.45.

1) Gender discrimination is a problem in British society, although the situation's gradually improving. Fixed ideas about men's and women's roles are slowly giving way to an acceptance that you shouldn't define people by gender, and that the idea of certain roles is unnecessary and bad for both genders.

2) Gender stereotypes — e.g. women being more emotional or men being more confident — are now seen by many people as false and damaging to both genders. For example, many people think it's bad that men might feel less able to show or express their emotions because it's thought not to be 'manly' to do so.

3) Some people argue there is still a long way to go before women are treated equally to men, e.g. as well below half of MPs are women. Others think the genders are now treated equally. A minority of people argue that it's now men who have it worse, e.g. because women are now more likely to go to university.

There are Problems with Equality in the Workplace

1) Women have always worked, but in the past they were prevented from doing many jobs, by law or by other people. Some had to stop work when they married.

2) Women were often paid less than men for the same job, or only offered jobs with less responsibility and lower pay. This is still the case, but it's less common now because it's been made illegal through various laws, which were brought together in the Equality Act 2010.

3) Despite these laws, there are professions in which one gender is underrepresented. Nursing or midwifery are seen as women's jobs, while building or firefighting are seen as men's. Women are also underrepresented in positions of authority, e.g. as politicians or company directors.

4) Many women still face discrimination at work, such as not being considered for promotion or being sexually harassed, although it's illegal. It can be hard to prove it happened because of their gender — or even to find out it's happening. E.g. it's hard to tell if you're being paid less than someone else in the same job.

Gender Equality All religions

The Bible is a bit Unclear on the Status of Women

1) The Bible gives different messages on the subject of gender discrimination. Some of Jesus's followers were women, e.g. Mary and Martha (Luke 10:38-42), and he treated them equally.

2) Galatians 3:28 says "There is neither ... male [nor] female, for you are all one in Christ Jesus" (NIV). But 1 Timothy 2:12 says: "I do not permit a woman to teach or to assume authority over a man; she must be quiet" (NIV), which suggests that men and women aren't equal.

> For most of Christian history, women weren't allowed to be priests. This is no longer the case — women can now be ministers in most Protestant denominations, and Anglican priests and bishops. But they can't be Roman Catholic or Orthodox priests.

3) The Bible also says wives should do as their husbands tell them. But many Christians say this reflects the ideas of society at the time, and doesn't correspond with Jesus's attitude towards women.

> "Wives, submit ... to your own husbands as you do to the Lord. For the husband is the head of the wife as Christ is the head of the church..." Ephesians 5:22-23 NIV

4) Many Christians now believe men and women should be equal. The Catechism of the Catholic Church 1938 mentions "sinful inequalities" and says Catholics fight against this.

5) Pope John Paul II said "society should create and develop conditions favouring work in the home" for women (Familiaris Consortio 23). Other denominations are less focused on traditional gender roles.

Jewish Men and Women are Often Seen as 'Separate but Equal'

1) Genesis 1:27 ("male and female he created them" NIV) is often used to state that men and women are seen as equals before God, although different, and with different responsibilities.

2) Judaism doesn't suggest that women should not be able to follow their chosen career. However, there is still a belief that motherhood is a privilege, and women should devote some of their life to it.

3) Orthodox Jews aim to uphold Jewish tradition, so are more likely to suggest women stay at home as wives and mothers. Women play an important role in celebrating Shabbat and teaching children about the faith. Many ultra-Orthodox women work at least part-time though, so their husbands can study the Torah.

4) Reform and Liberal Judaism are committed to full gender equality, e.g. they have female rabbis (p.26).

In Islam, Men and Women are Equal but have Different Roles

1) Men and women have an equal obligation to Allah in terms of prayer, fasting, pilgrimage and charity.

> "Indeed, the Muslim men and Muslim women, the believing men and believing women, the obedient men and obedient women ... the charitable men and charitable women, the fasting men and fasting women... and the men who remember Allah often and the women who do so — for them Allah has prepared forgiveness and a great reward." Qur'an 33:35

2) The Prophet Muhammad had several wives. He treated them equally, and told others to treat their wives well, but all his wives were expected to act modestly. His first wife worked before they were married.

3) Some teachings might suggest men are superior, e.g. "Men are in charge of women by [right of] what Allah has given one over the other and what they spend [for maintenance] from their wealth" (Qur'an 4:34). But they're usually taken to mean that men and women have different roles in the community — men are responsible for providing for the family, and women for the home.

4) Many Muslims believe it's OK for women to work. But some believe women should only work if essential or in traditionally female roles, e.g. midwifery. Some see it as a distraction from looking after the family.

5) Wearing modest clothing, often including a head covering, is an important part of Islam for many Muslim women. Many others don't consider it part of their faith. Some people see it as a way of oppressing women and believe Muslim women are forced to wear it. Many Muslim women argue it's their choice, and that any ban on head coverings would be just as oppressive, as it takes away that choice.

Hmmm... it's a tricky issue.

Learn specific examples to give in your answer, such as jobs where women or men are underrepresented.

Revision Summary

You might think you're done with this section... but I'm afraid there are a few questions for you to do first, just to see how much went in. These questions are similar to the questions you'll have in the exam, so you can get used to what you're meant to do and how much you should write.

If you're not sure about any of the answers, have another read of the section and then try again.

For some courses, you need to learn about the views of <u>different religions</u> on these topics. But for other courses, you need to know about them in the context of just <u>one religion</u> — if that's the case for your course, answer each of these questions <u>in the context of the religion you've studied</u>.

Let's start you off gently with 1 mark multiple choice questions.
1) Which of the following describes when an unmarried couple live together?
   a) Sex outside of marriage   b) Cohabitation   c) Heterosexuality   d) Promiscuity
2) Which of the following means preventing pregnancy?
   a) Conception   b) Celibacy   c) Contraception   d) Conscience

Some 2 mark questions now. All you need are two short points.
3) Give two religious beliefs about sexual relationships.
4) Give two religious beliefs about the significance of procreation.

These questions are worth 3 marks, so you need to write down three brief points.
5) Outline three ways in which the religious community supports families.
6) Outline three types of family.
7) Outline three religious beliefs about marriage.

If you want top marks in these 4 mark questions, you'll need to make sure your answers are well-developed.
8) Explain two contrasting religious beliefs in British society today about promiscuity.
9) Explain two ways that children can be introduced to their faith.
10) Explain two religious beliefs about non-traditional families.

And add 1 more — these are worth 5 marks. Your answer should refer to religious teachings or sacred texts.
11) Explain two ways in which religious believers respond to divorce.
12) Explain two religious beliefs about homosexuality.
13) Explain two religious beliefs about gender equality.

For the long answer questions, be sure to write a concise, well-organised answer — make your points clear to the examiner.

And the big one — this is a 12 mark question. There'll be additional marks for SPaG in some essay questions like this. Use the bullet point list below to help you plan your answer — the list gives you the things you need to include. Remember, you'll need to make sure you've covered arguments for and against the statement.

14) 'Marriage is a lifelong union between one man and one woman.'
   Evaluate this statement.
   Your answer should include the following:
   • religious arguments that support the statement
   • religious arguments that disagree with the statement
   • a conclusion
   You can also include non-religious points of view in your answer.

Take a look at the 'Do Well in Your Exam' section — it gives advice on writing essays.

The Origins of the Universe   All religions

No one saw exactly how the Earth came to be like it is... but science and religion both have their theories.

Scientific Arguments — There are Two Main Types

Cosmological Theories — How the Universe Began

Chief amongst these is the Big Bang theory. It says that the Universe began in an explosion of matter and energy. Matter from this explosion eventually formed stars, planets and everything else. The Universe still seems to be expanding — important evidence for this theory.

Evolutionary Theories — How Living Things Changed

Charles Darwin argued that life on Earth originated from simple cells. Life evolved (gradually changed) over millions of years into a huge variety of forms, and those best adapted survived — 'survival of the fittest'. According to this theory, people evolved from apes, not Adam and Eve.

Non-religious people look to science for answers. They believe that the universe and human life came about by chance. They say that since people evolved from apes, they can't have been created by God.

Religions have their own Ideas about all this...

Some religious people believe only in the stories written in scriptures. Others believe that science tells them how the world was created, but religion explains why. They believe that God caused the Big Bang, and evolution is the way he made humans.

Christian Ideas

1) Genesis chapter 1 says God created everything over six days. On the seventh day he rested. Genesis chapters 1 and 2 describe how God created people in his image, and made woman from man (see p.3).

2) Some believe the Bible gives a literal account of what happened. People who disagree with evolution claim there's a lack of proof backing up the theory — fossils don't show the full process of evolution.

3) However, lots of Christians view the creation story as symbolic and also believe in scientific theories. The Big Bang theory was actually first put forward by a Roman Catholic priest, Georges Lemaître, so religion and science don't have to be completely separate.

4) In fact, many believe that science and religious ideas can exist in harmony. Both the Church of England and the Roman Catholic Church have recognised the benefits of the two working together.

"Collaboration between religion and science is mutually beneficial..." General Synod of the Church of England, 2010

"Evolution in nature does not conflict with the notion of Creation..." Pope Francis, Pontifical Academy of Sciences, October 27 2014

Jewish Ideas

1) The Jewish creation story is in Genesis and is the same as the Christian one (see p.3).

2) Jews interpret this story in different ways. Ultra-orthodox Jews believe it is literally true, and would find it difficult to accept scientific arguments.

3) Others would argue that the Torah account is a metaphor, and are open to scientific evidence.

"So God created mankind in his own image..." Genesis 1:27 NIV

Islamic Ideas

1) The Muslim creation story is similar to that in Genesis: "It is Allah who created the heavens and the earth and whatever is between them in six days" (Qur'an 32:4).

2) The Qur'an says Allah "began the creation of man from clay" (Qur'an 32:7) and breathed life and a soul into the first man, Adam — and all humans descend from him.

3) Some see the descriptions of creation in the Qur'an as agreeing with science. E.g. the Qur'an says "Have those who disbelieved not considered that the heavens and the earth were a joined entity, and We separated them..." (Qur'an 21:30) — this could be understood to support the Big Bang theory.

No monkeying around now, there's a lot to learn here...

Jot down all the beliefs you've learnt about the origins of the universe.

| General | # The Environment and Stewardship |

Religious believers think people should <u>look after</u> the environment because it was created by God.

The World is a Way for God to Reveal His Presence

Many believers <u>appreciate</u> the world and what's in it because it is <u>God's creation</u>. They feel that he reveals himself constantly in the world through <u>experiences</u> that inspire <u>awe</u> and <u>wonder</u>, where someone can <u>feel God's presence</u> — e.g. a <u>beautiful sunset</u>, a <u>wild sea</u> or a <u>butterfly's wing</u> might convince someone there must be a creator. But people <u>don't</u> always take good <u>care</u> of the world we live in...

Humans have Damaged the Environment

Global Warming

- <u>Gases</u> in the atmosphere, called '<u>greenhouse gases</u>', help keep the Earth <u>warm</u>.
- Over the past century, the amount of greenhouse gas in the atmosphere has <u>increased</u>, and measurements show that the Earth has <u>got hotter</u>. This is called <u>global warming</u>. Higher temperatures make <u>ice melt</u>, which causes <u>sea levels</u> to <u>rise</u>. This could lead to <u>flooding</u> in low-lying areas.
- It is mainly caused by the <u>fuels</u> used to generate energy, like <u>oil</u>, <u>coal</u> and <u>gas</u>.

Natural Resources

- A <u>natural resource</u> is anything found naturally that's <u>useful</u> to humans.
- The Earth's population is <u>increasing</u> and people use more <u>raw materials</u> and more <u>energy</u> every year. If people carry on like this, many <u>natural resources</u> will eventually <u>run out</u>.
- <u>Fertile land</u> for growing crops is also rapidly <u>declining</u>. Each year, <u>overgrazing</u> and <u>irresponsible farming methods</u> turn more fertile land into <u>desert</u>.

Pollution

- Pollution from chemicals can <u>contaminate</u> the environment.
- <u>Sewage</u> and <u>chemicals</u> can pollute lakes, rivers and seas. These pollutants <u>harm</u> the plants and animals that live in and around the water, including humans.
- People use <u>toxic chemicals</u> for farming. They also bury <u>nuclear waste</u> underground, and dump a lot of <u>household</u> and <u>industrial waste</u> in landfill sites. The toxic chemicals can <u>kill</u> plants and animals, and cause <u>cancer</u> in humans.
- <u>Smoke</u> and <u>gases</u> from vehicles and industry can pollute the <u>air</u>, cause <u>health problems</u> in humans and damage the <u>ozone layer</u>.

There are Many Ways to Tackle these Problems

1) Many people, both religious and non-religious, work to <u>reduce</u> and <u>repair</u> the harm caused to the <u>environment</u>. They think that it's <u>important</u> to look after the planet for <u>future generations</u>.

2) Many religious believers feel it's their <u>duty</u> to <u>look after</u> the environment. God <u>gave</u> people the Earth, but expects them to <u>care</u> for it — this idea is called <u>stewardship</u>. See the next page for more details on different religious beliefs.

3) Lots of people try to be environmentally friendly by <u>recycling</u> things like <u>paper</u> and <u>plastic</u>. They may also take <u>public transport</u> or <u>walk</u> to cut down on pollution caused by vehicle fumes.

4) There's a <u>limit</u> to the <u>Earth's resources</u>, so many people believe it's <u>important</u> to be able to <u>manage</u> the resources currently available and to find alternative, <u>sustainable</u> options too.

5) Some also <u>campaign</u> to better inform others about the <u>damage</u> being done to the environment.

Recycle some of this information by using it in the exam...

You've probably been told this a hundred times, but always read the questions carefully. You might come across questions that ask for a specific number of points, so make sure you give the correct number.

The Environment and Stewardship | All religions

Christians Believe in Looking After the Environment

1) In Genesis 1:26, God said humans could "rule over the fish in the sea and the birds in the sky, over the livestock and all the wild animals..." (NIV). This power is known as dominion. Some people think it means humans can use the environment however they want.

> "humanity's dominion cannot be understood as licence to abuse, spoil, squander or destroy what God has made..." Christian Declaration on Nature, Assisi 1986

2) However, many Christians believe that God made them stewards of the environment. They have no right to abuse God's creation, and they have a responsibility to protect it.

> "The Lord God took the man and put him in the Garden of Eden to work it and take care of it." Genesis 2:15 NIV

3) Some Christians believe that everything is interdependent (i.e. everything depends on everything else), so driving species of animal or plant to extinction, or harming the planet, eventually ends up harming people.

4) The damage humans do to the environment clashes with their role as stewards. Christian organisations such as CAFOD, Christian Aid and Tearfund® are concerned with putting this responsibility into practice. They put pressure on governments and industry to think more about how people are abusing the planet.

Judaism also Teaches Stewardship

1) Jews value the world because it is God's and he created it: "The earth is the Lord's, and everything in it, the world, and all who live in it; for he founded it on the seas and established it on the waters" (Psalm 24:1-2 NIV).

2) Jews believe in the concept of stewardship. Concern for the natural world is often seen as being at the heart of Jewish teaching.

> "...it is our Jewish responsibility to put the defence of the whole of nature at the very centre of our concern." Jewish Declaration on Nature, Assisi 1986

3) God's creations should remain as he intended, and humans have no right to abuse them. The Jewish Declaration on Nature also stated that "humanity was given dominion over nature, but was commanded to behave towards the rest of creation with justice and compassion". Some think everything is interdependent, with trees being particularly important. Since the creation of Israel in 1948, millions of trees have been planted to aid the reclamation of the desert and help rebuild the nation.

4) Jews also believe that as custodians, they're responsible for making the world better — this is called tikkun olam ('mending the world'). Tikkun olam isn't just about the environment — it's a general ideal that includes helping the poor, and behaving morally.

Muslims are Khalifah of the Earth

1) The Earth is seen as being a product of the love of Allah, so Muslims should treat it with love.

2) Muslims believe they have been appointed khalifah (vice-regents or trustees) of the Earth. This is the idea that while they're on Earth they should take responsibility for the world (stewardship), and make it the sort of place Allah wants it to be.

3) This means Muslims have an obligation to protect the environment. Muslims might carry out their duty as khalifah by being careful with the resources they use, and encouraging others to take care of the environment too.

4) The Prophet Muhammad (called Allah's Apostle here) said that planting a tree is a good, charitable deed:

> "Allah's Apostle said, 'There is none amongst the Muslims who plants a tree or sows seeds, and then a bird, or a person or an animal eats from it, but is regarded as a charitable gift for him.'" Sahih al-Bukhari 39:513

5) At the Day of Judgement, Muslims believe questions will be asked of them. They will be required to answer for any ill-treatment of the planet and its resources.

Look after the environment — it's the natural thing to do...

Define stewardship in your own words, then write a few points about how people might carry it out.

All religions	# Animal Rights

There is a variety of views on whether animals should be used for the benefit of humans.

Animal Experimentation and Vegetarianism are Key Issues

1) Animals are sometimes used to test products used by humans or for medical experiments. Some people see this as cruel. Others look at the issue in a utilitarian way — utilitarianism is the idea that decisions should be made based on what has the best balance of good and bad outcomes. This can be used to argue that animal testing is acceptable if it could help many people, even if animals suffer.

2) Animals are also used for food. Some say that humans are built to consume meat. Other people argue that hurting animals is wrong, so it's better to be vegetarian or vegan.

Christians believe Animals should be Treated Well

1) Some people might argue that dominion gives humans the right to do what they want with animals, but others say stewardship means caring for God's creatures. Christianity teaches that animals should be treated with kindness, but that they can be used to benefit mankind (as long as their suffering is considered): "The righteous care for the needs of their animals" (Proverbs 12:10 NIV). Many would say only human life is sacred, as only humans were created in the image of God.

2) The Catholic Church tolerates animal testing, but only if it benefits mankind (e.g. if the experiments lead to the development of life-saving medicines).

"Medical and scientific experimentation on animals is a morally acceptable practice if it remains within reasonable limits and contributes to caring for or saving human lives. It is contrary to human dignity to cause animals to suffer or die needlessly." Catechism of the Catholic Church, 2417-2418

3) Some Christians think it's always wrong to cause suffering to animals to increase our scientific knowledge, particularly since medicines don't always have the same effect on humans as they do on animals. Some denominations, e.g. the Society of Friends (Quakers), are against any ill-treatment of animals.

4) Unlike some other religions, Christianity has no specific food laws. So vegetarianism (not eating meat) and veganism (not eating or using any animal products) are matters for individuals to decide about. The Bible talks about eating meat, so many Christians believe it's fine.

Judaism has Laws about Eating Meat

1) The Noahide Laws, a set of rules Jews believe people should follow, forbid cruelty to animals. The Torah contains specific food laws — only certain animals can be eaten, and the ones that are allowed must be slaughtered in a humane fashion. Foods that are allowed are called kosher (see p.32).

2) The Torah teaches people to treat animals in a sustainable way. Deuteronomy 22:6-7 says that a person can take young birds from a nest, but should not take the mother.

3) Experiments on animals may be tolerated if they result in a benefit for mankind, but only as a last resort. Jews believe in pikuach nefesh — the idea that human life must be saved, even if that means going against other Jewish laws (see p.28). This can be used to argue in favour of animal testing.

Islam Teaches that Animals Should Never be Mistreated

1) The idea of khalifah affects how Muslims treat animals (see p.49). Animals are part of Allah's creation, which Muslims are entrusted to look after.

2) Cruelty to animals is forbidden, as is their use simply for pleasure.

"It is Allah who made for you the grazing animals... you eat." Qur'an 40:79

3) Muslims believe in showing compassion for all creatures — animals must be slaughtered humanely for the meat to be halal (Arabic for 'allowed').

4) Muslims will generally only allow animal testing if it is done to produce genuine medical advances for humans. The animals should be treated humanely, and no unnecessary pain should be inflicted on them.

"Allah's Apostle said, 'Whoever keeps a dog, one Qirat of the reward of his good deeds is deducted daily, unless the dog is used for guarding a farm or cattle.'" Sahih al-Bukhari 39:515

Animal rights shouldn't be left out...

Summarise religious teachings about the treatment of animals. Try to mention sacred texts too.

Abortion and Euthanasia

Arguments about abortion and euthanasia revolve around who can decide when life begins and ends.

Abortion and Euthanasia are Controversial Issues

> Abortion is when a foetus is removed prematurely from the womb before it can survive. It's legal in England, Scotland and Wales and can take place until the 24th week of pregnancy. Abortions can take place after this time if there's a danger to the health of the mother or foetus.

> Euthanasia is killing someone to relieve suffering, often from an incurable illness. Active euthanasia is when a patient requests help to die, often using drugs — it is illegal in the UK, but legal in some countries, e.g. Belgium. In passive euthanasia, medical treatment that might extend someone's life is withdrawn — they might refuse further treatment, or a life-support machine might be turned off if there is no hope of recovery. This is legal in the UK.

1) Christianity, Islam and Judaism teach that all life is created by God. As God's creation, all life belongs to God and is therefore holy. This is the 'sanctity of life' argument.

2) Based on this, many religious people believe that people don't have the right to interfere with when life ends, or to prevent the beginning of a new life. Many support hospices — a hospice is a place where terminally ill people can be well cared for.

3) Other people take into consideration a person's quality of life (how able they are to live a normal life).

Many Christians see Abortion as Undesirable

1) Abortion is a very complicated and emotional issue, but generally speaking, Christianity teaches that abortion is undesirable as God "created mankind in his own image" (Genesis 1:27 NIV).

2) However, the Roman Catholic Church goes so far as to say that abortion is murder, as it teaches that human life starts as soon as the egg is fertilised at conception.

> "...all direct abortion... [is] to be absolutely excluded as lawful means of regulating the number of children." Humanae Vitae, section 14

3) Many argue abortion is wrong because God cares a lot about children. Jesus said "Let the little children come to me, and do not hinder them, for the kingdom of God belongs to such as these" (Luke 18:16 NIV).

4) Not all Churches see it in such black and white terms. The Church of England believes that abortion is permissible in certain circumstances, such as when the pregnancy puts the mother's life at risk. The Society of Friends (the Quakers) argues that the life of the unborn child cannot be valued above that of the woman. Many Christians argue that allowing a woman to choose is a way of showing Christian compassion — whether they agree with the choice made or not.

5) The Bible doesn't actually mention abortion, but it connects life with breath, e.g. in the creation of Adam — so it could be argued that the foetus is only alive when it breathes independently. Other Christian writings (e.g. the Didache, a 2nd century manual of Christian teaching) are quite specifically against it.

Some Christians are Strongly Against Euthanasia

1) Roman Catholics are the most strongly opposed to euthanasia. They believe that anything that intentionally causes death is wrong. So even those who are unlikely to recover consciousness should be kept alive.

> "...an act or omission which... causes death in order to eliminate suffering constitutes a murder gravely contrary to the dignity of the human person and to the respect due to the living God, his Creator." Catechism of the Catholic Church, 2277

2) Some Christians view euthanasia as going against the commandment "You shall not murder" (Exodus 20:13 NIV). Some might argue that only God should decide when a person's life ends, as he gave them life in the first place.

3) Many Christians believe suffering is part of life. Job was made to suffer by Satan, but refused to end his life: "Shall we accept good from God, and not trouble?" (Job 2:10 NIV).

4) Euthanasia could be seen to ruin the natural course of death, when a soul starts to make its way to God.

5) Many Christians feel they must care for sick people, and euthanasia goes against this. Local churches often have links with hospices — Christians would argue hospices allow a person to feel valued as they reach the end of their life.

Abortion and Euthanasia

Some Christians Support Passive Euthanasia

1) Some Christians suggest that the use of 'extraordinary treatment' (e.g. life-support machines which are keeping someone alive artificially) is not always the best approach — they suggest the easing of suffering through passive euthanasia is a way of demonstrating Christian compassion.

2) However, many only agree with euthanasia if the dying person chooses it for themselves.

3) Anglican denominations are against active euthanasia. However, they agree that terrible distress should not be suffered at all costs, and that death may be considered a blessing rather than continuing life-extending treatment. They argue that a person's quality of life must also be considered.

Judaism Allows Abortion in Some Cases

1) As a general rule, Judaism is opposed to abortion that is carried out for non-medical reasons. Human life is part of the universe that God created, and he "created mankind in his own image" (Genesis 1:27 NIV). An unborn child is part of that creation.

> "For you created my inmost being; you knit me together in my mother's womb." Psalm 139:13 NIV

2) Some Jews might argue that it is up to God to decide when life starts and ends (see below).

3) However, Judaism does not teach that the life of an unborn child is more valuable than that of the mother — the foetus isn't seen as a human until birth. Many Jews accept that, in certain cases, abortion should be allowed. Most rabbis allow abortion if pregnancy becomes physically or mentally dangerous for the woman concerned, or if the child is likely to be severely disabled and unable to lead a full life. But it cannot be carried out simply for convenience.

> "...anyone who saves a life is as if he saved an entire world." Mishnah Sanhedrin 4:5

Judaism Teaches That Only God Can Decide When People Die

1) Jewish teaching is generally opposed to the practice of euthanasia. There are some rabbis who have come out in support of it, but most Jews see life as a sacred gift from God. They believe people do not have the right to decide when a life should end.

2) Many see euthanasia as going against pikuach nefesh (see p.28) — Jews should do all they can to save human life, not bring about its end.

3) The relief of pain and suffering is a key part of Jewish teaching. So although euthanasia is seen as wrong if it involves actively doing something to cause someone's death, it may be possible to withhold treatment, if this treatment would cause further distress. Reform Jews would agree with this idea, but ultra-orthodox Jews are strongly against stopping treatment.

4) The words of Rabbi Moses Isserles are sometimes used to argue that it may be reasonable to switch off a life-support machine that's keeping someone alive: "If there is anything which causes a hindrance to the departure of the soul... then it is permissible to remove it."

5) The Jewish sacred text, the Nevi'im, contains an example of euthanasia. Abimelek is hit by a stone:

> "...a woman dropped an upper millstone on his head and cracked his skull. Hurriedly he called to his armour-bearer, 'Draw your sword and kill me, so that they can't say, "A woman killed him." ' So his servant ran him through, and he died." Judges 9:53-54 NIV

To avoid being killed by a woman, which would have been seen as embarrassing, he gets a man to kill him instead. This could be seen as supporting the right to die in a dignified way, but the text doesn't condone or condemn the action, and most don't see it as giving support for euthanasia.

It's tricky, emotional stuff...

Make sure you've got all the viewpoints straight by having a go at this exam-style question:
Outline three beliefs about euthanasia.   [3]

Abortion and Euthanasia

Islam Allows Abortion Before Ensoulment in some Circumstances

Muslims believe that people's lives are <u>sacred</u> (see p.51). The Qur'an teaches that "whoever kills a soul... it is as if he had slain mankind entirely" (Qur'an 5:32). This means that abortion is <u>generally</u> seen as wrong.

1) The passage on the right sums up Islamic teaching on <u>abortion</u>. But there are circumstances in which it is <u>permissible</u>.

> "And do not kill your children... We provide for them and for you. Indeed, their killing is ever a great sin." Qur'an 17:31

2) When the <u>mother's</u> life is in <u>danger</u>, abortion is <u>lawful</u>. The <u>potential</u> life in the womb is <u>not</u> as <u>important</u> as the <u>actual</u> life of the mother.

3) When a <u>foetus</u> gets its <u>soul</u>, this is called <u>ensoulment</u>. Islam teaches that this happens <u>after 120 days</u>, when "the soul is breathed into his body" (Sahih al-Bukhari 55:549).

4) This means that within the <u>first 120 days</u>, abortion can be allowed if the mother's life is <u>at risk</u>, or if the baby would be born with a serious <u>defect</u>, though not all Muslims agree with this. After 120 days, abortion is <u>only</u> allowed to save the <u>life</u> of the mother.

5) Some Muslim women argue that they should be <u>free</u> to <u>choose</u> what happens to their <u>bodies</u>. Those that disagree claim that Qur'an 81:8-9 says <u>unborn children</u> will want to know <u>why</u> they were <u>killed</u>.

Muslims are Usually Against Euthanasia

1) Euthanasia is seen as <u>wrong</u> by most Muslims: "do not kill yourselves [or one another]" (Qur'an 4:29).

2) Muslims believe that their lives are <u>Allah's</u> and he has a <u>plan</u> for every living person — he has decided <u>how long</u> each person will live on this Earth, and they do not have the right to <u>interfere</u> with that plan.

3) Islam teaches that <u>life on Earth</u> is a <u>test</u>. Allah knows <u>why</u> people <u>suffer</u>, and they do <u>not</u> have good reason to <u>end</u> their <u>own lives</u>, no matter how bad that suffering is. Instead, those who are suffering should turn to <u>Allah</u>, <u>pray</u> and <u>wait</u> — Allah is <u>merciful</u>, and all will be revealed on the <u>Day of Judgement</u>.

> "O you who have believed, seek help through patience and prayer. Indeed, Allah is with the patient." Qur'an 2:153

4) As a result, Muslims support <u>hospices</u>, but often they try to look after the ill person <u>at home</u> — this allows them to be surrounded and taken <u>care</u> of by their <u>family</u>, <u>friends</u> and <u>neighbours</u>.

5) However, when a patient has a terminal illness with <u>no hope</u> of <u>improvement</u>, Islam allows doctors to stop 'unnecessary' treatment.

> "...when disaster strikes them, [they] say, 'Indeed we belong to Allah, and indeed to Him we will return.' Those are the ones upon whom are blessings from their Lord and mercy." Qur'an 2:156-157

There are Many Non-Religious Views on Abortion and Euthanasia

1) Many atheists support abortion as it gives women <u>control</u> over what happens to their <u>bodies</u>. Humanists <u>prioritise</u> quality of life over sustaining life, and look at the <u>impact</u> on the <u>woman</u> first.

2) There is some <u>debate</u> surrounding the <u>time limit</u> on abortions. Since some babies born <u>prematurely</u> at 24 weeks or less are <u>surviving</u>, some feel that the <u>timeframe</u> for abortions should be <u>shortened</u>. Others feel that there <u>shouldn't</u> be a time limit on abortions at all.

3) There is more of a <u>divide</u> in opinions when it comes to <u>euthanasia</u>. Some support it when a person will <u>die</u> from an illness or where they are suffering from an <u>incurable</u> illness. They feel that ending someone's <u>suffering</u> through euthanasia is the <u>kindest</u> thing to do.

4) However, some people fear that <u>legalising</u> euthanasia would potentially lead to people feeling <u>pressured</u> into it. Some also feel that <u>doctors</u> should work to <u>protect</u> lives, not the opposite.

5) Some people might apply <u>situation ethics</u> — looking for the <u>most loving</u> option in each situation, rather than applying the same <u>rules</u> in <u>every instance</u>. This might lead them to <u>support</u> abortion or euthanasia where it seems to be the <u>kindest</u> option.

Abortion and euthanasia are complicated topics...

...so go back over the pages if you need to. Then try out this question when you're ready:
Explain two religious teachings on abortion.   [4]

All religions	# The Afterlife

There's <u>more information</u> on the afterlife on p.6 for Christianity, p.20 for Islam and p.29 for Judaism.

Most Religions Teach that there is an Afterlife

1) Many people believe that, although your <u>body</u> may die and decay, your <u>soul</u> can live on — in other words, you move on to a different kind of <u>existence</u>. This is the basic idea of <u>life after death</u>.

2) Most religions teach that something happens to the soul <u>after death</u>. Some religions teach that the soul is <u>rewarded</u> or <u>punished</u> for the <u>actions</u> of the person on Earth. Others believe the soul is <u>reincarnated</u>. Christians, Muslims and Jews believe that life on Earth isn't <u>everything</u> — a <u>better life</u> awaits them. It's still <u>important</u> though, and is <u>preparation</u> for the afterlife.

<u>CHRISTIANITY</u> teaches that people go to <u>heaven</u> or <u>hell</u>, depending on how God <u>judges</u> their actions — trying to live life according to Christian <u>teachings</u> and believing in <u>Jesus</u> will allow them to receive <u>God's grace</u> and go to <u>heaven</u>. Catholics believe that some go to <u>Purgatory</u> — a place where <u>sins</u> are <u>paid for</u> before going to heaven (see p.6).

"And God raised us up with Christ and seated us with him in the heavenly realms in Christ Jesus... For it is by grace you have been saved..." Ephesians 2:6-8 NIV

"...one who had repented, believed, and done righteousness, it is promised by Allah that he will be among the successful." Qur'an 28:67

<u>MUSLIMS</u> believe the afterlife means going to <u>jannah</u> (paradise) or <u>jahannam</u> (hell). After a person dies, their soul goes to <u>barzakh</u> to <u>await judgement</u> (see p.20). On <u>Yawm ad-Din</u> (the Day of Judgement), everyone's actions will be judged. Muslims believe Allah "...will assemble you for the Day of Resurrection..." (Qur'an 45:26). Those who Allah deems <u>good</u> go to <u>jannah</u>, and the <u>bad</u> to <u>jahannam</u>.

Lots of <u>JEWS</u> believe in <u>Gan Eden</u> (paradise) and <u>Gehinnom</u>, a place where people are <u>punished</u> for bad things they've done (see p.29). Most people will <u>move</u> from Gehinnom to Gan Eden, but <u>evil</u> people will stay for <u>eternity</u>. Some believe they'll eventually be <u>resurrected</u>, when God "will swallow up death for ever" (Isaiah 25:8 NIV). This is part of <u>Maimonides'</u> 13 principles of faith. However, Jews tend to <u>concentrate</u> on <u>this life</u>, rather than what might happen after death.

3) There are many <u>arguments</u> used by both <u>religious</u> and <u>non-religious</u> people to <u>support</u> life after death:

- The <u>paranormal</u> (things science can't explain, which are thought to have a spiritual cause, e.g. <u>ghosts</u>) is sometimes used as evidence. Some people (<u>mediums</u>) claim they can <u>talk</u> to the <u>dead</u>.
- Some people claim to have evidence of <u>reincarnation</u> (they lived a previous life, died, and were reborn in a new body). Lots of research has been carried out with young <u>children</u> who claim to remember <u>past lives</u>.
- People say they've had a <u>near-death</u> or <u>out-of-body experience</u> where they've spoken to long-dead <u>family members</u>.
- Some believe there must be <u>more</u> after <u>life on Earth</u>. They might see going to heaven or paradise as a <u>reward</u> for people who've been <u>good</u> all their lives — it must exist to <u>compensate</u> for the <u>unfairness</u> of life on Earth.

Some People Don't Believe in Life After Death

1) Many people believe that when you die, that's it — you <u>cease to exist</u>. They might argue that there isn't any <u>concrete evidence</u> that there is life after death, so the <u>logical</u> answer is that it <u>doesn't exist</u>. They think people's <u>memories</u> of previous lives <u>aren't real</u> — they could've been <u>suggested</u> to the person.

2) They might say that believing in an afterlife is just a way of <u>helping</u> people deal with <u>death</u> — the idea provides <u>comfort</u>.

3) They could also argue that the idea of an afterlife is used by religions to put <u>pressure</u> on people to <u>follow</u> their teachings and <u>live</u> their lives in a certain way.

4) Believers would <u>disagree</u> with these arguments, since their own beliefs come from <u>sacred texts</u>.

5) Christians might argue that Jesus's <u>resurrection</u> shows that there's life after death: "He was put to death in the body but made alive in the Spirit" (1 Peter 3:18 NIV). However, <u>non-believers</u> may say that the stories of Jesus's resurrection are <u>made up</u>.

It might not seem like it now, but there is life after exams...

Be sure to finish essay questions with a conclusion, based on the arguments you've considered.

Section 5 — Life and Death

Revision Summary

Those were some pretty big issues that you've just read about — now let's see how much you can remember. These questions will let you get a feel for how the exam will be, and how much writing is involved.

If there's anything you can't answer, go back through the section and have another go when you've re-read it.

For some courses, you need to learn about the views of <u>different religions</u> on these topics. But for other courses, you need to know about them in the context of just <u>one religion</u> — if that's the case for your course, answer each of these questions <u>in the context of the religion you've studied</u>.

Getting the ball rolling with some 1 mark questions — they're even multiple choice.

1) Which of the following is the idea that believers must look after God's creation?
   a) Veganism   b) Dominion   c) Stewardship   d) Pikuach nefesh

2) Which of the following is the theory that includes the idea that humans evolved from apes?
   a) The Big Bang   b) Reincarnation   c) Ensoulment   d) Evolution

3) Which of the following words means to terminate a pregnancy?
   a) Abortion   b) Euthanasia   c) Conception   d) Purgatory

Let's make things a little trickier. Write down two brief points for the marks.

4) Give two examples of what religious people could do to protect the environment.

5) Give two religious beliefs about dominion.

6) Give two religious beliefs about how people might experience God's presence through the natural world.

Pressing on with some 3 mark questions. 3 marks = 3 short points.

7) Outline three religious beliefs about how the world was created.

8) Outline three ways in which people damage the environment.

Moving up to 4 marks. Make two points, but this time develop them further to get an extra mark for each.

9) Explain two religious beliefs about the sanctity of life.

10) Explain two ways in which believers might respond to animal experimentation.

11) Explain two reasons why religious people might accept scientific arguments about creation.

5 marks up for grabs now. You'll need to refer to a source of wisdom and authority for top marks.

12) Explain two religious beliefs about stewardship.

13) Explain two religious beliefs about life after death.

Make sure that you write clearly and organise your answer well for the longer answer questions.

And last but not least — the 12 mark question (with extra marks for SPaG). The question will often come with bullet points that you should include in your answer, so use them to make a plan before you begin. Think about arguments in favour of and against the statement, and pack your answer full of information.

14) 'Euthanasia can be the most compassionate way to help someone who is terminally ill.'
   Evaluate this statement.
   Your answer should include the following:
   • religious arguments that support the statement
   • religious arguments that disagree with the statement
   • a conclusion
   You can also include non-religious points of view in your answer.

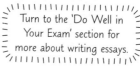

Turn to the 'Do Well in Your Exam' section for more about writing essays.

Section 5 — Life and Death

All religions	Justice, Good and Evil

Working for justice and trying to live good lives are important for many religious believers.

Justice is Important for Many People

1) Justice is the idea of each person getting what they deserve and maintaining what's right. It includes punishing the guilty and protecting the innocent. For victims of crime, justice might mean seeing the offender pay for what they did through punishment, and being made to realise the impact of their actions.

2) Justice is important to religious and non-religious people. Most believe justice is essential for countries to run properly and to ensure that people follow the law. Religious people believe that God/Allah is just:

> CHRISTIANS believe justice is important — everyone should be treated fairly as God created people to be equal. Christians see God as just, and think that they should be too: "And what does the Lord require of you? To act justly..." (Micah 6:8 NIV). They believe that, after a crime is committed, justice can be restored by giving the offender a punishment for their actions.

> ISLAM teaches Muslims to work for justice, and to treat others justly and equally. It is an important part of shari'ah (Islamic law). Muslims believe that they should always strive for justice to take place: "O you who have believed, be persistently standing firm in justice, witnesses for Allah, even if it be against yourselves or parents and relatives" (Qur'an 4:135). Many also believe that those who fight for justice will be rewarded in the afterlife, but those who don't will be sent to jahannam (hell).

> JEWS must follow the mitzvot set out in the Torah, and there have been courts (Bet Din) ensuring these laws are followed since long ago. Jews believe that everyone is equal, and they are encouraged to work for justice: "You must purge the evil from among you... Show no pity: life for life, eye for eye, tooth for tooth, hand for hand, foot for foot" (Deuteronomy 19:19-21 NIV). This means that the victim needs to be compensated by the criminal for justice to truly be done.

People Should Do Good and Avoid Evil

1) Christianity, Islam and Judaism all teach people to live good lives. This includes following religious teachings, e.g. by helping other people. The good things that people do will please God/Allah. Religious people believe they should avoid sin and evil, as their actions will be judged when they die.

2) Many believe that there are two types of evil. Moral evil is when suffering occurs because of human actions, e.g. murder and rape. Natural evil is suffering caused by the world, e.g. floods and earthquakes.

3) Both crime and punishment are connected to suffering. Religious people are normally against most crimes because of the suffering they cause. In some sacred texts, suffering is described as a punishment for the sins people have committed or as a test from God — read the second part of p.79 for more information.

> • In CHRISTIANITY, the sheep and goats parable (Matthew 25:31-46) says that everyone will be judged and separated into the good (the sheep) and the bad (the goats). Jesus said that helping another person is like helping him. If you ignore someone in need of help, it's like ignoring him: "...whatever you did not do for one of the least of these, you did not do for me" (Matthew 25:45 NIV). The people who haven't helped will suffer because of this.
> • Many Christians believe that evil and suffering is caused by humans misusing their free will — they believe that the original sin people are born with makes them capable of sin (see p.7). Some say Satan tempts people to sin.

> • ISLAM teaches that Allah is merciful and those who have done good things will be rewarded, but he will make people who do bad things suffer for them.
> • If people intend to do something good, that will help them on the Day of Judgement, but if they intend to do something bad, it won't count against them (see p.20).
> • Many Muslims believe that the devil, Iblis, tries to make humans turn to evil.

> "He admits whom He wills into His mercy; but the wrongdoers - He has prepared for them a painful punishment." Qur'an 76:31

> • The JEWISH sacred texts explain how to behave in a good way.
> • Jews believe that evil and suffering is the result of humans taking advantage of the free will they were allowed by God.
> • But God will forgive people if they commit sin: "I will have mercy on whom I will have mercy, and I will have compassion on whom I will have compassion" (Exodus 33:19 NIV).

4) Non-religious people reject the idea that God causes suffering. They might feel religion isn't worth the suffering it can sometimes cause, e.g. as an excuse for terrorism, or through persecution of believers.

Why is justice important? Just is...

...that won't get you any marks. Summarise why justice is important to religious believers.

Crime

Crime happens on a <u>daily</u> basis for many reasons. Many <u>religious organisations</u> work to put an <u>end</u> to it.

Many Crimes Break Religious Laws and Teachings

1) There are many <u>different types</u> of crime, including <u>murder</u>, <u>theft</u> and <u>hate crimes</u>.

2) Christianity, Islam and Judaism are against these as they break <u>religious moral laws</u>.

3) <u>Christians</u> and <u>Jews</u> are strongly against <u>murder</u> and <u>theft</u> as they <u>break</u> two of the <u>Ten Commandments</u>. In <u>Islam</u>, the Qur'an also <u>condemns</u> murder and theft.

4) Murder, often seen as the <u>worst</u> crime, goes against the idea of <u>sanctity of life</u> (the belief that life is <u>sacred</u>) held by <u>all</u> three religions.

5) Crimes such as <u>theft</u> and <u>hate crimes</u> disregard religious teachings that people should be treated <u>equally</u>, as the offender shows <u>no concern</u> for the victim.

A hate crime is any type of crime committed against someone because of their ethnicity, religion, etc.

Crime is Caused by Lots of Different Factors

Most religious believers would agree that if someone does something <u>illegal</u>, they <u>deserve</u> to be <u>punished</u>. But the cause of crime <u>isn't</u> as simple as someone just being <u>bad</u> — there are many different <u>reasons</u> why a person might <u>commit</u> a <u>crime</u>:

1) POVERTY — People who are poor might turn to <u>crime</u> out of <u>desperation</u>. They might <u>steal food</u> or <u>money</u>, or earn <u>money</u> illegally, e.g. selling stolen goods.

2) UPBRINGING — Some people might become criminals if they've had a <u>troubled childhood</u>, or if they've <u>grown up</u> around crime and it's become <u>normal</u> to them.

3) MENTAL ILLNESS — This can lead people to commit crimes because, e.g. they may not fully <u>understand</u> the <u>difference</u> between what's <u>legal</u> and <u>illegal</u>. Others may be easily <u>persuaded</u> into committing a crime.

4) ADDICTION — Being dependent on something such as <u>drugs</u> or <u>alcohol</u> can lead to people doing illegal things to <u>fund</u> their <u>addiction</u>.

5) GREED — Someone might <u>steal</u> or <u>earn</u> money <u>illegally</u> to get something they <u>want</u> but can't afford.

6) HATE — A person might do something illegal because someone else has <u>treated</u> them <u>badly</u>, or because they're driven by <u>prejudice</u>, e.g. racism.

7) OPPOSITION TO UNJUST LAW — A law might be <u>broken</u> as a <u>protest</u> if it's seen as unfair. In the 1950s and 60s many people, such as <u>Rosa Parks</u>, broke laws that treated black people <u>unfairly</u> in the <u>USA</u>.

Many feel that the <u>reason</u> behind the crime should be taken into <u>consideration</u>, and many religious people would want to <u>help</u> the <u>individual</u> as well as tackle the <u>bigger issues</u> that cause crime. However, certain causes would be more likely to get <u>sympathy</u> than others, e.g. <u>poverty</u> would be seen as more <u>reasonable</u> than <u>greed</u>. Many think that breaking a law that is <u>unfair</u> or that goes <u>against</u> religious law is <u>acceptable</u>.

Christians Work to Prevent Crimes

1) Christians are <u>strongly against</u> crime — they're told to <u>care</u> for others: "Love your neighbour as yourself" (Mark 12:31 NIV). Committing a crime such as <u>theft</u> or a <u>hate crime</u> doesn't treat the victim as an <u>equal</u>. Murder is seen as <u>destroying</u> something <u>created</u> by God.

2) Christians have <u>defied laws</u> to fight for what's <u>right</u>, e.g. Martin Luther King (see p.66). In this case, Christians may <u>support</u> breaking laws: "We must obey God rather than human beings!" (Acts 5:29 NIV).

3) Many Christians would <u>help</u> people who are e.g. struggling in <u>poverty</u>, in order to tackle the <u>source</u> of crime. They might donate to <u>charity</u> or help out in <u>food banks</u>, among other things.

4) <u>Christian groups</u> also play their part to try to <u>prevent</u> crime:

The <u>Prison Fellowship</u> is a Christian organisation in England and Wales that helps prisoners by <u>praying</u> for them, through <u>group activities</u>, and helping maintain <u>contact</u> with their <u>families</u>. They try to make prisoners see how they have <u>affected victims</u> of their crimes and <u>stop</u> them from <u>committing crime</u> again when they leave prison, e.g. through <u>restorative justice</u> (see p.59).

<u>Street Pastors</u>, who help people out at night (see p.13), have helped to <u>lower</u> crime rates and <u>prevent violence</u>.

Islam & Judaism | Crime

Elements of both Islam and Judaism help to <u>prevent</u> crime.

Muslims Believe Crime Interrupts the Relationship with Allah

1) Muslims believe that on <u>Yawn ad-Din</u> (the Day of Judgement — see p.20), those who've committed crimes might <u>not</u> be sent to <u>jannah</u>.

> "Allah orders justice and good conduct and giving to relatives and forbids immorality and bad conduct and oppression." Qur'an 16:90

2) Many Muslims also believe that a life of crime <u>doesn't</u> allow believers to <u>focus</u> on what really <u>matters</u> — their <u>faith</u> and connection with <u>Allah</u>.

3) <u>Murder</u> is seen as one of the <u>worst</u> crimes: "whoever kills a soul... it is as if he had slain mankind entirely" (Qur'an 5:32). Crimes such as <u>theft</u> and <u>hate crimes</u> defy Islamic <u>teachings</u> about people being <u>equal</u>.

4) Muslims hope that <u>key elements</u> of their religion help to <u>reduce</u> the likelihood of <u>crime</u>. For example, <u>compulsory</u> charitable donations (<u>zakah</u> — see p.22) help to tackle poverty. Alcohol, drugs and gambling are <u>banned</u>, reducing the chance of <u>addiction</u>. Parents are taught to follow <u>teachings</u> in the Qur'an to give their child the best possible <u>upbringing</u>, which should <u>prevent</u> them from turning to crime. Some <u>mosques</u> offer help for families too.

5) Islam teaches Muslims to <u>speak out</u> against <u>unjust laws</u> that go against Allah's teachings, so many would <u>understand</u> someone breaking an unjust law in <u>protest</u> against it.

6) In <u>shari'ah courts</u>, the <u>circumstances</u> surrounding the crime are looked into <u>thoroughly</u>, so the defendant is punished <u>accordingly</u>.

7) Some Muslims work to try to <u>reduce</u> crime by <u>helping prisoners</u> and <u>ex-offenders</u>:

> The <u>Muslim Chaplains Association</u> offers <u>religious guidance</u> in <u>prisons</u> in the UK. It aims to <u>reform</u> prisoners and <u>stop</u> them from committing crimes after they are <u>released</u>, e.g. by helping them to <u>reintegrate</u> into society again. It also tries to keep ex-offenders <u>connected</u> to <u>chaplaincies</u> in their local <u>community</u> so they continue to receive <u>support</u> after prison.

> <u>Mosaic</u> is a charity that pairs <u>young people</u> approaching the <u>end</u> of their prison sentence with a <u>mentor</u>. As they adjust to life outside of prison, the mentor will <u>help</u> them with things like finding a <u>job</u> and somewhere to <u>live</u> — with the aim that this should <u>prevent</u> them from returning to a life of <u>crime</u>.

Judaism Forbids Murder and Theft in the Noahide Laws

1) The <u>Noahide Laws</u>, which Jews believe that <u>everyone</u> in the world should follow, state that <u>murder</u> and <u>theft</u> are <u>forbidden</u>. Crimes such as <u>hate crimes</u> go against Jewish teachings on <u>equality</u>.

> "...the Lord's anger will burn against you, and he will shut the heavens so that it will not rain and the ground will yield no produce, and you will soon perish..." Deuteronomy 11:17 NIV

2) Crime goes against <u>God's teachings</u> — Judaism teaches that people who <u>disobey</u> God will be <u>punished</u> by him.

3) Some <u>aspects</u> of Judaism work to <u>reduce</u> the chances of crime. For example, Jewish <u>financial aid</u> (<u>tzedakah</u>) is donated to charity and helps to combat <u>poverty</u>. Jewish parents are told to <u>guide</u> their <u>children</u> and to make sure they know what's <u>right</u> and <u>wrong</u>.

4) Many Jews would <u>protest</u> against <u>unjust laws</u>, and perhaps <u>break</u> them, as there are <u>examples</u> in the <u>Torah</u> of defying the law for what is right. In Exodus 1:16-17, two <u>midwives</u> were told by the king to <u>kill</u> Hebrew baby boys, but they <u>didn't</u> follow his instructions.

5) Some <u>rabbis</u> work with the <u>Jewish Prison Chaplaincy</u> in order to provide support for Jewish prisoners. The <u>support</u> offenders receive can help them to <u>turn their backs</u> on crime when they leave prison.

There's lots to learn here, so have another read if you need...

Then have a go at writing a short summary of religious teachings about crime, and what religious people do to try to prevent crime.

Forgiveness

Forgiveness is important to many religious believers — seeking God/Allah's forgiveness, and forgiving others.

Forgiveness can Reunite People and Prevent Reoffending

1) Forgiveness means stopping being angry with someone who's done something wrong. It is very important for many religious believers. They believe God is merciful towards people who genuinely seek his mercy and that they should reflect God's forgiving nature in their own behaviour.

2) Many believe it's important to forgive criminals so they can be reconciled with the community. If they leave prison isolated from others, with no job and little prospects, reoffending might seem like the only option. Forgiveness allows both victims and perpetrators to move on. However, most religious people believe that criminals should still be punished for what they've done.

3) Forgiveness can be shown in many ways. Lesser offences no longer stay on people's records permanently, and there are schemes that give ex-offenders skills and a job when they're released.

4) Restorative justice is where an offender might meet people who've suffered because of the crime they committed. Actually meeting the people they've hurt can help offenders to realise the extent of the damage they've done, try to make up for their actions and discourage them from reoffending. It helps the victim to work towards forgiving the offender.

Christianity Teaches that Forgiveness Comes from Love

1) Jesus taught that God is always ready to forgive and that Christians must accept that forgiveness, and forgive others in turn. The Lord's Prayer includes a verse about forgiveness (Matthew 6:12).

2) Jesus told people to seek reconciliation in any disagreements before offering a gift to God at the temple: "First go and be reconciled to them; then come and offer your gift" (Matthew 5:24 NIV). He also taught people to forgive "not seven times, but seventy-seven times" (Matthew 18:22 NIV).

3) Forgiveness is closely related to repentance. Christians believe that God's forgiveness can only come when they repent of their sins (i.e. say sorry, and turn their backs on them).

Islam Teaches that Allah is Forgiving

1) Muslims can seek retribution (see p.60) for injuries, but they're encouraged to forgive instead. Whenever the Qur'an describes punishment, it talks about forgiveness too.

2) Muslims believe that they must be merciful so that Allah will do the same to them on Yawm ad-Din (the Day of Judgement).

> "But if you pardon and overlook and forgive - then indeed, Allah is Forgiving and Merciful." Qur'an 64:14

3) They believe that wrongdoing should be forgiven if the offender is sorry and tries to make amends.

4) The Prophet Muhammad was forgiving, as told in the Hadith — Muslims believe in following his example.

5) But some crimes are seen as so awful that forgiveness isn't an option, e.g. shirk (see p.17).

Jews Should Follow God's Example and Be Forgiving

1) Jews believe that God is forgiving and merciful, so they must forgive other people too: "...for with the Lord is unfailing love and with him is full redemption" (Psalm 130:7 NIV).

2) For the festival of Yom Kippur, Jews ask for forgiveness, both from people they've hurt and from God (see p.34). Jews believe that you can only be forgiven by the one you've hurt, so God can only forgive a sin against God, not another person.

3) Jews should allow criminals to repent for what they've done and seek forgiveness:

> "Let the wicked forsake their ways and the unrighteous their thoughts. Let them turn to the Lord, and he will have mercy on them, and to our God, for he will freely pardon." Isaiah 55:7 NIV

Forgive and forget (but not your revision)...

Explain two religious beliefs about forgiveness. Include a sacred text reference in your answer. [5]

General, Christianity, Catholic Christianity — # Punishment & Treatment of Criminals

Punishment can be used to 'get back' at someone for committing a crime, or to prevent crime in the future.

Criminals Have the Right to Be Treated Fairly

1) The European Convention on Human Rights gives the accused the right to have a fair trial. A trial is considered fair when it is carried out publicly in an unbiased court, and the accused has the opportunity to present their version of events. In the UK, the person is considered 'innocent until proven guilty'.

2) Being tried before a jury (a panel made up of members of the public) is not compulsory in the UK under the Human Rights Act, but many consider it to be one of the main ways to ensure a trial is fair.

3) If found guilty, the sentence given varies depending on the severity of the crime — these include prison and community service. Believers are often in favour of community service — it allows the offender to repay their debt to society yet still lead a normal life, which should help to ensure they don't reoffend.

4) In some countries corporal punishment and torture are forms of punishment:

- Corporal punishment is when physical pain is delivered by e.g. beating or flogging the offender. It's not used in Europe.
- Torture is illegal in the UK under the European Convention on Human Rights, but it is used as a punishment in some countries. Torture is often carried out to extract information or confessions from suspected criminals
- Many religious people would say that torture goes against the sanctity of life argument — life comes from God and is sacred.
- People who use situation ethics may decide torture is justified in some cases if the information it provides could save many lives.

Punishment can have Various Aims

Retribution

Some people think of punishment as a way of taking revenge on a criminal, of making them 'pay' for what they've done. Critics of this way of thinking argue that revenge doesn't put right the wrong — that it's better to look for a more constructive solution.

Protection

If a criminal is considered dangerous, this is the idea that their punishment should protect the rest of society, e.g. imprisonment. Not many people would disagree with this, but some would argue that you protect society best by reforming offenders.

Reformation

Punishment should aim to change criminals so they won't reoffend again — the idea being that nobody is inherently bad. Many religious people feel this allows offenders to repent and seek forgiveness from God for their actions. Programmes to reform criminals include counselling and giving them work in the community.

Deterrence

The idea that if a punishment is sufficiently bad in some way (e.g. expensive, embarrassing, restricting, painful) it will put people off committing the crime — they understand the consequences. Critics argue that people don't stop to think about punishment before they commit a crime, especially if they've taken drugs or alcohol, so deterrence doesn't work.

Christianity Supports Fairness and Human Rights

1) Christians believe people should be given a fair trial — which could be through trial by jury: "Speak up and judge fairly; defend the rights of the poor and needy" (Proverbs 31:9 NIV).

2) Jesus told people to look at their own behaviour before criticising others. In John 8, a woman who was accused of adultery was saved by Jesus when he said: "Let any one of you who is without sin be the first to throw a stone at her" (John 8:7 NIV). No-one did, and it reminds Christians that everyone sins.

3) Christians believe in treating criminals mercifully: "...if someone is caught in a sin, you who live by the Spirit should restore that person gently" (Galatians 6:1 NIV).

4) Christians think that criminals should be punished for what they've done in a just way, but some think that life in prison should be difficult in order to make offenders think twice about crime. Some think punishment should be "eye for eye" (Leviticus 24:20 NIV), so focus on retribution. Others believe they should "turn... the other cheek" (Matthew 5:39 NIV), and so look more towards reformation.

5) Many Christians don't support torture or corporal punishment because Jesus was against violence (Matthew 26:52), and many support human rights. Christians are particularly aware of the cruelty of physical punishment, as Jesus was beaten and made to wear a crown of thorns before his death.

Punishment & Treatment of Criminals

There are many different views on punishments, but most Muslims and Jews believe in treating people fairly.

Islamic Law is Different to UK Law

1) Some Muslim countries have legal systems that are similar to many Western countries, but some use shari'ah. Shari'ah courts are different to UK courts. Juries aren't used — instead, the judge decides if the accused is guilty. Solicitors often aren't present — the accused represents themselves in court.

2) The Qur'an says that the punishment should fit the crime: "...an eye for an eye..." (Qur'an 5:45). But Qur'an 2:178 explains that the offender can sometimes compensate the victim financially.

3) Many Muslims believe in reformation, and punishment should give criminals the opportunity to see the error of their ways.

> "Allah wants to make clear to you [the lawful from the unlawful] and guide you to the [good] practices of those before you and to accept your repentance." Qur'an 4:26

4) The Qur'an teaches that prisoners should be treated fairly:

> "And they give food in spite of love for it to the needy, the orphan, and the captive" Qur'an 76:8

5) However, some argue that treating prisoners harshly can be more effective in reforming them. Some Muslims are against community service as they believe it's too easy and doesn't stop reoffending.

6) Shari'ah allows corporal punishment. The Qur'an mentions punishments such as whipping that are carried out publicly — the aim of this is to deter the criminal, but some believe this form of punishment can reform offenders too, and offers retribution. However, some Muslims believe corporal punishments are too severe, and don't respect the offender's human rights.

7) Most Muslims don't agree with torture, but some might allow it if it could prevent greater suffering.

Fairness is Important in Judaism

1) Human rights are important to many Jews, and Judaism teaches that offenders should be treated fairly:

> "One witness is not enough to convict anyone accused of any crime or offence they may have committed. A matter must be established by the testimony of two or three witnesses." Deuteronomy 19:15 NIV

2) Fair trials are important in Judaism, and many Jews support having juries involved in trials.

3) In Israel, juries aren't used — the case is decided by one judge, or sometimes three judges. Solicitors defend the accused in court, and can help those arrested before they talk to the police.

4) Jewish people believe that punishment is important. They value punishment in terms of deterrence, protection and retribution: "When justice is done, it brings joy to the righteous but terror to evildoers" (Proverbs 21:15 NIV). But the majority of Jews also believe that punishment should give offenders the chance to reform.

5) The Torah says that the punishment should match the crime: "Anyone who injures their neighbour is to be injured in the same manner: fracture for fracture, eye for eye, tooth for tooth" (Leviticus 24:19-20 NIV). The Torah also explains that "Whoever sheds human blood, by humans shall their blood be shed" (Genesis 9:6 NIV). This might suggest that corporal punishment is appropriate, but many Jews are against it.

6) Many think the punishments set out in the Torah are too harsh — most understand "eye for eye" as meaning that the severity of the sentence given to the offender should be appropriate for the crime committed, rather than that violence should be used.

7) Lots of Jews are concerned about the condition of prisons and prisoners' wellbeing. Most disagree with torture, but some might argue that it's tolerable if the information uncovered could protect lots of people. Pikuach nefesh requires that Jews do all they can to save lives (see p.28).

Don't do the crime if you can't do the time...

Have another read of the last couple of pages if you want, then try out this exam-style question:
Explain two religious beliefs about physical punishment.   [4]

EXAM QUESTION

All religions	# The Death Penalty

The death penalty is killing someone as punishment for a crime — it's also called capital punishment.

The Death Penalty Isn't Used Much Nowadays

1) Capital punishment has been abolished in many countries, including most of Europe and South America. Elsewhere, it only tends to be used for very serious crimes, e.g. murder, espionage (spying) and treason.

2) Religious and non-religious people might make some of these arguments for and against the death penalty:

For the Death Penalty	Against the Death Penalty
• The risk of death might act as a better deterrent to violent criminals than a prison sentence. • If you execute a murderer, it's impossible for them to kill again. Imprisoned murderers have been known to order killings from jail, or to reoffend when released on parole. In cases like these, the suffering of the criminal could potentially protect many people. • Utilitarianism (or the principle of utility) is the idea that the best course of action creates the best balance of good and bad results, e.g. it could be used to argue that killing criminals, although bad for them, would be good for the majority of society.	• Killing as punishment is just as bad as murder — many religious people and Humanists are against any form of killing. • It doesn't give the offender the chance to reform. • There have been cases where someone has been proved innocent after having been executed. • Life is special and should be preserved — many religious people believe in the sanctity of life. • Many religious believers think God alone can decide when to end someone's life.

3) Christians and Jews might be against the death penalty because the Ten Commandments forbid killing.

4) Some people might use situation ethics to decide on a case-by-case basis if the death penalty should be applied. This could lead to people being for the death penalty in some cases, but against it in others, depending on, e.g. the severity of the crime and the background to the case.

Christians have Mixed Views on Capital Punishment

1) Many Christians are opposed to capital punishment, as it doesn't allow for reform, or show mercy. Jesus said to set aside "eye for eye" (Matthew 5:38 NIV) and told people to "love your enemies" (Matthew 5:44 NIV). Many are against the violent nature of the death penalty.

2) However, some Christians in the United States (where capital punishment is legal) believe that the death penalty is a good thing. They say it protects the innocent. They might refer to biblical texts such as "Whoever sheds human blood, by humans shall their blood be shed" (Genesis 9:6 NIV) and "Anyone who strikes a person with a fatal blow is to be put to death" (Exodus 21:12 NIV).

Islamic Law Allows the Death Penalty

1) The Qur'an outlines crimes punishable by death, but encourages victims' families to take compensation.

2) Muhammad said that death could be a punishment in three cases: "the married adulterer, a life for life, and the deserter of his Din (Islam)" (Sahih Muslim 16:4152). This is reflected in shari'ah law.

3) However, some Muslims believe that Allah, not humans, should decide when life ends — they don't agree with capital punishment.

Many Jews are Against Capital Punishment

1) Exodus 21:12-17 outlines crimes punishable by death, such as kidnapping. Someone who "schemes and kills someone deliberately" (Exodus 21:14 NIV) could face the death penalty. Many Jews disagree with this — people can pay for their actions and seek forgiveness. The death penalty is an option in Israel, but is hardly used.

2) Mishnah Makkot 1:10 suggests that the death penalty should be avoided. A court "that would execute somebody once in seven years would be considered destructive". The Talmud put many restrictions on using the death penalty so it was nearly unusable.

Learn all the different arguments about the death penalty...

You must discuss both sides of the argument for the essay question — don't just stick to your own views.

Revision Summary

And that wraps up another section — time to see how you got on. The questions below are similar in style to the questions you'll be answering in the actual exam. If there's anything you can't answer, go back through the section and have another go when you've re-read it.

For some courses, you need to learn about the views of <u>different religions</u> on these topics. But for other courses, you need to know about them in the context of just <u>one religion</u> — if that's the case for your course, answer each of these questions <u>in the context of the religion you've studied</u>.

Jumping right in with some 1 mark multiple choice questions.

1) Which of the following is the idea that punishment should try to change the criminal for the better?
   a) Protection   b) Reformation   c) Retribution   d) Deterrence

2) Which of the following is where an offender might meet their victim?
   a) Corporal punishment   b) Prison   c) Community service d) Restorative justice

For these 2 mark questions, keep it short and snappy with two brief points.

3) Give two arguments against capital punishment.

4) Give two examples of causes of crime.

Time for some 3 mark questions — don't spend too much time on them, just three short points will do.

5) Outline three aims of punishment.

6) Outline three ways that forgiveness can be shown.

7) Outline three conditions that make a trial fair.

These 4 mark questions require you to develop your points for full marks.

8) Explain two religious beliefs about evil and suffering.

9) Explain two religious beliefs about preventing crime.

10) Explain two religious attitudes to the aims of punishment.

Make sure your longer answers are well organised and clearly written so the examiner can easily see your points.

And the questions continue — this time for 5 marks. Refer to sacred texts for full marks.

11) Explain two reasons why justice is important to many religious believers.

12) Explain two religious beliefs about the treatment of people accused of crimes.

13) Explain two religious beliefs about why people should live good lives.

Saving the best for last — the 12 mark question, with extra marks for SPaG. The question will often have bullet points that you need to include, so you can use these to make a plan. Jot down arguments for and against the statement so you don't forget any when you actually start writing your answer.

14) 'The death penalty is never a suitable punishment.'
    Evaluate this statement.
    Your answer should include the following:
    • religious arguments that support the statement
    • religious arguments that disagree with the statement
    • a conclusion.
    You can also include non-religious points of view in your answer.

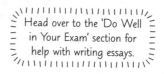
Head over to the 'Do Well in Your Exam' section for help with writing essays.

General	Peace and Conflict

World peace — a pretty tall order, but there are a lot of people <u>striving</u> for it...

Peace is the *Absence* of *Conflict* and *Violence*

1) <u>Peace</u> means that everyone in the world lives in <u>harmony</u>, and there is <u>no conflict</u>.

2) Many organisations, such as the <u>United Nations</u> (UN), work to find <u>peaceful solutions</u> to disputes and to <u>end all wars</u>, all over the world.

3) Christianity, Islam and Judaism all <u>encourage</u> believers to work towards <u>achieving peace</u> in the world.

Pacifism

- A <u>pacifist</u> is someone who has strongly held beliefs that <u>war</u> and physical <u>violence</u> are <u>wrong</u>. Pacifists believe that <u>all</u> disputes should be settled <u>peacefully</u>.

- There were pacifists in Britain who <u>refused</u> to fight in the world wars. These '<u>conscientious objectors</u>' went to prison rather than go against their beliefs — they were <u>prisoners of conscience</u>. They suffered <u>humiliation</u> in prison, and after they'd been released.

- There are different <u>degrees</u> of pacifism — some people are against violence <u>under any circumstances</u>, whereas others may <u>disagree</u> with violence, but understand that sometimes violence is the <u>least horrible</u> option.

Violence Has *Many Different Forms*

1) <u>Crime</u> is a source of a lot of violence, e.g. <u>assault</u> or <u>murder</u>.

2) Violence can occur during <u>protests</u> — a protest is when a group of people join together to <u>campaign</u> for a cause they support. While many protests occur <u>peacefully</u>, some protests become <u>violent</u> if protesters don't feel their views are being heard.

3) <u>Terrorism</u> is when a person or group deliberately seeks to cause <u>fear</u> and inflict <u>suffering</u> on other people through <u>violence</u>, sometimes for <u>political</u> reasons. The attack on the <u>World Trade Center</u> by the terrorist organisation <u>al-Qaeda</u> in New York in September 2001 was the <u>worst</u> terrorist attack in history.

4) <u>War</u> is when two or more groups or countries <u>fight</u> one another. It's <u>usually</u> decided by <u>governments</u>.

5) War and terrorism have caused many <u>deaths</u>. Lots of religious people believe in the <u>sanctity of life</u> argument, that life is given by <u>God</u> and is <u>sacred</u>, so war and terrorism are in <u>direct conflict</u> with this.

Wars Can Have Many Causes

Most wars have causes that are a <u>combination</u> of lots of different factors:

1) <u>RELIGION</u> — this has been the cause of many <u>conflicts</u> in the past and the present (see p.65-68).

2) <u>SELF-DEFENCE</u> — wars started to <u>combat</u> a threat from another country or to <u>stop</u> them from attacking first, e.g. a <u>pre-emptive strike</u>.

3) <u>TRIBALISM</u> — this tends to trigger wars where a <u>group</u> of people fight for their own <u>independent</u> state.

4) <u>HONOUR</u> — wars fought to defend the <u>honour</u> and <u>dignity</u> of a country, or to <u>save face</u>.

5) <u>GREED/ECONOMICS</u> — <u>acts of aggression</u> (attacking without provocation) are <u>condemned</u> by the UN, so purely economic wars driven by greed (e.g. raids and invasions to gain territory or goods) are few and far between. Economic factors still have an impact though — <u>poverty</u> and <u>economic imbalances</u> can make wars <u>more likely</u>.

6) <u>RETALIATION</u> — a war might be started in <u>revenge</u> for something, e.g. <u>World War One</u> started after Franz Ferdinand, Archduke of Austria, was <u>assassinated</u>.

I'll give you a peace of advice...

In some of the questions in your exams, you can scoop extra marks for spelling, punctuation, grammar and specialist terms. Brush up on these by heading over to the 'Do Well in Your Exam' section.

Peace and Conflict

Some wars are seen as necessary and 'just'. Others are sometimes seen as being fought for God.

Many People Think There Can Be 'Just Wars'

1) Although most people see peace as being ideal, many recognise that sometimes a war has to be fought. Just War theory is a philosophical theory, developed from ideas of Christian philosophers — such as St Thomas Aquinas in the 13th century. The ideas have now been adopted by people of many different beliefs. The theory explains the conditions that must be met for a war to be classed as necessary:

- There must be a good reason for the war, e.g. self-defence or to help innocent people under threat.
- All other options have been attempted to avoid war.
- It must be started by a proper authority — such as an elected government or president.
- A war must have a reasonable chance of success. Fighting an unwinnable war is considered a waste of lives.
- Any harm caused by fighting the war mustn't be as bad as the harm it's trying to prevent.

There are also conditions for fighting a war justly. These are:

- Discrimination: war should discriminate between combatants and civilians — it's not seen as 'just' to deliberately target civilians.
- Proportionality: the military advantage gained by an attack must outweigh any harm to civilians.

2) Religious and non-religious people might turn to situation ethics to decide if a war is 'just'. They'd look at all the factors surrounding the case, and choose what they think would most likely bring about peace.

People Who Fight in Holy Wars Believe They're Supported by God

1) A holy war is one where people believe that God is 'on their side'. Wars are mentioned in both the Old Testament and the Tenakh, and in the Qur'an.

2) In the past, holy wars have been fought over territory or to convert people, e.g. the crusades in the 11th to 13th centuries. However, holy wars can be declared for different reasons, such as to protect a religion.

3) Religion has been a factor in modern wars too (though often not the only factor). Although the civil war in Syria didn't start over religion, Sunni and Shi'a Muslims have fought on opposite sides. Jews and Muslims are on opposing sides in the conflict in Palestine.

4) Atheists and humanists, who don't believe in God, have criticised religion for causing conflict and wouldn't support starting a war over religion — but neither would many religious people. Some atheists and humanists also identify as pacifists, and don't agree with conflict being used at all.

Christians Believe People Should Be Peaceful

1) Many of Jesus's teachings show that peace is the ultimate goal for all human beings.

2) Isaiah 9:6 referred to the Messiah as the "Prince of Peace" (NIV) — Christians believe Jesus was the Messiah and God wanted him to create peace on Earth.

3) For Christians, Jesus's command to "Love your enemies" (Luke 6:27 NIV) is very important in the way they live their lives. He said that people shouldn't follow the Old Testament teachings about retaliation:

"You have heard that it was said, 'Eye for eye, and tooth for tooth.' But I tell you... If anyone slaps you on the right cheek, turn to them the other cheek also." Matthew 5:38-39 NIV

This implies that Christians shouldn't meet violence with violence.

4) This is evident in Matthew 26:47-56. Even though Judas had betrayed him, Jesus didn't condone anyone being violent. Jesus said "all who draw the sword will die by the sword" (Matthew 26:52 NIV), suggesting that people who engage in conflict will die because of it.

5) In his Sermon on the Mount, Jesus said "Blessed are the peacemakers" (Matthew 5:9 NIV). He also told his followers "Peace I leave with you; my peace I give you" (John 14:27 NIV).

Peace and Conflict

Many Christians Follow Jesus's Teachings and Work for Peace

1) Some Christians put Jesus's teachings into action and work to put an end to violence in the world.

> Dorothy Day was a Catholic activist who followed Jesus's pacifist teachings. She protested against the Spanish Civil War, WW2, violence and nuclear weapons in the USA (see p.69). She co-founded 'The Catholic Worker', a newspaper which was firmly anti-war and eventually evolved into a pacifist group of campaigners.

> The Catholic Archbishop Óscar Romero worked for peace during turbulent times in 1970s El Salvador. He raised awareness of the suffering and violence people were being subjected to by the military and the police. He helped those affected by the cruelty, fought for their rights and promoted peace between opposing groups. He was killed for his beliefs in 1980.

2) Some, such as Dorothy Day, believe that Jesus's teachings mean Christians should be pacifists. The Society of Friends (Quakers) is opposed to war under all circumstances.

3) Because of their belief in peace, Christians tend to use passive resistance against injustice — campaigning without violence.

> Dr Martin Luther King was a Baptist minister who dedicated his life to trying to change the way black people were treated in the USA. He organised peaceful marches, rallies and boycotts, and in 1965 blacks were given equal voting rights with whites.

> Thomas Merton was a Catholic monk and a famous pacifist. In the 1960s, his writings influenced many in the civil rights movement for racial equality and he was against the violence of the Vietnam War.

4) Most Christians wouldn't support violent protests, but some might think it's sometimes justified — when Jesus saw that some people were exploiting the temple, he "overturned the tables of the money changers and the benches of those selling doves" (Matthew 21:12 NIV) in protest at what they were doing.

Some Christians Recognise Just Wars

1) Although war goes against the teachings of Jesus, most Christian denominations accept that there can be such a thing as a 'just war'. They would agree with the conditions of the Just War theory (see p.65). It doesn't mean that the war is right — it's just not the worst option.

2) Some interpret this verse as meaning the government has the right to use violence to ensure peace:

> "...if you do wrong, be afraid, for rulers do not bear the sword for no reason. They are God's servants, agents of wrath to bring punishment on the wrongdoer." Romans 13:4 NIV

Some believe that sometimes war is the only way to find peace, e.g. against an evil regime. Christians are taught to "Love your neighbour" (Mark 12:31 NIV) — this could involve defending people in war.

3) The Catechism of the Catholic Church (2265) says that "Legitimate defence can be not only a right but a grave duty for one who is responsible for the lives of others". However, due to the advanced weaponry used in modern-day wars (see p.69) and the horrendous impact that war has had in Syria, the Catholic Church is reconsidering its stance on just war.

4) Christians are strongly against the indiscriminate killing involved in terrorism.

Holy Wars are Now Rejected By Nearly All Christians

1) In the 11th, 12th and 13th centuries, Christians went on crusades to 'free' the Christian holy places in Palestine. The wars caused a lot of devastation.

2) In the past, holy wars were fought to convert other people to Christianity. Jesus told his disciples "Do not suppose that I have come to bring peace to the earth. I did not come to bring peace, but a sword" (Matthew 10:34 NIV). Many think Jesus wasn't actually talking about violence here — he meant that spreading the Christian message would cause divisions between believers and non-believers.

3) The vast majority of Christians don't believe in the idea of a holy war any more. Although it's for different reasons, their stance on holy war would be the same as an atheist's (see p.65).

Just war — just learn it...

Explain two Christian beliefs about just war. Refer to sacred texts.   [5]

Peace and Conflict

Islam Teaches People to be Peaceful

1) Islam promotes living a peaceful existence — the Qur'an teaches that people should be <u>kind</u> to others, even if they <u>don't</u> treat them well. Muslims believe Allah sees <u>everything</u> and will <u>judge</u> people.

> "And the servants of the Most Merciful are those who walk upon the earth easily, and when the ignorant address them [harshly], they say [words of] peace." Qur'an 25:63

> "If you should raise your hand against me to kill me - I shall not raise my hand against you to kill you. Indeed, I fear Allah, Lord of the worlds." Qur'an 5:28

2) Muslims believe they should play their part to bring about <u>peace</u>. They can do this through <u>prayer</u>, <u>campaigns</u> or by working with people from <u>other religions</u> to create peace in the <u>community</u>.

3) The <u>majority</u> of Muslims <u>disagree</u> with <u>pacifism</u>, as war is sometimes <u>justified</u> in the Qur'an: "Fight in the way of Allah those who fight you but do not transgress. Indeed. Allah does not like transgressors" (Qur'an 2:190). It means they can fight in <u>self-defence</u>, but should <u>only</u> do what's absolutely <u>necessary</u>.

4) Some are <u>against</u> all war and violence as they believe <u>peaceful action</u> is always best, and is key to Islam.

5) The <u>Arab Spring</u> in 2011 saw many Muslims in countries such as Egypt demanding more <u>political power</u> for ordinary people. Many demonstrations were carried out <u>peacefully</u>, with a focus on <u>passive resistance</u>. Islam teaches people to protest against <u>injustice</u>, but <u>not</u> in <u>violent</u> ways.

In Islam, a Just War is Known as Military Jihad

1) Jihad means '<u>striving</u>' or '<u>struggle</u>', and the concept is often <u>misunderstood</u>. There are two types of jihad — <u>greater</u> and <u>lesser</u> jihad (see p.23). Lesser jihad is the 'struggle' to <u>improve</u> the <u>world</u>, and war is an example of it, but it must be fought only as a <u>last resort</u>. The Qur'an teaches that people can <u>fight</u>: "Allah will punish them by your hands and will disgrace them and give you victory over them..." (Qur'an 9:14).

2) The part of jihad involving <u>military action</u> is known as <u>Harb al-Maqadis</u> (holy war). It's a war considered to be justified by God to <u>protect</u> Muslims and their <u>religion</u>. Some believe the Qur'an says that war is an <u>acceptable</u> option to <u>defend Islam</u>: "Those who believe fight in the cause of Allah" (Qur'an 4:76).

3) Sunni and Shi'a Muslims have <u>similar views</u> on jihad nowadays. Both consider it a <u>key part</u> of their religion as it's covered in the <u>Qur'an</u> — in Shi'a Islam it's also <u>formally</u> recorded as one of the <u>Ten Obligatory Acts</u> (see p.21). In the past, <u>Twelver</u> Shi'a Muslims believed that jihad could <u>only</u> be declared when the <u>last Imam</u> came out of <u>hiding</u> (see p.16), but jihad for <u>defensive</u> purposes was still <u>allowed</u>.

4) Military jihad has very strict <u>rules</u> — these are the <u>conditions</u> in Islam for a just war. There are many <u>similarities</u> with <u>Just War theory</u>:

> * It is justified to bring about <u>freedom</u> from tyranny, restore <u>peace</u>, combat <u>oppression</u>, or right <u>injustice</u>.
> * Jihad must be in the name of <u>Allah</u>, and according to his <u>will</u>. It must be <u>declared</u> by a <u>religious leader</u>.
> * If an <u>Islamic country</u> has been assaulted, then war is justified.
> * In the past, jihad was used to <u>spread Islam</u> and gain more <u>land</u>. However, now many Muslims believe jihad must <u>not</u> be used to <u>colonise</u>, suppress or impose Islam on non-believers.
> * The hadith Muwatta Malik 21:10 also sets out some <u>conditions</u> for battle: "Do not kill women or children or an aged, infirm person. Do not cut down fruit-bearing trees. Do not destroy an inhabited place".
> * If the <u>opposition</u> wants to <u>end</u> the war, then Muslims must <u>accept</u> it: "And if they incline to peace, then incline to it [also]..." (Qur'an 8:61).

5) Some believe that if they do <u>fight</u> for Allah, they'll be <u>rewarded</u> in the afterlife "And he who fights in the cause of Allah and is killed or achieves victory — We will bestow upon him a great reward" (Qur'an 4:74).

6) Some Muslims <u>believe</u> that just wars can no longer exist because of, e.g. the use of WMDs (see p.69).

7) The term 'jihad' is sometimes used by Islamic <u>terrorists</u> to <u>justify</u> their acts of terror. However, nearly all Muslims are <u>strongly against</u> this — they don't consider the terrorists to be <u>real Muslims</u>.

Learn all the conditions for a just war in Islam...

Explain two Muslim beliefs about just war. Refer to sacred texts.   [5]

Peace and Conflict

Judaism Teaches that Peace is Very Important

1) The universal greeting among Jews is 'shalom' (peace). Jews don't support war unless it's essential — the Torah teaches that peace should be the first approach, and war shouldn't be started without good reason.

2) Trying to bring about peace is very important in Judaism, and it features in many Jewish prayers. Peace is believed to be given by God.

3) Jews expect that a Messiah will come and bring peace to Earth (see p.29). Micah 4:3 prophesies that when this happens, weapons will be unnecessary and will be turned into ploughshares (the blade of a plough): "They will beat their swords into ploughshares and their spears into pruning hooks" (NIV). Isaiah 2:4 demonstrates how Jews hope that war will end: "Nation will not take up sword against nation, nor will they train for war any more" (NIV).

4) Jews are against terrorism, and hope God will defend the weak from terrorists: "defending the fatherless and the oppressed, so that mere earthly mortals will never again strike terror" (Psalm 10:18 NIV).

5) Most Jews aren't pacifists, but non-violence is seen as a good choice if it's the only way to survive, or if using violence would be pointless. This is why Jews generally don't respond violently to anti-Semitism. Only non-violent protest against injustice would be encouraged.

Emanuel Ringelblum provided food and tried to improve conditions in the ghettos of Warsaw (under German control at the start of WWII). He collected accounts of the atrocities that happened and hid them underground — some information eventually reached other countries in Europe. He defied the Germans without resorting to violence.

Violence is Sometimes Allowed

1) Pikuach nefesh (the duty to save life) means Jews must try to save someone who's in danger of being murdered — even if they must kill the murderer. However, they should use the minimal necessary force.

2) According to the Talmud and the Torah, a person can kill someone else in self-defence if their own life is under threat: "Whoever sheds human blood, by humans shall their blood be shed" (Genesis 9:6 NIV).

3) These ideas can apply to war, and many Jews believe that sometimes war is needed to bring about peace.

There are Two Types of War — Obligatory and Optional

1) War is split into two types — milchemet mitzvah (obligatory war) and milchemet reshut (optional war).

2) Milchemet mitzvah are thought to be commanded by God, so could be thought of as holy war. In the Old Testament, God supported the Israelites in war — King David praised God for his help: "The Lord... shot his arrows and scattered the enemy" (2 Samuel 22:14-15 NIV). Milchemet mitzvah might be:

- a war fought in self-defence, or a pre-emptive strike in order to avoid being attacked.
- a war to help neighbouring countries — so that your own country is not invaded.

These conditions are similar to Just War theory.

3) In recent times, wars have been fought by the state of Israel. Many Jews see these as milchemet mitzvah. Some see them as defending the Promised Land that was given to Abraham by God.

4) Milchemet reshut refers to wars described in the Tenakh to expand Israel's territory. Maimonides said they could only be fought while the Temple existed — many think they can't be fought today.

5) There were conditions on milchemet reshut, e.g. in Deuteronomy 20. One condition was peace must be offered first: "When you march up to attack a city, make its people an offer of peace" (Deuteronomy 20:10 NIV). It includes rules about the treatment of women and children, and cutting down trees too.

6) Although some of these aren't in line with Just War theory, they've been developed into modern ideas about just war, such as protecting non-combatants and not causing unnecessary destruction.

Mitzvah or reshut? Make sure you know which is which...

Explain two Jewish beliefs about when war is justified.
Include an example from a source of wisdom and authority. [5]

Weapons of Mass Destruction | All religions

Another heavy topic I'm afraid...

Weapons of Mass Destruction Cause a Huge Amount of Damage

1) Some wars have used <u>weapons of mass destruction</u> (WMDs). These are weapons that can destroy large areas of land and/or lots of people all at once, e.g. <u>chemical</u>, <u>biological</u> and <u>nuclear</u> weapons. They're <u>indiscriminate</u> — they harm soldiers and civilians alike.

2) <u>Chemical</u> and <u>biological</u> weapons are <u>banned</u> by international law — using them is considered a <u>war crime</u>. There are many arguments <u>for</u> and <u>against</u> possessing <u>nuclear weapons</u>:

- Nuclear weapons serve as a <u>deterrent</u> to ensure peace — a country might <u>not</u> attack another if that country has nuclear weapons. Many countries give this as the <u>reason</u> for <u>keeping</u> nuclear weapons. In the 1900s, several conflicts were <u>settled</u> or <u>sidestepped</u> because nuclear weapons posed too big a <u>risk</u>.
- Some have a <u>utilitarian</u> perspective — the best course of action is the one that brings about the best <u>balance</u> of positive and negative results. The <u>USA</u> bombed Hiroshima and Nagasaki in Japan in <u>WW2</u> as they thought that using nuclear weapons would <u>save</u> the most <u>lives</u> overall, and <u>end</u> the war <u>faster</u>.
- Nuclear weapons could be used by a country in order to <u>defend</u> itself if under attack.

- Nuclear weapons are <u>costly</u>. Many people argue that <u>funds</u> could be <u>better spent</u>, e.g. on healthcare.
- Many religions believe in the <u>sanctity of life</u> — life was given to humans by God and should be <u>respected</u>. <u>Widespread suffering</u> caused by nuclear weapons completely goes against this.
- Believers who agree with <u>Just War theory</u> might argue that the <u>indiscriminate nature</u> of nuclear weapons (they would kill innocent people) could <u>never</u> be classed as <u>just</u>.
- Earth is <u>God's creation</u> — using nuclear weapons would <u>destroy</u> what God trusted humans to take <u>care</u> of.

Many Religious Believers are Against WMDs

Christian views

- Some Christians use <u>Jesus's teachings</u> about peace to argue against nuclear weapons. <u>All</u> Christian denominations are <u>against</u> using them.
- However, some think nuclear weapons help to <u>keep the peace</u> as countries are afraid of starting a nuclear war.

Muslim views

- Many Muslims are against WMDs as they don't follow the conditions of <u>lesser jihad</u> (see p.67) — <u>innocent people</u> would get hurt or killed.
- <u>Pakistan</u> (a Muslim country) has nuclear weapons, but other Muslim countries have come out <u>against</u> possessing WMDs.

"...whoever kills a soul... it is as if he had slain mankind entirely." Qur'an 5:32

Jewish views

- The Talmud says that if something will inflict harm on over a <u>sixth</u> of the population, then it's <u>not allowed</u>.
- The <u>Purity of Arms</u> rule is followed by the <u>Israeli Defence Forces</u>. It says they will only use their weapons as much as is considered <u>reasonable</u>, they <u>won't hurt</u> people who aren't involved in the conflict and will try <u>not</u> to <u>damage</u> buildings. The sweeping damage caused by WMDs <u>doesn't</u> fit with these constraints.
- Although actually using WMDs <u>couldn't</u> be <u>justified</u>, Jews believe that a country could <u>say</u> that they'll use nuclear weapons, but <u>without</u> ever intending to <u>use</u> them, to <u>stop</u> something <u>bad</u> happening. They might support this idea with the <u>sanctity of life</u> argument. Israel has <u>never</u> revealed <u>whether</u> it has nuclear weapons.

1) Both <u>Christians</u> and <u>Jews</u> might turn to Deuteronomy 20. It suggests that <u>women</u> and <u>children</u> should be <u>spared</u>, and <u>unnecessary damage</u> shouldn't be caused: "When you lay siege to a city for a long time... do not destroy its trees by putting an axe to them, because you can eat their fruit" (Deuteronomy 20:19 NIV). The <u>total destruction</u> that WMDs would cause goes <u>against</u> this.

2) Some <u>atheists</u> are in favour of WMDs to <u>deter</u> an opponent and to potentially <u>use</u> — they don't believe their <u>actions</u> will be <u>judged</u>. Others are strongly <u>anti-WMDs</u> as they believe people only live <u>one life</u> on Earth. <u>Humanists</u> have <u>opposed</u> the use of WMDs due to the <u>huge number</u> of people that would <u>suffer</u>.

Make sure you know arguments for and against WMDs...

...plus non-religious views and ethical arguments too. These can help edge you closer to top marks.

All religions

Peacemaking

Finding peace and resolving conflicts is important to Christians, Jews and Muslims.

Justice, Forgiveness and Reconciliation are Key to Peacemaking

1) Justice is the idea of each person getting what they deserve, and maintaining what's right. Believers think that God is just — he treats and judges people fairly as he created everyone equally. Justice leads to a fairer society — if people feel they're treated equally, there's more chance of peace.

2) Forgiveness is when a person stops feeling hurt by something another person has done to them. Another of God's characteristics is that he is merciful — he forgives people for the things they've done wrong. As God is merciful towards them, believers feel that they should forgive other people, and that forgiveness is the only way true peace can be achieved.

3) Reconciliation is bringing people together that previously were in conflict to make peace.

Christians Believe That God is Fair and Forgiving

1) Christians believe that justice is very important, since people are equal in the eyes of God. Christians have a duty to look after other people, and try to guide them to do what's right and repent of their sins.

2) They believe they should follow God's example and be just to others: "...what does the Lord require of you? To act justly and to love mercy and to walk humbly with your God" (Micah 6:8 NIV). The parable of the sheep and goats shows God treats people well if they've done the same to others.

3) Forgiveness is important to Christians — read p.59 to learn more about it. They believe they should seek God's forgiveness and forgive people who've hurt them.

> "Blessed are the merciful, for they will be shown mercy." Matthew 5:7 NIV

4) If they repent, and put their faith in God, God forgives people and they are reconciled with him. Christians believe the same sort of reconciliation is needed between people to create peace.

Muslims Try to Forgive and Reconcile as Muhammad Did

1) Muslims believe strongly in justice and that they should treat all people fairly and equally. They consider maintaining justice to be part of their role as 'khalifah' — vice-regents of Allah's creation.

2) Islam teaches that Allah and the Prophet Muhammad are forgiving — have a read of p.59.

3) Muslims are encouraged to work to restore peace. They believe it's important to reconcile fractured relationships — this is something that the Prophet Muhammad did.

> "And not equal are the good deed and the bad. Repel [evil] by that [deed] which is better; and thereupon the one whom between you and him is enmity [will become] as though he was a devoted friend." Qur'an 41:34

Jews Must Work for Justice and Ask for Forgiveness

1) Justice is a major part of Judaism — Jews believe in fairness. Pirkei Avot 1:18 (part of the Talmud) says that "By three things is the world sustained: law, truth and peace."

2) Many Jews believe that true peace can only happen when everyone is treated fairly and any people in conflict are reconciled.

> "Learn to do right; seek justice. Defend the oppressed." Isaiah 1:17 NIV

3) Seeking forgiveness from God and people you've wronged is very important in Judaism. In conflict situations, asking for forgiveness and forgiving others is an important step to reconciliation. Turn to p.59 to find out more about forgiveness in Judaism.

Learn it all — the examiner isn't as forgiving as God...

Write 'Justice', 'Forgiveness' and 'Reconciliation' along the top of a piece of paper. Underneath, write down the religious views that you've learned from this page.

Peacemaking

Many religious organisations work towards <u>peace</u> and help people in countries devastated by war.

Religious Believers Can Work for Peace Directly and Indirectly

1) Many religious believers feel they must act to create <u>peace</u> — see p.66 for some examples. Some might be <u>directly</u> involved in peacemaking by working for organisations which offer <u>relief</u> to war-torn areas.

2) Some religious charities <u>campaign</u> for help for groups in conflict to <u>rebuild</u> their <u>relationship</u>. For example, <u>Christian Aid</u> has urged governments to find a <u>compromise</u> in the Israel/Palestine conflict.

3) Religious people can also help to create peace <u>indirectly</u>, e.g. by <u>donating</u> money to charitable causes and by holding <u>protests</u> and <u>demonstrations</u> against conflicts. Some may work to ensure that people have equal <u>human rights</u>, which could help to <u>avoid</u> conflict.

Christian Charities Work for Peace and Help Victims of War

In the <u>Sermon on the Mount</u>, Jesus says "Blessed are the peacemakers, for they will be called children of God" (Matthew 5:9 NIV). Many feel that it's important to <u>help people</u> caught up in <u>conflict zones</u> and to try to bring <u>peace</u> to the area.

- <u>Pax Christi</u> is a Catholic organisation that works for peaceful conflict <u>resolution</u>. They try to bring people back <u>together</u> who've been in <u>conflict</u> with one another.
- They believe in <u>avoiding</u> conflict and the <u>violence</u> that comes with it. They campaign for governments to spend <u>less money</u> on weapons and armed forces. They also disagree with <u>nuclear weapons</u>, and work for nuclear <u>disarmament</u>.

Muslims Can Give Money to Support Peacemaking

1) Muslims believe it's important to try to create a <u>peaceful world</u>. They believe that this is part of their role as <u>khalifah</u>.

2) Individuals can help to make the world more <u>equal</u> through <u>zakah</u> — <u>2.5%</u> of their yearly savings should be given to the <u>needy</u>, no matter how rich or poor they are. Zakah could be <u>donated</u> to a number of different <u>charities</u> which are involved in <u>peacemaking</u> and supporting <u>victims of war</u>.

- The <u>Muslim Peace Fellowship</u> is a group of Muslims who want to promote <u>peace</u>, <u>justice</u> and <u>non-violence</u>.
- It strives to do <u>good</u> through <u>Islam</u> — the group promotes peace <u>through</u> faith, and works to bring about changes that make society <u>fair</u> and <u>compassionate</u> to <u>everyone</u>. They do this by <u>raising awareness</u> through events, prayer and working with other faiths.

- <u>Islamic Relief UK</u> is a group inspired by their <u>faith</u> to try to help as many people as possible.
- They help people affected by <u>war</u> — in <u>Syria</u> they've given people essentials such as <u>food</u> and <u>healthcare</u>. They also help people in <u>neighbouring countries</u> who've <u>fled</u> their homes because of the <u>conflict</u>.

Many Jews Work for Peace in Israel

1) Jews believe that <u>peace</u> is something that God gives the <u>world</u>. Many Jews <u>protest</u> for peace and try to create a <u>fairer world</u>, since they believe that peace is only really possible when <u>everyone</u> is treated <u>justly</u>.

2) Charity through <u>financial aid</u> is called <u>tzedakah</u>. Everyone is expected to contribute <u>10%</u> of their wealth — this money can <u>help</u> people <u>affected</u> by war and help to create <u>equality</u> to <u>avoid</u> war.

The <u>Jewish Peace Fellowship</u> is a pacifist organisation, founded to help <u>conscientious objectors</u> in WWII. The organisation believes that military action <u>never</u> solves conflicts, and that <u>active non-violence</u> (e.g. negotiations, promoting social justice) is the only way to settle disputes. They're helping to <u>resolve</u> the conflict in <u>Israel</u> and <u>reconcile</u> the people there.

<u>Natal</u> (Israel Trauma Center for Victims of Terror and War) helps people in <u>Israel</u> who've been affected by the <u>conflict</u> there. It aims to <u>care</u> for and <u>treat</u> people suffering from <u>health problems</u> related to <u>war</u>, e.g. post traumatic stress disorder.

Peace, love, charity... and a nice revision task to end with...

How do religious believers work for a more peaceful world? Jot down as many ways as you can.

Revision Summary

That was a lot of information to take in there, so now test yourself to see how you got on. These questions are similar to the ones that you'll be answering in the exam, so you know what it'll be like on the day.

If there's anything you can't answer, go back through the section and have another go when you've re-read it.

For some courses, you need to learn about the views of different religions on these topics. But for other courses, you need to know about them in the context of just one religion — if that's the case for your course, answer each of these questions in the context of the religion you've studied.

Let's start with some nice 1 mark multiple choice questions.
1) Which of the following is the idea that everyone should get what they deserve?
   a) Justice   b) Peacemaking   c) Reconciliation   d) Forgiveness

2) Which of the following is the act of deliberately causing suffering and fear through violence?
   a) Passive resistance   b) Pacifism   c) Holy war   d) Terrorism

3) Which of the following might involve starting a war in revenge for something?
   a) Tribalism   b) Retaliation   c) Self-defence   d) Honour

Moving up to 2 marks now, no biggy. Two short points are all you need.

4) Give two causes of conflict.

5) Give two religious beliefs about reconciliation.

Now see how you get on with some 3 mark questions.

6) Outline three conditions of Just War theory.

7) Outline three ways that charities work for peace and help victims of conflict.

4 marks now — make two points, but this time develop them for full marks.

8) Explain two ways in which religious people can work for peace.

9) Explain two religious teachings about forgiveness.

10) Explain two religious attitudes to pacifism.

Make sure your writing is well structured and accurate in the longer questions — your points have to be clear to the examiner.

Next up, a 5 mark question. You need to refer to religious texts in order to get all 5 marks.

11) Explain two religious teachings about conflict.

12) Explain two religious beliefs about holy war.

A 6 mark question now — remember to include examples from sources of wisdom and authority.

13) Explain why peace is important to believers.

Hang on to your hat — it's the 12 mark question, with additional SPaG marks. The question usually comes with a list of things to include, so use it when you start planning your answer. Write a list of arguments for and against the statement and make sure you've included them all.

14) 'Nuclear weapons deter countries from attacking each other and ensure peace.'
    Evaluate this statement.
    Give arguments that support the statement and arguments that disagree with the statement.
    You must include:
    • examples of religious teachings
    • different religious opinions
    • appropriate ethical arguments
    • a conclusion.

If you need advice on writing essays, have a look at the 'Do Well in Your Exam' section.

Design and Causation All religions

The belief that God created the world is an important part of many religions, and often strengthens faith.

Different People Believe for Different Reasons

1) About 84% of the global population belongs to a religion (source Pew Research Centre). The rest don't have specific religious beliefs, or have no spiritual beliefs. There are many reasons for being religious:

- People want to find out why life is as it is. Some people are convinced the 'design' or 'causation' arguments explain this.
- Some are drawn to the purpose, structure and comfort religion provides, or simply by the desire to have something to believe. Some people's faith is strengthened by the feelings they experience during worship and as part of a religious community.
- People brought up by religious parents or in a religious community are more likely to believe in a god.

2) There are various reasons why people might reject religion: they believe there's no proof there's a god, or that religion causes too much strife between people, or that the evil in the world shows there's no god.

3) Atheists reject the idea of a divine being. Agnostics believe it's impossible to know either way for certain.

The Design Argument: 'The Universe Must Have Had a Designer'

1) Belief that God created the universe is a central part of belief in God — not only does the universe's existence prove God's existence, but believers think it shows some of his characteristics, e.g. his power.

2) Many Christians, Muslims and Jews believe a god exists because of 'design' arguments. The idea is that the intricate workings of the universe can't have come about by chance. There must have been some kind of designer — a god. The Bible, the Qur'an and the Torah support this argument:

> The Qur'an says aspects of nature are evidence Allah is the creator. "In the creation of the heavens and earth, and the alternation of the night and the day ... and ... the winds and the clouds ... are signs for a people who use reason." (Qur'an 2:164)

> The Bible's argument is similar. Romans 1:20 says "since the creation of the world God's invisible qualities — his eternal power and divine nature — have been clearly seen, being understood from what has been made" (NIV).
>
> "God created the heavens and the earth" Genesis 1:1 NIV — Torah/Bible

3) Some think aspects of nature support this idea. For example, snowflakes form complex shapes that are unique to each individual snowflake. The distribution of petals and seeds on many plants and the spiral shape of some shells follow mathematical rules.

4) William Paley's watchmaker argument says that if you came across an intricate watch, you wouldn't think it was made by chance — you would assume it had been designed. The same must be true of complex structures in nature. A common example people give is the human eye, which is made up of many parts — it's so sophisticated, they believe it must have had a designer.

5) Scientists say the conditions that led to the creation of the universe and life were extremely specific. The fine-tuning argument says this shows there was a designer — they couldn't have occurred by chance.

Some People Aren't Convinced by These Arguments

1) Charles Darwin explained how species developed by adapting themselves to the conditions around them through 'survival of the fittest'. Species or individuals that have characteristics that are beneficial for survival are more likely to live, while those that aren't well-adapted are more likely to die out. This helps to explain how species have developed their characteristics through time — known as evolution.

2) In 2009, a survey found 37% of people in Britain thought evolution was 'beyond reasonable doubt'.

3) Some Christians, Muslims and Jews believe evolution doesn't contradict the design argument — God or Allah must have 'designed' evolution. Darwin didn't see it as conclusive proof against God's existence.

4) Some disagree with evolution. They may struggle most to reconcile evolution with the belief that God created humans in his own image — it may seem unlikely he did so by slowly evolving humans from apes.

5) Scientists can explain things such as why plants and shells often have spiral patterns — shells have evolved to do so because it means the animal inside a shell can keep living in it as it grows.

6) Some people believe God created the universe but has not had any further involvement with it. Some believe that there's no evidence the 'designer' and creator still exists.

Design and Causation

Ideas about <u>causation</u> have been used over the <u>centuries</u> as evidence that a divine being <u>exists</u>.

Causation: 'There Must Have Been a First Cause'

1) The <u>cosmological argument</u>, also known as the <u>First Cause</u> argument, is founded on a <u>chain of logic</u>.

2) Everything that <u>happens</u> is <u>caused</u> by <u>something else</u>. An event <u>now</u> was caused by an <u>earlier</u> event, that was caused by an <u>even earlier</u> event, etc. If you trace this <u>chain</u> back in time, there are <u>two</u> possibilities:
   - The chain goes back <u>forever</u> — i.e. the universe has <u>always</u> existed, it's <u>eternal</u>.
   - You eventually reach a <u>starting point</u> — an <u>uncaused</u> cause or 'First Cause'.

3) Some think the '<u>First Cause</u>' was <u>God</u>, as only he is <u>eternal</u> and has enough <u>power</u> to create the universe.

4) The <u>scriptures</u> in Christianity, Islam and Judaism describe how <u>God</u> created the <u>universe</u>. Believers may use the <u>cosmological</u> argument (along with the design argument) as <u>evidence</u> to <u>support</u> this idea.

Christians Believe God Created the Universe

1) <u>Christian</u> teachings on creation are taken from Genesis 1-2, which says God created <u>everything</u> — see p.3. Some take the description in Genesis <u>literally</u>. Others think it's more <u>symbolic</u>, and might look to <u>science</u> too.

2) <u>Thomas Aquinas</u>, a 13th century monk, developed <u>Five Ways</u> to prove God <u>exists</u>. They've been <u>influential</u> in <u>Christianity</u>. Three of them have a <u>similar logic</u> to the <u>cosmological</u> argument:

• <u>Nothing</u> can <u>move</u> by itself — everything needs <u>something</u> to <u>move</u> it. • This means the <u>first</u> thing that <u>ever</u> moved needed something to <u>move</u> it. • This <u>first mover</u> is <u>God</u>.	• <u>Nothing</u> can <u>create</u> itself. • There can't be a <u>chain</u> of <u>creation</u> that's been happening <u>forever</u>. • So there must have been a <u>first cause</u> — God.	• <u>Contingent</u> beings are beings that are <u>caused</u> to <u>exist</u>. • It's <u>necessary</u> for there to be a <u>being</u> which has <u>created</u> contingent beings. • This <u>necessary being</u> must be God.

The Qur'an States that Allah Created the Universe

1) <u>Muslims</u> believe <u>Allah</u> created the world — Qur'an 79:27 says "Allah constructed it". The Qur'an says <u>Allah</u> made Adam from <u>clay</u> and breathed <u>life</u> and a <u>soul</u> into him — and that all humans <u>descend</u> from Adam.

2) The Muslim theologian <u>al-Ghazali</u> wrote in his book al-Iqtisad fil'Itiqad that <u>everything</u> that starts to exist was <u>caused</u> to <u>exist</u>. The <u>universe</u> started to exist, so it had a <u>cause</u> — <u>Allah</u>. The focus on the universe having <u>started</u> to exist (i.e. not being <u>infinite</u>) is a <u>key part</u> of the theory, known as the <u>kalam cosmological argument</u>. Al-Ghazali believed the <u>universe</u> was made up of <u>chains of events</u> that Allah had <u>predetermined</u>.

The Torah says God Created the Universe

1) <u>Jewish</u> teachings about <u>creation</u> come from Genesis 1-2, which says God created <u>everything</u> — see p.3 for more.

2) <u>Ultra-Orthodox</u> Jews, who see the Torah as the <u>literal</u> word of God, tend to <u>accept</u> the account in Genesis. <u>Others</u> may argue the story <u>isn't exact</u> but just a way of <u>understanding</u> how it happened, though they think God created everything. Other parts of the Tenakh <u>support</u> this, e.g. God says "It is I who made the earth" in Isaiah 45:12 NIV.

3) The theologian <u>Maimonides</u> wasn't sure about <u>creation</u> — "the world cannot but be either eternal or created in time. If it is created in time, it undoubtedly has a creator". He came up with forms of the <u>cosmological argument</u> too.

There are Differing Opinions on the Cosmological Argument

1) Some people question its <u>logic</u>. They argue that the argument <u>contradicts</u> itself — it says <u>everything</u> has to have a <u>cause</u>, but then says there must be an <u>event</u> that <u>didn't</u> have a <u>cause</u> — the <u>first cause</u>.

2) There's <u>no evidence</u> that if there is a <u>first cause</u>, it has to be a <u>divine being</u> — a <u>god</u>. Some say that even if a <u>god</u> was the <u>first cause</u>, it doesn't mean they <u>still</u> exist now. It also doesn't give any <u>indication</u> that the god has the <u>characteristics</u> of the <u>Christian</u>, <u>Jewish</u> or <u>Muslim</u> god.

3) Some <u>believers</u> think the <u>Big Bang theory</u> (p.47) <u>supports</u> the argument — God <u>caused</u> the Big Bang.

Blimey, it's enough to make your head spin...

It's a good idea to read these two pages again now to get them in your head — they're pretty complex.

Miracles

Miracles are a form of revelation (p.76-78) — believers may think they prove God exists and reveal his nature.

Many Believe Miracles Prove There is a God

1) Miracles are seemingly inexplicable events, such as people with apparently incurable illnesses being healed.

2) Christianity, Islam and Judaism all involve some belief in miracles, though to differing extents. These include events in their scriptures, though some people believe miracles also happen nowadays. Others argue that the miracles in religious texts should be interpreted symbolically rather than literally.

3) People believe miracles offer proof there is a god because they go against the laws of nature — only God would have the power to do so. They also show God's benevolence, as many miracles are beneficial, e.g. healing someone who is ill. Healing people also shows that God can decide who lives or dies.

Christians Read Stories of Miracles in the New Testament

1) Jesus performed miracles to show he had the power of God, and to show the importance of faith. These included feeding 5000 people with very little food, and walking on water (Matthew 14:13-21 and 22-33).

2) He was known for curing people of their illnesses, e.g. John 4:43-54. Healing miracles are important in Christianity, e.g. the water at the Catholic pilgrimage site Lourdes is thought to cure people (see p.77).

3) Christians believe the birth and resurrection of Jesus were miracles in their own right (see p.4).

Miracles are Important in Judaism

1) Many miraculous events are described in the Torah. A well-known example is God sending down manna (miraculous food) from heaven so the Israelites could eat while they were in the desert — see Exodus 16.

2) Some Progressive Jews say the stories are spiritual messages and aren't literally true. More orthodox Jews may think they did happen. Many Jews prefer to focus more on God, the Torah and creation than miracles.

3) The word 'nes' is used for 'miracle' in Hebrew — it means 'sign' or 'marker', as miracles are signs of God. But the Torah warns Jews not to be influenced by miracles alone — it's more important to focus on God.

> "If a prophet ... announces to you a sign or wonder, and if the sign or wonder ... takes place, and the prophet says, '... follow other gods ...,' you must not listen to the words of that prophet ... It is the Lord your God you must follow." Deuteronomy 13:1-4 NIV

Muslims Believe the Qur'an is a Miracle in Itself

1) Muslims believe the Qur'an is a miracle — the direct word of Allah, with a style that's impossible to copy. Qur'an 17:88 says "If mankind ... gathered ... to produce the like of this Qur'an, they could not".

2) Some think the Qur'an contains 'scientific miracles' — it describes facts discovered centuries later, e.g. how human embryos develop (Qur'an 23:13-14). Others disagree, as it's not detailed enough to be sure.

3) Many Muslims think that the prophets performed miracles in order to show they had been sent by God. For example, some believe Muhammad split the moon in two — Qur'an 54:1 says "the moon has split".

Some People Don't Believe in Miracles

1) Some believers prefer to focus on God and living their life in a moral way rather than on miracles.

2) Atheists and humanists don't tend to believe in miracles. They think they can be explained by science, or are fakes or misunderstandings. They might explain someone being cured of a terminal disease by saying they had been misdiagnosed, or the hope of a religious figure healing them had stimulated their recovery.

3) It can be a matter of perspective — a religious person might seek a miraculous explanation for something atheists and humanists would call a coincidence, e.g. something happening soon after you prayed for it.

Don't rely on a miracle to pass your exam — revise well...

... and do exam questions. Miraculously, there's one here:
Explain two different religious attitudes to beliefs in miracles. [4]

All religions	Revelation

For many religious people, revelation is an important factor in proving God's existence.

Revelation is How God's Presence is Revealed

1) It's difficult to conclusively prove God exists. So Christians, Muslims and Jews look for evidence to reveal God's presence. They believe he is revealed in different ways, including through the scriptures, the world around us and religious experiences.

2) Revelation doesn't just involve knowing God exists, but also what he's like and what he expects of people. Revelations can give rise to or strengthen people's belief in a god. There are two main types of revelation:

Special Revelation

1. Special revelations are revelations to specific people. The scriptures of all three faiths include accounts of these, sometimes about the same people — e.g. God (Allah) appearing to Noah (Nuh) and Abraham (Ibrahim). Jews and Christians believe God made agreements (covenants) with them — he gave them rules for how to live, in return for him caring for them.
2. Special revelations include revelations through prophethood (sometimes written down as scriptures), visions and miracles (see p.75).
3. They're direct and personal, so they can be powerful experiences. However, they're hard to prove because they're personal.
4. Some think they still occur today, while others disagree.

General Revelation

1. General revelations are revelations available to everyone. They're more indirect and therefore have to be interpreted.
2. Many think the world is an example of general revelation. Believers think God created the world, so it proves he exists.
3. Many think our conscience proves God exists, as people all over the world have similar morals, e.g. that killing is wrong. God must have created this within every person.

The Scriptures are Important Revelations

1) Christians, Muslims and Jews believe God's nature and will are revealed in their holy books. Many believe they were either inspired by God or came directly from him. They contain knowledge of God and the faith.

2) Most religious people believe that all or parts of them were special revelations, as they were revealed to specific prophets. In their written form, they also have some features of general revelation — they are available to everyone, all the time, and they need to be interpreted to be understood.

The Bible

The Bible is a collection of books written by various authors. Some Christians think the authors were inspired and guided by God as they wrote, but he didn't directly reveal it to them. The New Testament describes Jesus's life — Jesus is seen as the completion of God's revelation to people. Hebrews 1:1-2 says "God spoke to our ancestors through the prophets at many times and in various ways, but in these last days he has spoken to us by his Son" (NIV). Jesus is seen as the 'new covenant' — he died for people's sins, but in return people should worship God.

The Torah

Orthodox Jews believe the five books of the Torah were directly revealed to Moses by God. Progressive Jews tend to believe it contains God's message but the text was written by people.

The Qur'an

Muslims believe Allah revealed the Qur'an directly to Muhammad. It's a fully accurate record of Allah's final revelation to humankind. Muslims believe he gave earlier revelations to prophets such as Musa (Moses) and Isa (Jesus) but the texts have been altered.

3) Many atheists and humanists think the scriptures just depict their authors' ideas about God, and that many of the events in them didn't occur. They may see these ancient texts as largely irrelevant to life today.

Revelations Show God's Nature

For more about the nature of God, see p.1 for Christianity or p.27 for Judaism. For more on Allah, see p.17.

1) Christians, Muslims and Jews have similar beliefs about God's characteristics. Many believe he is just, omniscient, omnipotent, loving, eternal, transcendent and immanent. See p.1, 17, and 27 for definitions.

2) Revelation can give people ideas about what God is like, though people may see him in different ways. For example, many believe they can have a relationship with God, e.g. through prayer, showing he is a personal god. Others see him as distant from people as he rarely acts in the world — so he's impersonal.

3) The scriptures can show God's characteristics, e.g. Qur'an 57:4 says "He is with you wherever you are", while Psalm 139:1 says "Lord ... you know me" (NIV). This suggests to believers that God is personal.

4) Believers think God shows his compassion through his intervention in the world — e.g. showing people how to live a better life through the prophets in all three faiths, and through Jesus as Messiah in Christian belief.

Revelation

Some See Nature as Revelation

A beautiful sunset may be seen by some as a numinous experience.

1) Christians, Muslims and Jews believe God created the world — it shows he exists. The natural world can provide numinous (spiritual) experiences, by inspiring awe and a sense of God's presence. Interventions in nature, e.g. miracles, show God's immanence.

2) Nature may show God's transcendence — he created it but isn't present in it — as well as other aspects:

Many Christians believe characteristics such as God's intelligence are revealed through the complexity of nature. The Catechism of the Catholic Church says "The beauty of creation reflects the infinite beauty of the Creator" (341). Nature is often cruel, which can be hard to explain. Some believe nature became cruel after the Fall — when Adam and Eve sinned. So nature no longer fully shows what God is like.

Many Jews see the universe's existence as proof enough that God exists — no more proof is needed. The wonders of creation may deepen their relationship with God — Jews may offer blessings to God if they see something beautiful in nature. Jews believe all of nature comes from God, even the negative parts — Isaiah 45:7 says "I bring prosperity and create disaster" (NIV). Jews have a responsibility to look after his creation.

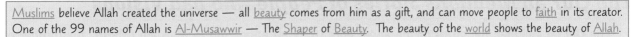

"The heavens declare the glory of God; the skies proclaim the work of his hands." Psalm 19:1 NIV

Muslims believe Allah created the universe — all beauty comes from him as a gift, and can move people to faith in its creator. One of the 99 names of Allah is Al-Musawwir — The Shaper of Beauty. The beauty of the world shows the beauty of Allah.

3) Atheists and humanists don't believe that nature reveals God. They argue that even aspects of nature we don't fully understand, e.g. how animals navigate as they migrate, will one day be explained by science.

God can be Revealed Through Religious Experiences

1) Religious experiences are personal experiences of God — they're a form of special revelation.

2) They can take many forms — a vision, a dream, hearing a voice, a feeling of ecstasy or peace, or feelings of being loved, forgiven or guided. They can take place during prayer or worship, or at other times. They can be so powerful they change the life of the person, or they might be more gentle experiences.

3) Other religious believers may take inspiration from someone who's had such an experience. Some people who have had religious experiences become well known — see below and the next page.

Visions are a Dramatic Form of Religious Experience

1) A vision is a religious experience in which a person sees something sacred — such as an angel. Visions usually tell the receiver about God and his will, or about the receiver's own life.

2) Visions are direct and powerful forms of religious experience. They often change how believers live their lives — they can strengthen people's faith or even induce them to believe in something they didn't believe in before. They can convince people that God exists — only he could have made them happen.

There are Many Examples of Visions in Christianity

For Old Testament examples, see the top of p.78.

1) Some visions are reported in the Bible, which gives them authority, as they're part of the scripture.

- At the transfiguration, the disciples saw a vision of Moses and Elijah with Jesus, who was covered in light. God said "This is my Son ... Listen to him!" (Matthew 17:5 NIV). This and the presence of Moses and Elijah showed Jesus was important.
- St Paul was originally named Saul. He persecuted Christians. One day he saw a light, and heard Jesus asking why Saul was persecuting him. This transformed Saul's life — he became Christian and spent the rest of his life preaching the gospel.

2) Other visions of Mary or angels appeared to people later. The Churches confirm if they think they're authentic. Belief in this type of vision is more significant in Catholicism than in Protestant Christianity.

- Joan of Arc was a French peasant. She had visions of the archangel Michael, among others. These encouraged her to lead France against England in the Hundred Years' War. She was captured and killed by English allies. The Catholic Church declared her a saint — Catholics think her visions were genuine.
- Many Catholics report visions of Mary. One example is Bernadette Soubirous, who claimed she saw Mary several times in 1858 near Lourdes (France). Lourdes is now a popular pilgrimage site — many think people can be healed by visiting it.

All religions	# Revelation

Judaism was Founded by Men who had Visions of God

1) Many visions are recorded in the Torah, and elsewhere in the Tenakh.

2) Abraham and his wife were old and childless. God's word came to him in a vision, promising him a son and countless descendants. He believed God — and what God promised happened.

> "...the word of the Lord came to Abram in a vision" Genesis 15:1 NIV

3) Jacob had a vision of a ladder with angels on it reaching from Earth to Heaven — see Genesis 28:10-22.

4) God first spoke to Moses from within a burning bush — see Exodus 3. This is an indirect or veiled revelation — another example is God appearing as a pillar of cloud in Deuteronomy 31:15.

5) Moses is the only person to have seen God — he spoke to "Moses face to face, as one speaks to a friend" (Exodus 33:11 NIV). These were direct revelations — a direct experience of God.

6) Many Jews believe in the visions of God in the Tenakh, but some Progressive Jews may see them as metaphorical stories. Visions in more recent times aren't really a key part of Judaism.

The Qur'an Mentions Stories of People who had Visions

1) The Qur'an includes the story of the angel Jibril (Gabriel) appearing to Maryam (Mary), the mother of Isa (Jesus) — see Qur'an 19:16-22. Jibril told her she would bear a son, even though she was a virgin.

2) The angel Jibril appeared to Muhammad while he was meditating in a cave outside Makkah. Muhammad recited the verses Jibril gave to him — these were the first verses of the Qur'an to be revealed.

3) Sufi Muslims are Muslim mystics who seek to be filled with knowledge and love of Allah through direct experience of him, which can include visions. This affects them spiritually at a deep level.

4) Sufis can be Sunni or Shi'a, but many Muslims are sceptical of the Sufis' religious experiences.

5) There are other examples of seemingly miraculous events or visions in Islam. Qur'an 2:118 says "We have shown clearly the signs to a people who are certain [in faith]", showing how Allah reveals himself.

Prayer Can Help Belief in God

You only need to read this if you're studying Christianity. For a reminder of how Christians pray, see p.8 and 11.

1) Prayers are an important part of life for Christians. They believe God hears their prayers and responds. If someone prays for something and it then happens, they may see it as confirmation that God exists, as it can only have been him who heard their prayer and responded.

> "if we ask anything according to his will, he hears us. And if we know that he hears us ... we know that we have what we asked of him." 1 John 5:14-15 NIV

2) Praying on a regular basis can help keep people connected to the faith. Many see prayer as a 'conversation' with God — this personal aspect helps them feel close to God.

Upbringing Can Influence People's Belief

Only learn this if you're studying Christianity.

1) Many Christians bring up their children as Christians too — they may want to pass on their belief in God and their values, or think it's the only way their children will reach heaven.

> "Start children off on the way they should go, and even when they are old they will not turn from it." Proverbs 22:6 NIV

2) Children can be introduced to the faith in several ways, including at church and at home — see p.42.

3) Rituals such as prayer and attending church may help inspire children's respect and dedication to God. Activities at home, e.g. reading Bible stories, may help children believe as they're more fun and accessible.

4) Atheists and humanists may think it's better to let their children decide for themselves when they grow up.

5) If parents are too strict and insistent about their child being Christian, the child may reject the faith.

Branches of the same faith may have different views...

...so make sure you revise different opinions, as you'll often be asked to give multiple beliefs or views in the exam. Meanwhile, try this exam-style question:

Explain two religious beliefs about visions. Refer to sacred texts in your answer. [5]

Arguments Against the Existence of God All religions

Many People Don't Believe in Religious Experiences

Religious experiences are private, so it's impossible to provide proof of them. Atheists and humanists don't believe in God, so think religious experiences can be explained in other ways. Their arguments include:

1) Some religious experiences may happen because of wish fulfilment — the person wants the experience so much that their subconscious makes it happen. Religious people tend to have visions consistent with their own religious beliefs, and not of figures or ideas from another religion, which casts doubt on their validity.

2) The person involved may be lying about their experience, perhaps because they might profit from being believed.

3) Some religious experiences may result from things which affect the brain, such as mental illness, or physical illness such as brain tumours, or drugs. An example is the 12th century nun Hildegard of Bingen, who saw visions all her life, but some people think she was actually suffering from migraines.

4) Some might misinterpret their experience, or choose to interpret it in a religious way. If you were ill and dreamt you'd be cured the next day, and then you felt better, you might think God helped, or just see it as a coincidence.

5) Religious experiences can bring up contradictions in the ideas people have about God. It's hard to understand why, if God is capable of acting in the world, he doesn't do it more often. Miracles (see p.75) show God's power as they break the laws of nature, but this doesn't explain why he doesn't use his power to prevent suffering.

Some believers may not believe in these experiences either, particularly ones not written in their sacred text. They might prefer to focus on God and living a good life instead of events which may or may not be true.

Evil and Suffering Make People Doubt There is a God

1) Christians, Jews and Muslims all believe in a God who is omniscient (all-knowing), omnipotent (all-powerful), and benevolent (kind). So they believe he knows what happens in the world, doesn't want people to suffer, and is powerful enough to do something about it.

2) However, there's a lot of suffering in the world, which seems to contradict these ideas. Some people find it hard to see how God could allow it to happen, and therefore doubt he exists.

3) Some may think suffering can't be explained by humans. In the Torah and Bible, Job endures many hardships, but despite this, he decides suffering must be accepted as we can't understand God's plan.

4) In the scriptures, suffering is also often described as punishment for people's sins.

5) However, suffering is widespread and affects everyone, so atheists and humanists might argue that justifying suffering as punishment doesn't make sense. They might also argue that it doesn't seem to add up because animals and plants suffer too, even though they can't be being punished for their sins.

6) Believers might explain it by saying that humans need to be able to choose between good and evil as a test of their character — that's why they have free will. Without bad things happening, good can't exist.

7) Religious people try to relieve the suffering of others, e.g. through charity and prayer.

Many Christians believe the concept of original sin can explain suffering (see p.7). God gave people free will — they choose to create suffering or good. St Augustine said suffering was the price people pay for free will. St Irenaeus thought people were created with faults because they had to develop into being children of God — so they needed evil and suffering to exist, else they'd have no concept of what's right. Christians try to follow God's example of goodness — Psalm 119 asks for his help to do so. Isaiah 45:7 says "I bring prosperity and create disaster" (NIV), which suggests God isn't only responsible for good — he creates suffering as a punishment.

Jews believe suffering is a test from God. A lot of Jewish thought doesn't try explaining evil, and the Holocaust makes it particularly hard to do so. Many Jews struggle to understand why God let it happen, especially as Psalm 103:17-18 says "the Lord's love is with those … who keep his covenant" (NIV). Many believe evil needs a response, not an explanation — e.g. helping those who are suffering.

Muslims believe suffering can be a test from Allah. Everything is part of Allah's plan and there are good reasons for it, even if we can't see them. Evil gives people the chance to do good and help those in need. If we ourselves are suffering, Muslims believe we must bear it with patience and faith. Qur'an 2:155-156 says: "good tidings to the patient, Who, when disaster strikes them, say, 'Indeed we belong to Allah' ".

Revise thoroughly for the exam — else you'll suffer...

In the exam, read each question carefully. You need to know exactly what the questions are asking.

Revision Summary

A whole page of exam-style questions — just what you've been waiting for. They'll test whether you remember what you've learnt in the section, and give you an idea of what you'll be asked to do in the exam. If there's anything you're not completely sure about, go back through the section and have another read of the relevant pages, then give the questions another go.

For some courses, you need to learn about the views of different religions on these topics. But for other courses, you need to know about them in the context of just one religion — if that's the case for your course, answer each of these questions in the context of the religion you've studied.

To get you warmed up, let's start with these 1 mark multiple choice questions.
1) Which of the following believe it's impossible to know for certain if God exists or not?
   a) Atheists   b) Humanists   c) Theologians   d) Agnostics
2) Which of the following is not a type of revelation?
   a) Vision   b) God   c) Miracle   d) Scripture

You can get 2 marks for these, so make two short points in your answer.
3) Give two aspects of the First Cause argument.
4) Give two religious beliefs about special revelation.
5) Give two examples of people who have had visions.

These questions are worth 3 marks — all you need to do is write three brief points.
6) Outline three reasons for belief in a god.
7) Outline three aspects of the cosmological argument.
8) Outline three non-religious explanations for religious experiences.

Moving up to 4 marks. Make two points, but this time develop them further to get an extra mark for each.
9) Explain two ways believers respond to the theory of evolution.
10) Explain two religious beliefs about the scriptures as revelation.
11) Explain two religious beliefs about the revelation of God in nature.

To make sure your longer answers are clear, make sure your answer is well-structured.

5 marks available now. You'll need to refer to religious texts for top marks.
12) Explain two ways religious people respond to the problem of God allowing evil and suffering.

6 marks up for grabs. You should include examples from sources of wisdom and authority.
13) Explain why many religious people believe creation proves the existence of God.

Finish on a high with this 12 mark question — you could even grab some extra marks for SPaG. Before you begin, use the bullet points in the question to make a plan and structure your answer. Have a quick brainstorm of arguments for and against the statement.
14) 'God doesn't exist.'
    Evaluate this statement. Give arguments that support and arguments that disagree with the statement.
    You must include:
    • examples of religious teachings
    • non-religious views
    • appropriate philosophical arguments ← *Don't be put off by this reference to 'philosophical arguments' — it just means things such as the cosmological argument, or the belief that miracles prove God's existence.*
    • a conclusion.

Attitudes to Equality

General, Christianity,
Catholic Christianity

Equality is something that many people work towards — for example, in terms of race, sexuality and gender.

Prejudice and Discrimination Prevent Equality

Difference in wealth is another
form of inequality — see p.87-89.

1) Prejudice is judging something or someone for no good reason, or without full knowledge of a situation. Discrimination is treating someone unjustly or differently, often because of prejudice.

2) Prejudice comes in different forms. Sexism is the belief one gender is inferior to the other. Racism is prejudice against people of other races. Homophobia is prejudice against people who are homosexual.

3) The Equality Act 2010 says it's illegal to discriminate on the grounds of 'protected characteristics', which include race, gender, age and sexual orientation. The Act aims to ensure everyone is treated equally.

4) Positive discrimination is when someone in a group that often suffers discrimination is given an advantage. This often relates to job applications — it's only legal if they're as well qualified as the other applicants.

Christianity teaches Equality

Jesus said the second most important commandment, after loving God, is "Love your neighbour as yourself" (Mark 12:31 NIV).

1) 'Do to others what you would have them do to you' is a fundamental part of Christian teaching, often called the 'Golden Rule'. Many Christians think everyone was created equal, so try to avoid discrimination.

2) Jesus said "A new command I give you: love one another" (John 13:34 NIV) — i.e. don't mistreat others.

3) The Catechism of the Catholic Church 1935 says "...discrimination ... on the grounds of sex, race, colour, social conditions, language, or religion must be ... eradicated as incompatible with God's design".

The Good Samaritan parable is an important teaching on prejudice. Two holy men ignore a man who's been beaten and robbed. He's then helped by a Samaritan, a group who were despised at the time. The story shows how prejudices can be wrong.

Christian Attitudes to Gender Equality have Shifted

For more on this, see p.45.

1) Traditionally, Christians believed women's roles were to look after the home and children, while men earnt money and led the family. Some still believe this, but most now think both genders can do either role.

2) Women traditionally had less authority in religion — there were no female church leaders for centuries. There are now female ministers in most Protestant denominations, though not Catholic or Orthodox ones.

Christian Teaching on Racism is Clear

"From one man he made all the nations" Acts 17:26 NIV

1) Christianity teaches that racism is unacceptable, and God made everyone equal — "you are all one in Christ Jesus" Galatians 3:28 NIV. This means many Christians believe it's their duty to fight racism.

2) This can be done by an individual, e.g. by welcoming someone of another ethnicity to the community, or at an institutional level, e.g. a church asking its members to treat everyone equally. The Church of England recommends that people make "neighbours out of strangers" in its report Faithful Cities.

3) Racial equality can be difficult to achieve. The Church of England has been criticised for not having enough ethnic minority people among its clergy — it's now making efforts to increase diversity.

4) Desmond Tutu is an Anglican archbishop who fought against apartheid in South Africa, in which the white minority population oppressed everyone else. After apartheid ended, he led the Truth and Reconciliation Commission, which investigated the crimes of the apartheid era and focused on unity between everyone.

There's a lot of Debate on Homosexuality in the Christian Churches

For more, see p.37 and 39.

Homosexuality is a divisive topic in Christianity. The idea of loving your neighbour seems to contradict the Bible teachings forbidding homosexuality, such as 1 Corinthians 6:9-10. Many Christians focus on loving your neighbour and therefore accept homosexuality. Others focus on the fact it's seen as a sin.

The Anglican Church is split on the issue. Church of England bishops issued a report in 2017 saying they wouldn't change the Church's definition of marriage as being between one man and one woman (Canon B30), but many members of the Church disagree with this.

The Catholic Church is in a similar position — its Catechism says homosexual acts are "contrary to the natural law" (2357) but many individual Catholics accept homosexuality.

Judaism | Attitudes to Equality

Equality is important in Judaism — the Torah says God made everyone equal.

Different Jewish Traditions Have Different Views on Gender Roles

1) Jews believe that men and women are equal, based on Genesis 1:27, which says "So God created mankind in his own image ... male and female he created them" (NIV).

2) Men and women tend to have different roles in Orthodox Judaism — but they're still seen as equal in God's eyes. Men are obliged to pray 3 times a day, but women aren't (but they should say the Amidah twice daily — see p.31). Only men can read the Torah in synagogue and make up a minyan (the group of at least 10 people needed for some prayers). Traditionally, only men can be rabbis, but this is changing.

3) Women are exempt from such duties as it's expected they'll be looking after the home and children. They have religious duties in the home, such as lighting the Shabbat candles while saying a blessing. Traditionally, 'Jewishness' is passed on via the mother — a child with a non-Jewish mother isn't a Jew.

4) In Liberal, Reform and Masorti Judaism, religious duties can be carried out by women too. All three have male and female rabbis. Liberal, Reform and some Masortis have developed gender-neutral liturgy, e.g. avoiding calling God 'Father' or 'King'. They have equivalent rites of passage for boys and girls (p.32-33).

The Torah Preaches Racial Equality

1) Genesis 3:20 says all of humanity comes from the same source, so Jews see people as equal before God. The Torah makes it clear that people of different ethnicities should be treated the same as each other:

> "When a foreigner resides among you in your land, do not ill-treat them. The foreigner residing among you must be treated as your native-born. Love them as yourself, for you were foreigners in Egypt." Leviticus 19:33-34 NIV

2) Most Jews believe that Jewish people are God's chosen people. This doesn't mean they think they're better than anyone else — just that God gave them extra responsibilities in the covenants (see p.27-28).

3) Jews have often faced anti-Semitism (discrimination against Jews), particularly during the Holocaust, when 6 million Jews were killed. This means many are vocal about racism and make efforts to try to reduce it.

4) Ahavat ha-beriot means loving all of God's creations. It's a mitzvah (commandment) to do so, so it's important. This encourages Jews to accept everyone, regardless of their ethnicity.

5) The Jewish Council for Racial Equality (JCORE) works for racial equality, focusing especially on attitudes to asylum seekers and refugees. It campaigns against negative attitudes to immigrants in the UK.

Views on Homosexuality Also Vary Between Jewish Traditions

1) Orthodox Jews tend not to approve of homosexuality. They're against homophobia, but tend to see being in homosexual relationships as a sin. Sex between men is forbidden in Leviticus 18:22 (so it's assumed sex between women is banned too). Orthodox synagogues don't hold same-sex weddings.

2) Attitudes are beginning to change within the Orthodox community though. Efforts are being made to welcome and support homosexual Orthodox Jews in the community.

3) Progressive Jews accept homosexuality and welcome homosexual people into their communities. They argue that as God created everyone in his image (Genesis 1:27), homosexuality can't be wrong.

4) Both Liberal and Reform Judaism campaigned for the legalisation of same-sex marriage in the UK, and hold same-sex weddings now they're legal. Homosexual people can become Liberal and Reform rabbis.

5) Many Masortis accept homosexuality. They have a shutafut (partnership) ceremony for same-sex marriages or civil partnerships, different from the traditional kiddushin.

Remember, there are usually different opinions...

You'll often be asked to discuss different beliefs in the exam, so make sure you learn both sides of the argument — be sure to know any contrasting opinions that are held in a religion.

Attitudes to Equality

Islam teaches that Allah <u>created</u> everyone to be <u>equal</u>, even though people are <u>different</u> from each other.

Men and Women have *Different Roles* within Islam

1) The <u>Qur'an</u> makes it <u>clear</u> that men and women are <u>equal</u> when it comes to their <u>religious obligations</u>, e.g. prayer, fasting, hajj and charity — have a look at Qur'an 33:35 on p.45, which also has more information on <u>gender equality</u>. All that counts is how good a <u>Muslim</u> they are, not their <u>gender</u>:

> "O mankind, indeed We have created you from male and female and made you peoples and tribes that you may know one another. Indeed, the most noble of you in the sight of Allah is the most righteous of you." Qur'an 49:13

2) Women don't <u>have</u> to attend mosque for <u>prayer</u>, but it is <u>permitted</u>. If women do go to the mosque, they must pray in a <u>separate</u> group — behind (or otherwise out of sight of) the men. Like in <u>Judaism</u>, this is because it's thought it might be <u>distracting</u> for both genders to pray in a mixed group.

3) Women can't lead prayers in <u>mixed groups</u>, but they can lead prayers being said by groups of <u>women</u>.

4) There is a growing movement working for women to have a more <u>prominent role</u> in Islam. Several women have led <u>mixed-gender</u> prayers across the world. Their actions have been <u>condemned</u> by some Muslims as not following the teachings of Islam. There are plans for a <u>mosque</u> run by women in Bradford.

5) Some say it's <u>part of Islam</u> for Muslim women to wear <u>modest clothing</u> — Qur'an 24:31 says "tell the believing women ... to wrap [a portion of] their headcovers over their chests and not expose their adornment". Others argue it doesn't say they have to cover up <u>completely</u> and that their <u>faith</u> and <u>piety</u> are more <u>important</u> than clothing — Qur'an 7:26 says "the clothing of righteousness — that is best".

Islam says People are *Created Equal*, but not *Identical*

1) Islam teaches that <u>all people</u> were created by <u>Allah</u>, and were created <u>equal</u> (although <u>not</u> the <u>same</u>). He intended humanity to be created with <u>differences</u>. But this just means we're all <u>individuals</u>.

2) Muslims all over the world are united by the <u>ummah</u> — the <u>community</u> of Islam. The ummah consists of <u>all Muslims</u>, regardless of <u>nationality</u>, <u>tradition</u> (i.e. Sunni or Shi'a) and so on. This helps promote <u>racial</u> and <u>social harmony</u>, as in theory no one's <u>excluded</u> or <u>discriminated</u> against.

> The final sermon of Muhammad is clear that <u>no race</u> is <u>superior</u> to another: "you are all descended from Adam and none is higher than the other except in obedience to Allah. No Arab is superior to a non-Arab. Between Muslims there are no races and no tribes." The only <u>important</u> thing is whether someone's a <u>good Muslim</u> or not.

3) People on <u>hajj</u> all wear <u>simple white clothes</u>, showing everyone's <u>equal</u> — race, gender etc. <u>don't matter</u>.

4) Sahih al-Bukhari 56:681 says everyone should be <u>treated</u> the <u>same</u> way, regardless of <u>who</u> they are.

> <u>Malcolm X</u> was a <u>prominent Muslim figure</u> in the struggle for <u>civil rights</u> for <u>African Americans</u> in the <u>US</u>. He initially advocated <u>black supremacy</u> and <u>separatism</u>, but later supported <u>interethnic dialogue</u>. He inspired many with his campaigning for <u>human rights</u>.

Homosexuality is *Controversial* in Islam

For more on this, see p.40.

1) Many <u>Muslims</u> believe that the Qur'an <u>forbids</u> homosexuality — for example, Qur'an 7:81 says "you approach men with desire, instead of women ... you are a transgressing people" (the quote is addressed to men). This means they're <u>against</u> the <u>legalisation</u> of <u>same-sex marriage</u>.

2) Some Muslims disagree, arguing that as <u>Allah</u> created all people, homosexuality is part of his <u>creation</u>.

3) Muslims often speak against <u>homophobia</u>, as Muslims should be <u>tolerant</u> towards others. Some Muslim organisations state that they are <u>against</u> homosexual acts but believe homosexual people should be <u>respected</u>. Others, such as <u>Imaan</u>, <u>support</u> homosexual Muslims and campaign for their <u>rights</u>.

So, now you know these pages off by heart and backwards...

...try this exam-style question. If you don't feel you know the topic well enough, read the pages again. Explain two beliefs about the status of women in religion. [4]

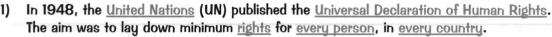

| All religions | # Human Rights |

Human rights are moral, legal and political rights that should give people freedom and protection worldwide.

The United Nations Defined Human Rights

The European Court of Human Rights. (I think.)

1) In 1948, the United Nations (UN) published the Universal Declaration of Human Rights. The aim was to lay down minimum rights for every person, in every country.

2) It states that all human beings are born free and equal in dignity and rights. It also lists specific rights, e.g. the right to life, freedom from slavery, freedom from imprisonment or exile without good reason, freedom of opinion and expression, the right to have an education and to seek work.

3) The Universal Declaration of Human Rights stated how things should be, but meant nothing in a court of law. So in 1953, the Council of Europe brought into effect the European Convention on Human Rights, which is a similar list of rights to the UN declaration. It's enforced by the European Court of Human Rights (ECHR). These rights became part of the UK's domestic law in 1998, with the Human Rights Act.

4) Most religious believers agree that all human beings should be treated fairly and with respect. This is based on a belief in human dignity — all human life is valuable, because people are created in the image of God — and a belief in justice, the idea everyone should be treated fairly. Everyone should be free to think and to choose how to act (though hopefully they'll live a good moral life).

5) People applying situation ethics look for the most loving outcome to a situation. They may often support human rights, but in some cases they may feel going against a right gives the best overall outcome.

Many Christians Support Human Rights

1) The Catholic Church highlights the role of the individual as well as the state in protecting human rights. It says human rights aren't just defined by states putting them into law, but "Every member of the community has a duty … in order that the rights of others can be satisfied and their freedoms respected" (The Common Good and the Catholic Church's Social Teaching: 37).

> "So God created mankind in his own image, in the image of God he created them; male and female he created them." Genesis 1:27 NIV

> "You … were called to be free. But do not use your freedom to indulge the flesh; rather, serve one another humbly in love." Galatians 5:13 NIV

2) Christians may find their views contradict others' ideas about rights. E.g. many think women should have the right to abortion, but some Christians disagree, believing the foetus's right to life is more important.

Human Rights are Important for Most Jews

1) Most Jews support human rights — Deuteronomy 16:20 asks Jews to "Follow justice and justice alone" (NIV). Teachings such as the two below ask Jews to protect the rights of specific people:

> "Whoever oppresses the poor shows contempt for their Maker, but whoever is kind to the needy honours God." Proverbs 14:31 NIV

> "When a foreigner resides among you in your land, do not ill-treat them … Love them as yourself" Leviticus 19:33-34 NIV

2) However, Jewish beliefs can sometimes clash with human rights. For example, many Orthodox Jews think homosexuality is wrong, which may lead to discrimination.

The Qur'an says Justice is Very Important

1) Most Muslims are supportive of human rights. The Qur'an frequently emphasises the importance of justice, saying for example "O you who have believed, be persistently standing firm for Allah, witnesses in justice … Be just; that is nearer to righteousness" (Qur'an 5:8).

> "Indeed, Allah orders justice and good conduct and giving to relatives and forbids immorality and bad conduct and oppression. He admonishes you that perhaps you will be reminded." Qur'an 16:90

2) Some Muslims argue that Islamic law sometimes undermines Muslim women's rights, e.g. they don't have equal rights in divorce to men.

The right to drink tea is part of British law... I think...

Shut the book and write down as many ideas about human rights as you can remember.

REVISION TASK

Freedom of Belief

The UK is a Diverse, Multi-Faith Society

Estimates vary, but between a quarter and a half of the population say they have no religious belief.

1) Freedom of religion and belief is a legal right in the UK — it gives the freedom to follow any or no religion.

2) People are protected from being discriminated against because of their beliefs. The beliefs they hold as part of their religion are protected, e.g. religions can choose not to hold same-sex marriages in their places of worship if it doesn't fit with their beliefs. Freedom of belief is sometimes a tricky area though:

- Some people feel there isn't enough recognition of those who don't hold religious beliefs, e.g. in religious studies in schools.
- There can be a fine line between educating people about a faith and influencing them too much. Some may think that e.g. religious charities have too much influence, while the charities would argue they're not trying to convert people, just help them.
- Some people, including religious believers, object to the Church of England being the state church. For example, 26 bishops are peers in the House of Lords, which many see as unfair now that the country is more religiously diverse and many people don't have a religion at all. Others say the UK is a Christian country so it's acceptable — it's part of the culture.
- A religious person saying homosexuality is sinful clashes with homosexual people's right not to be discriminated against and could be seen as hate speech (a crime) — but stopping people from expressing their views undermines their freedom of belief.

3) Most religious believers happily live alongside others in the UK and enjoy the different perspectives it gives them. The Inter Faith Network for the UK promotes mutual understanding and combats prejudice.

4) Living in a multi-faith society can make it harder for some believers to practise their faith — e.g. some Christian festivals are UK bank holidays while other faiths' festivals aren't, making it harder to celebrate.

Many Christians Think People Can Follow Any Faith

1) Though many Christians think Christianity's the true religion, they think people have the right to practise any faith. It's "an inalienable requirement of the dignity of man" (Catechism of the Catholic Church 1747).

2) Some Christians think the only way to reach heaven is by being Christian, so they try to convert people.

3) But generally they support the right to choose — the Bible shows that Jesus didn't make people follow him.

Jews Accept Other Religions

1) Jews are a people as well as a religious group. Jews don't try to convert people, although people can convert if they want after a period of study. Once they've converted, they're seen as Jewish for ever.

2) Freedom of belief is important to Jews as they have often been persecuted, most horrifyingly during the Holocaust, when six million Jews were killed. They're often inspired by the Torah story of Esther, who saved the Jewish people from being killed by Haman. Esther risked her life to beg for mercy. The story shows the importance of allowing everyone to live without persecution, and having faith in the face of it.

The Qur'an Says People are Free to Choose Their Religion

1) The Qur'an says "There shall be no compulsion in [acceptance of] the religion" (Qur'an 2:256) — people are free to choose. Muslims believe that Islam is the only true faith — but some also believe that all righteous people will be favoured by Allah. Most Muslims don't try to convert others to Islam.

- However, Muslims' freedom of belief is often restricted by the common belief that converting to another religion from Islam or becoming an atheist is unacceptable in Islam — it's known as apostasy. Some hadiths say it deserves the death penalty.
- Some Muslims disagree, as the Qur'an leaves judgement up to Allah — Qur'an 3:85 says "whoever desires other than Islam ... he, in the Hereafter, will be among the losers". It can be hard for ex-Muslims — they're often cut off from their family.

2) Muslims call Muslims, Christians and Jews 'people of the book', as they're linked by a shared religious heritage. They all believe in prophets such as Ibrahim (Abraham) and many Muslims believe the Torah and New Testament contain important messages. Qur'an 29:46 says "our God and your God is one".

I can't do GCSEs, exams are against my religion...

...sorry, that won't wash. Get yourself prepared by trying this question:

Explain two religious ideas about freedom of belief.   [4]

Social Justice

Social Justice is the Idea that Everyone should be Treated Fairly

1) Social justice is putting into practice the principles of human rights. Working for social justice includes:

> • Trying to ensure different groups of people aren't discriminated against or more disadvantaged than others. This includes discrimination on the grounds of race, gender, religion, social class, poverty, age or disability.
> • Trying to redistribute wealth so everyone can afford to live comfortably. Some members of society are very wealthy while others struggle to meet their basic needs for food, shelter, warmth, etc.

2) Social justice efforts often focus on wealth, as a lack of it can deprive people of other opportunities and rights. Higher taxes for people on high incomes and free healthcare and education are ways to help.

3) Many people try to work for social justice. It's an important part of Christianity, Islam and Judaism. People using situation ethics would often support social justice as the most compassionate thing to do.

Christianity Teaches that People Should Help Those in Need

1) Christians follow Jesus's teaching to "Love your neighbour as yourself" (Mark 12:31 NIV). The parable of the sheep and goats is often used to teach about social justice — see p.14 for more.

> Jesus was known for helping poor people and for healing the sick. In Luke 16:19-31, he teaches that people who don't help others when they're able to will be punished — the story is about a rich man who repeatedly ignores a poor man, and ends up in hell for not helping him. Jesus healed a man with leprosy by touching him, at a time when lepers were outcasts from society. Christians should therefore follow Jesus's example — by helping those who need it, they can express God's love.

2) The Catholic Church emphasises the importance of human dignity in social justice. It says people should be allowed "to obtain what is their due, according to their nature and their vocation" (Catechism 1928) — people should be given opportunities to make the most of their lives and their abilities.

3) Catechism 1928 also says social justice is better for everyone — it's for "the common good".

Islam Encourages Helping Others

1) Muslims should work for social justice as part of their faith. Qur'an 76:8-9 says the righteous "give food in spite of love for it to the needy, the orphan, and the captive, [Saying] ... We wish not from you reward or gratitude". This means people should give help without expecting anything in return.

2) Zakah, charitable giving to redistribute wealth, is central to Islam — it's one of the five pillars (see p.22). The Qur'an says those who "give zakah ... will be the successful" (Qur'an 7:156-157).

3) It promises that those who have wealth to spare and give it away will be rewarded:

> Those who spend their wealth [in Allah's way] ... — they will have their reward with their Lord." Qur'an 2:274

Jewish Teachings say Jews Should be Generous to Others

1) Many Jewish teachings support working for social justice. According to Deuteronomy 15:11, God told Jews "to be open-handed towards your fellow Israelites who are poor and needy in your land" (NIV). Jews should give generously and willingly, "without a grudging heart" (Deuteronomy 15:10 NIV).

2) Jewish ideas of charity (tzedakah) focus on justice — it's not only kind to give to charity, but it's righting a wrong. Amos 5:24 NIV says "let justice roll on like a river, righteousness like a never-failing stream!".

3) The concept of tikkun olam — repairing the world — is linked to this. Jews should be active in improving things that are wrong in the world. This doesn't only mean personally giving to charity and helping others, but also campaigning on a political level to make sure that society is fair and just for everyone.

4) If Jews oppress those who are disadvantaged, God "will certainly hear their cry" (Exodus 22:23 NIV).

Basically, everyone should help people who need it...

There are quite a few different teachings on this page, so as a fun test (or maybe just a test...), write down as many as you can remember without looking at the page. Don't forget to give the source.

Wealth and Poverty

How wealth is used, and how it's distributed among people, is a big issue today.

Wealth Inequality is a Big Problem Today

In the UK, the poorest 50% of people own 8.7% of wealth, while the richest 10% own 45%.

1) The gap between the poorest and richest people is huge, and growing. In 2017, Oxfam estimated that the richest 8 people in the world had more wealth than the poorest half of the world (3.6 billion people).

2) Poverty is not having enough resources (money, etc.) to meet your basic needs, e.g. food or heating.

3) Poverty has many causes. In the UK, these causes often include low wages, high costs (e.g. renting a house or paying for childcare), a lack of skills so people can't get better-paid jobs, and unemployment.

- Fair pay is an issue. Many in poverty have low-paid jobs, so they work long hours to try to earn enough to live on. In some areas, well-paid jobs aren't available. Part-time work's often low-paid.
- By law, people have to be paid the National Minimum Wage, but many people think it isn't enough. Over-25s must be paid the National Living Wage, which is a bit higher than the minimum wage. However, many say it still isn't enough to live on — it's not a true living wage.
- Businesses are often reluctant to pay people more as it's expensive for them to do so — some try to avoid paying even the minimum wage. Some say increasing wages will mean they can't afford to pay people so they would have to cut the number of jobs, which wouldn't help.

4) Worldwide, poverty is also caused by things such as war, rapid population growth, natural disasters and exploitation. The Fairtrade Foundation works to ensure people in developing countries are paid a fair price for the products they sell and that they have decent working conditions.

Finding a Solution is Difficult

1) Helping poverty caused by disasters (e.g. war) often involves emergency relief during the disaster and long-term help afterwards, e.g. rebuilding houses. It can take years before things get back to normal.

2) In other situations, some people think giving money (e.g. benefits or donations) to people in poverty makes them too reliant on that money — they don't help themselves get out of poverty as they prefer to keep receiving the money. Others argue that this isn't the case, and that people living in poverty need financial help, because not giving it to them means they might not be able to eat or heat their home.

3) Some say it's people's own responsibility to get out of poverty — they should work harder and use money more responsibly. Others say that poverty is a result of many factors and that many do work hard — in 2016, 1 in 8 people employed in the UK were living in poverty (source Joseph Rowntree Foundation, 2016).

4) They say society should help those who face many issues such as illness, or a lack of skills or opportunities. Charities often try to help people learn new skills on top of giving them money or food.

Utilitarian ethics say the correct course of action is the one which has the largest balance of good against bad outcomes for those involved. Utilitarians often think people with excess wealth should give to people with less wealth. But if the money could be spent on another cause that would have a greater benefit (e.g. preventing more climate change), then giving the money to people in poverty would be wrong.

There are Other Problems Often Linked with Poverty

Excessive Interest on Loans

1) People sometimes need extra money, e.g. to pay for something unexpected, or just to afford food until the next payday. One way of covering this is take out a loan. A quick and seemingly easy way to do so is to borrow from a money lender, but money lenders often lend money at rates that go up to thousands of percent of interest (called usury). People might take out small loans, but they soon become so big that they can't repay them.

2) This was a big problem in the UK, so the government introduced some regulations to limit how much people have to repay. Now, people don't have to repay more than twice what they borrowed.

People-trafficking

1) People living in poverty are often more vulnerable to people-trafficking. People are forced to work for little or no money, after they've been transferred to a new place (often abroad) by the traffickers.

2) People are often persuaded to move willingly by the promise of a better life elsewhere, but once they get there the traffickers force them to work to pay back the money they owe for the move.

Wealth and Poverty

Christians Believe It's What You Do With Your Money that Counts

1) Christians shouldn't be fixated on wealth — Jesus said "You cannot serve both God and Money" (Matthew 6:24 NIV) and "It is easier for a camel to go through the eye of a needle than for someone who is rich to enter the kingdom of God" (Mark 10:25 NIV). Wealth should be used to help others who are less well off.

2) Many Christians think money should only be earnt in moral ways, not in ways that might harm others, such as working for arms manufacturers or running a business that pays people unfair wages.

3) They also try to avoid using their money in a way that harms others, which includes usury.

> The Church of England has launched an initiative to combat lenders who charge lots of interest. The Church is offering workshops to educate people about money matters, as well as promoting credit unions, which lend money at low rates of interest. The Church campaigned for the introduction of the Modern Slavery Act, which helps protect victims of people-trafficking.

Charity is Important to Christians

1) Giving to charity and helping others is important to many Christians, following the teaching to "Love your neighbour" (Mark 12:31 NIV). It's important to give in a way that helps people to help themselves — the parable of the talents (Matthew 25:14-30) says those who make most of what they have are rewarded.

2) Christians should give to charity as part of their faith. There are many Christian charities — see p.14.

> "If anyone has material possessions and sees a brother or sister in need but has no pity on them, how can the love of God be in that person?" 1 John 3:17 NIV

Checking your donation's gone to a worthy cause is a good idea...

3) It's best to give donations quietly and without boasting about it — Matthew 6:2 tells Christians that "when you give to the needy, do not announce it with trumpets" (NIV).

4) How much you give isn't important — what's important is giving as much as you can. Jesus taught that a poor woman giving a small amount of money she couldn't afford to lose was more important than rich people giving large sums they could easily do without (Mark 12:41-44).

5) Over 7500 churches are involved with the Fairtrade movement. For more on Christian charities, see p.14.

Charity is One of the Five Pillars of Islam

1) Charity plays an important role in Islam — zakah (financial aid) is one of the five pillars of Islam, which every Muslim has to follow. Qur'an 2:177 says "righteousness is [in] one who ... gives zakah".

2) With zakah, 2.5% of your yearly wealth should be given as charity, unless your wealth is below a minimum threshold. It's usually given to charities or mosques, or to Muslims who are less well off.

3) Muslims think wealth is given to people by Allah, so they should use it to help others. Being wealthy or poor is Allah's test of people — they should try to help themselves or others, depending on the situation.

> "A man is not a believer who fills his stomach while his neighbour is hungry." Al-Adab al-Mufrad 6:112 (collection of hadith)

4) Sadaqah is another kind of charity. It includes a wide range of charitable acts, from simply smiling at someone to cheer them up, to giving money to help those in need. Sadaqah is seen as a duty, but it involves any amount of effort, time or money — it's up to the individual to decide how much they do.

5) There's a particular emphasis on 'ongoing charity' — actions that will have a long-term effect. It's seen as best to help people become able to support themselves, rather than relying on donations. This means the benefits of sadaqah are long-lasting and help the community — known as sustainable development.

6) There are Islamic charities that help people globally and in the UK, including Muslim Aid and Islamic Aid.

Muslim Aid	Islamic Aid
1. Muslim Aid provides disaster relief and development aid around the world. The charity works in over 70 countries.	1. Islamic Aid is an international organisation dedicated to reducing poverty and deprivation.
2. It provides not only initial emergency aid after a war or natural disaster, but ongoing help. This help includes building new housing, sanitation and schools, and offering interest-free loans to help start-up businesses.	2. It focuses on a long-term approach to helping communities and employs people from the communities it works in.

Wealth and Poverty Islam & Judaism

How Money is Used is Important in Islam

1) Muslims shouldn't use money in ways that harm people — Islamic law says Muslims shouldn't harm others.

2) Islam forbids alcohol, so it's seen as immoral to make money from it. Islam is often focused on sexual modesty, so profiting from sex is forbidden (either directly or indirectly, e.g. sexually suggestive adverts).

3) Qur'an 2:275 says "Allah ... has forbidden interest" and that those who charge it will go to jahannam (hell). In Islam, money doesn't have a value in itself, so it shouldn't be used to make more money. This stops richer people profiting from poorer people, and ensures wealth is spread more fairly.

4) Muslims use Islamic bank accounts and run businesses that don't involve charging interest.

Jews Should Use Their Wealth to Help Others

1) Judaism teaches that there's nothing wrong in being wealthy, so long as you're not obsessed by it, and you give money to others. Wealth is seen as a gift from God. Jews should try to avoid being dependent on others if at all possible — although if they are really in need there's no shame in receiving charity.

2) Unfairness and dishonesty in business are condemned — you're answerable to God for any wrongdoing. All money should be earnt morally, so any job that's harmful in any way is forbidden. Jews particularly frown on work that is damaging to God's creation (e.g. unsustainable tree felling).

3) Jews shouldn't charge interest on loans to other Jews (Leviticus 25:37). This doesn't apply to loans made to non-Jews: "You may charge a foreigner interest, but not a fellow Israelite" (Deuteronomy 23:20 NIV).

4) Jews try to avoid talking about or handling money on Shabbat — the day of rest.

Charity is Important in Judaism

1) This passage from the Torah sums up Jewish teaching on charity:

> "If anyone is poor among your fellow Israelites in any of the towns of the land ... do not be hard-hearted or tight-fisted towards them. Rather, be open-handed and freely lend them whatever they need." Deuteronomy 15:7-8 NIV

2) The Jewish scholar Maimonides said the best way to give was to do so in a way that meant the recipient could help themselves. He also said giving anonymously was recommended, so the charity is given for the good of it alone, and not so the giver can be rewarded — they shouldn't expect anything in return.

3) There are two important charitable principles in Judaism — tzedakah and gemilut hasadim:

> Tzedakah: tzedakah means charity, but with a sense of justice — it's not just generous to give tzedakah, it's right as it makes society fairer. Everyone, even those in need, is expected to contribute 10% of their wealth. Deuteronomy 14:29 says people should donate some of their produce so "the foreigners, the fatherless and the widows who live in your towns may come and eat" (NIV), showing the importance of helping those in need.
> Gemilut hasadim: this means 'acts of loving kindness' — it refers to any compassionate actions towards others.

4) Many Jewish homes have collection boxes (called pushkes) in which money for charity can be placed.

5) Donating clothing and food to people who need them or visiting someone who's sick are considered gemilut hasadim (acts of loving kindness). There are Jewish charities that help people, including Tzedek:

> 1. Tzedek is a Jewish charity in the UK that seeks to get the Jewish community involved in helping to reduce poverty worldwide.
> 2. Their focus is on helping local projects, that improve a community's ability to get itself out of poverty.

All Three Faiths Work To End People-Trafficking

1) Leaders of Islam, Christianity and Judaism have got together to combat people-trafficking worldwide. They've created the Global Freedom Network, an organisation which aims to end slavery.

2) It works with governments to get them to pass laws to combat slavery and people-trafficking.

I hope you feel richer (in knowledge) after these pages...

Make sure you've learnt the technical terms for different kinds of charitable acts, such as zakah.

90

Revision Summary

Now here's the fun bit — let's see if you can remember what you've just read in the section. The questions below will give you an idea of what you might come across in the exam and how much you'll need to write.
If you're struggling with anything, have another read of the section and give the questions another go once you're re-read it.

For some courses, you need to learn about the views of <u>different religions</u> on these topics. But for other courses, you need to know about them in the context of just <u>one religion</u> — if that's the case for your course, answer each of these questions <u>in the context of the religion you've studied</u>.

Let's start off with some straightforward 1 mark multiple choice questions.
1) Which of the following means equality of rights and opportunities?
   a) Social justice   b) Freedom of belief   c) Discrimination   d) Gender inequality
2) Which of the following is the principle the Fairtrade Foundation campaigns for?
   a) Wealth inequality   b) Utilitarian ethics   c) Low pay   d) Fair pay

Right, now you need to write a bit. These are worth 2 marks, so give two short points.
3) Give two forms of prejudice.
4) Give two religious beliefs about working for social justice.

These questions are worth 3 marks, so give three short points.
5) Outline three examples of human rights.
6) Outline three issues surrounding freedom of belief.
7) Outline three factors that can lead to poverty.

Now on to 4 marks. Make two points and develop them more to get 2 marks for each.
8) Explain two religious beliefs about making money.
9) Explain two ways that believers can work for social justice.
10) Explain two reasons why many religious people believe human rights are important.

5 marks available for these questions. You need to refer to religious texts in your answers.
11) Explain two religious ideas about racial equality.
12) Explain two religious beliefs about giving to charity.
13) Explain two reasons why many religious people support social justice.
14) Explain two different religious attitudes to homosexuality.

Make sure your longer answers are clear by structuring your answer well and writing clear points.

And finally... the 12 mark question (with extra marks for SPaG). Make a plan with arguments for and against the statement before you start — it'll help you organise things. Don't forget to finish off with a conclusion.
15) 'To make the world fairer, the best thing to do is donate money to charity.'
   Evaluate this statement.
   Give arguments that support the statement and arguments that disagree with the statement.
   You must include:
   • examples of religious teachings
   • a conclusion.

Have a look at the 'Do Well in Your Exam' section for help with writing essays.

Section 9 — Equality

Christianity in British Society
All religions

In Britain, Christianity has long had a prominent role in many areas, from government to education. Some question its status in modern British society, which is both religiously diverse and increasingly non-religious.

Christianity is Seen by Many as Part of the UK's National Identity

1) Christianity has been present in Britain for over 1500 years, so much of British culture has been influenced by it. However, there are many other religions in Britain today and many people no longer follow any religion at all. This means the place of Christianity in British society is being questioned.

2) The UK as a whole has no official state religion or church. Historically, each UK country had a Christian state church, but only in England is this still the case. The situation is therefore different in each country:

- The Anglican Church of England (C of E) is the established (state) church in England. This means that Anglicanism is the official religion and the Church has a role in governing the country.
- The Church of Scotland is Presbyterian and independent of the state. The Church in Wales and the Church of Ireland are both Anglican but are independent of the state and of the Church of England.

3) There are many Christian denominations in the UK in addition to Anglicanism, including Methodism and Roman Catholicism. Many British people also follow Islam, Judaism, Sikhism, Hinduism or Buddhism. Estimates vary quite a lot, but between a quarter and a half of the population isn't religious at all.

The Monarch is the Supreme Governor of the Church of England

1) The British monarch has the title 'Supreme Governor of the Church of England' — this means they're technically the leader of the Church, though it's mostly a symbolic role. It's still important though — it demonstrates the UK's identity as a Christian country, as the head of state is head of a Christian Church.

2) The monarch appoints the Church's senior clergy, though the Church and the prime minister recommend who should get the roles. All the Church's clergy swear a vow of loyalty to the monarch.

3) The monarch often also engages with other religious groups to promote inter-faith harmony.

Christianity has an Influence on Many Aspects of British Life

1) Many UK public holidays are Christian festivals, including Christmas Day and Easter. School holidays are arranged around them. Some think other religious festivals, e.g. Diwali (a Hindu festival) or Id ul-Fitr (a Muslim one, see p.24), should be public holidays too, to recognise their significance in British society.

2) Various key national events are marked by Christian services. The coronation of a new monarch and ceremonies to commemorate those who have died fighting in wars are examples of this.

3) Some state schools are connected to a particular religion — there are many Church of England and Roman Catholic schools. Some, including the National Secular Society and Humanists UK, object to this, particularly as in many areas there is limited choice — see p.92 for more.

The Church of England and Parliament

- The House of Commons and the House of Lords start each day with prayers led by Church of England clergy.
- The Church of England has 26 positions in the House of Lords in Parliament reserved for its clergy. They are known as Lords Spiritual and are made up of the most senior and longest-serving bishops and archbishops.
- Humanists UK and the National Secular Society have campaigned to remove the Lords Spiritual — they argue that religious figures have no place in governing the country. Other groups argue that seats should be allotted to leaders of other faiths too — it's unfair only the Church of England is represented.
- The C of E says its Lords represent all faiths, though it would like other religious leaders to be peers too.

The other Lords are named Lords Temporal — Time Lords...

EXAM TIP

...well, that's sort of what it means. In the exam, try to be clear whether you're talking about the whole of the UK or just one country within it, e.g. England — they have different set-ups in relation to religion.

Challenges for Religion

A secular country is one in which religion and the state are separate. Some believe the UK should be secular.

Secularism is Based on Two Key Principles

For religious views on secularism, see p.97.

1) The first principle is that religion and the state should be separate — neither should be involved in running the other. The second is that everyone's beliefs, whether religious or not, should be equally protected.

2) Freedom of belief is very important in secularism — people are free to believe whatever they want, and non-religious views are just as important as religious ones. Freedom of belief is a right in the UK (p.85). However, freedom to express these beliefs can be limited if doing so may cause harm to others.

3) Secularism can come in different forms:

  - A complete separation — the state doesn't support any religious activity. France comes close to this — e.g. people are forbidden to wear obvious religious symbols, like a big cross, in state schools. This can undermine people's freedom of belief.
  - A more pluralist approach, in which the state supports religions (e.g. financially) but without giving priority to one religion. People can practise their religion as they choose. Some aspects of the British state reflect this, e.g. state-funded faith schools.

4) Some people argue that the UK is already essentially a secular country, and the Church of England's role within the state is just symbolic and doesn't significantly change anything. Others say the UK is Christian.

Education is a Key Area of Debate

See p.94 for religious opinions on the topics discussed over the next couple of pages.

1) There are sometimes debates over what pupils should be taught, as it may go against their beliefs.

2) Humanists UK campaigns against creationism (the belief God created the world) being taught as science, saying it's not fact. The government made changes so it's not taught as science.

3) Sex education is controversial — faith schools are allowed to adapt it to fit their beliefs. This has been criticised as it may allow faith schools to ignore topics such as homosexuality or contraception, or teach that they're wrong. Faith schools argue it's wrong to ask them to teach topics that go against their views.

4) By law, schools have to teach religious education, including non-religious views. Religious education qualifications have been criticised as religious views are studied in more detail than non-religious ones. Humanists UK supported court action to ensure the inclusion of non-religious views in the syllabus.

5) The 1988 Education Reform Act made 'daily collective worship' in state schools compulsory. The worship is meant to be mostly or completely Christian, though schools can be exempted from this. In practice, the requirement is often ignored, but some object to it being obligatory for children to worship.

Faith Schools can be Controversial

1) The majority of the schools in England are non-religious, but around a third of state schools in England are faith schools. The figure is higher in Northern Ireland but lower in Scotland and Wales.

2) A large proportion of English state schools are Church of England (C of E) schools — 1 in 4 primary and 1 in 16 secondary schools. They're run on Christian principles and aim to teach pupils Christian values.

3) There are also quite a few Catholic schools — 1 in 10 state secondary schools are Catholic. There are some Jewish, Muslim and other Christian schools too, and a small number of Hindu and Sikh schools.

4) Secularists, atheists and humanists, as well as some religious people, believe state-funded schools should be free from religious influence. They argue that faith schools give children a biased view of the world before they are old enough to make their own choices about their beliefs.

5) They also argue that faith schools discriminate against non-religious children, as they are allowed to choose religious children over others if the school doesn't have enough places for everyone.

6) It can be hard for non-religious children or children of a different religion in a faith school — they may have to choose between missing out on activities with religious aspects, e.g. assemblies, or taking part in something they don't believe in. There isn't always the option to go to a non-religious school.

7) However, many people welcome faith schools as they believe the schools teach children good values. Faith schools are often well-regarded academically, though why they do well is debated.

Challenges for Religion

There are some topics in which some people's religious beliefs may clash with modern values or developments in science. These can lead people to challenge the place of religion in society.

Ideas about Marriage have Changed in Society

See p.94 for religious views on these issues.

1) Some people's religious beliefs clash with what society now sees as normal. For example, same-sex marriage was welcomed by many in the UK, but some disagree with it as they see homosexuality as wrong.

2) In an arranged marriage, families help decide who their child should marry — but the child has a say too. Arranged marriages are more common in some cultures and religions than others, which can lead to tension if some see them as positive and others see them as wrong. For many, they're a way of finding a partner with shared values, but they may be misunderstood in the UK as they're not the norm.

3) Forced or child marriages are usually also arranged by the family. A forced marriage is when at least one party doesn't consent to marrying — they're illegal in the UK. Child marriages are when minors (under-18s) marry — they often involve girls more than boys. In most of the UK, people can marry from 16 with their parents' consent and from 18 without parental consent.

4) Some issues can lead people to question the place of religion in society. For example, the state church (the Church of England) campaigned against legalising same-sex marriage, despite the majority of the population wanting it legalised. Some think secularism is a solution, as it would stop religions having too much of an influence on topics that affect everyone. But religious figures think it would marginalise religious values — it would be unfair to believers for society to be organised on the basis of secularism.

Equality is Important in Religious Teachings

1) In Christianity, Islam and Judaism, women and men have traditionally been considered to have different roles, meaning some believers' views clash with modern ideas of equality. Some may think homosexual people shouldn't have equal rights. However, religious teachings are strongly in favour of racial equality.

2) It can be difficult to decide whose values should have priority in areas of disagreement:

> • A religion teaching that women can't be religious leaders is thought by many to undermine women's right not to be discriminated against, but preventing the religion from teaching this would undermine the faith's freedom of belief.
> • In 2014, a homosexual activist in Northern Ireland asked a bakery to make a cake with the slogan 'Support Gay Marriage'. The bakers refused, saying it was against their religious beliefs. A judge ruled that the bakers couldn't provide a service only to people who shared their beliefs. This was a significant case affecting the relationship between religious values and secular law.

Medical and Scientific Issues have Led to Tricky Debates

1) Abortion is accepted by most in British society, though the laws on it are very strict in Northern Ireland. It goes against many people's religious beliefs (p.51-53). It's an emotional issue which has led to debates about freedom of speech — anti-abortion groups are criticised for protesting outside abortion clinics, as some say they intimidate the clinics' visitors. But the groups say they have a right to express their views.

2) We can now keep more seriously ill people alive for longer, even if for example they can't breathe by themselves. This has led to debates about when or if it's OK for people to choose to die — euthanasia.

3) There are also debates about creating life — procedures such as artificial insemination and in vitro fertilisation (IVF) mean that women can now conceive if they are unable to conceive naturally.

4) Scientists can now manipulate genes (often called 'genetic engineering') to produce certain characteristics. For example, genetic engineering is used to produce insulin for diabetic people, whose bodies don't produce enough. Crops can be modified so they're more resistant to pests or taste better.

5) These issues can be challenging for religious people. Many object to people creating, changing or ending life on the grounds that it's God's role to determine when and how these things happen, not people's. Others may focus on compassion — many of these developments help people, e.g. people in pain.

6) Religious objections to these issues can lead to criticism of religion's role in society, especially if religious views differ from more widely held ones. E.g. Northern Ireland's controversially strict abortion laws are often attributed to the prevalence of religion there, which some would use as an argument for secularism.

Challenges for Religion

The Faiths have Different Views on these Areas of Debate

Christian Views
For views on marriage, see p.37 and 39, on abortion and euthanasia, p.51-53, and on equality, p.44-45 and p.81.

1. Some Christians support faith schools as they see it as important that children are educated in a Christian environment, especially when the UK is becoming less Christian. They may see it as important for promoting Christianity — Matthew 28:19 says "make disciples of all nations" (NIV). Others agree with secularists and humanists that education should be separate from religion.
2. There are other cases when Christian opinions may be similar to general views in society. For example, the Church of England has helped to work against forced marriage, which shows how religion can help support society's views and laws.
3. Some Christians' opposition to things which are accepted in society means Christianity can be viewed more negatively by some. For example, the Catholic Church's opposition to fertility treatment can clash with others' values. However, other Christians see fertility treatment more positively — they welcome it as it allows people to have children when they couldn't do so otherwise.
4. Some support genetic engineering if it benefits people's health. Others are against it, especially if it affects future generations.
5. Most Christians support sex education — the Church of England and the Catholic Church have welcomed it being made compulsory. Some may worry it covers topics that go against the Churches' teachings, but faith schools can adapt it to their beliefs.

Muslim Views
For views on marriage, see p.37 and 40, on abortion and euthanasia, p.51 and 53, and on equality, p.44-45 and p.83.

1. Some Muslims support faith schools as they uphold religious values. The C of E has said some Muslim parents see C of E schools as a chance for their children to understand other faiths and attend a school that takes faith seriously. Others may prefer for schools to be non-religious, especially as so many UK faith schools are Christian — there are less than 30 Muslim state schools.
2. Some Muslims disagree with the type of sex education given in schools, as they feel it goes against Muslim principles.
3. As some believe the UK's identity is Christian, it can be challenging for Muslims if they hold views seen as different from Christian cultural norms — a few think this means Muslims don't 'fit in'. An example is arranged marriages, which are common in many Muslim cultures — they're seen as more stable as they ensure the couple have shared values and involve both partners' families. Some Muslims see arranged marriages more negatively, especially as they may increase the likelihood of forced or child marriages. Forced marriages aren't supported by the Qur'an — Qur'an 4:19 says "it is not lawful for you to inherit women by compulsion".
4. Other Muslim views may be more similar to general views in UK society, e.g. many Muslims welcome genetic engineering if it can be put to positive use such as helping fight diseases. Many support fertility treatments, so long as they only involve a married couple.

Jewish Views
For views on marriage, see p.37 and 41, on abortion and euthanasia, p.51-53, and on equality, p.44-45 and p.82.

1. Some Jews welcome faith schools as an opportunity for their children to have a Jewish education. Others, particularly some Progressive Jews, are more wary of them as they believe faith schools may hinder integration between those of different faiths.
2. Arranged marriages are common for Ultra-Orthodox Jews but not so much among other Jews. These marriages focus on the couple fitting with each others' families — family is important in Judaism. Others in the UK may see arranged marriages more negatively.
3. Many Progressive Jews' opinions are similar to those accepted in wider UK society, and in the law, e.g. Progressive Jews work for gender equality and campaigned for same-sex marriage. It may be more challenging for Orthodox Jews, whose views may differ — their attitude to gender roles may be more traditional than many people's in the UK, for example.
4. Most Jews tend to support genetic engineering because of the principle of pikuach nefesh (p.28). They support even genetically modified crops under this principle, as a better supply of crops can help support human life. Many Jews also broadly support fertility treatments such as IVF because Jews believe Genesis 1:28 says they should have children: "Be fruitful and increase in number" (NIV).

Humanism is Becoming More Prominent in the UK

Humanists believe in humans' ability to improve their lives, both individually and collectively. Humanists are therefore guided by reason and empathy. They use science to explain things, and tend to reject belief in a god, though a few may take part in some religious activities.

1) Humanism is becoming more popular partly because religious belief has decreased — it's now socially acceptable not to be religious, and many see no place for religion in modern society.
2) People may choose humanism because while it shares some values with religions, e.g. compassion and empathy, some of its values are in line with more liberal values. Unlike atheism, it offers an alternative outlook to religion on how people should live their lives, as well as rituals for things such as marriage.

Answer in the context of the religion you've studied...

Compare religious and secular views about marriage. Refer to sacred texts.   [6]

EXAM QUESTION

Dialogue Between Different Groups | All religions

Dialogue between different religions and with non-religious groups is important in a multi-faith society.

There are Various Concepts Related to Religious Dialogue

1) In the UK, people are free to choose and express their beliefs, so long as they don't harm anyone else.

2) Many in the UK embrace the concept of diversity. This is the idea that difference is something to be celebrated, as everyone gains from living in a society with people of different backgrounds and cultures. The opposite of diversity is uniformity, when people generally have the same culture, beliefs and values.

3) Consensus is the idea that, despite any differences, people can agree on some fundamental principles that are generally important (e.g. democracy), which help them live together in harmony.

4) Inter-faith dialogue is co-operation and positive interaction between different religious traditions. Intra-faith dialogue is between different branches of the same religion, e.g. Sunni and Shi'a Islam.

5) Pluralism is the idea that those with differing religious views or no religious views can exist side by side — it recognises that all beliefs are valid for their respective followers.

6) Inclusivism is the idea that while a believer thinks their religion is the true one, they recognise that other religions have some validity. Exclusivism is when someone rejects any beliefs but their own as valid.

7) Proselytisation is trying to convert people to a faith. For more on freedom of belief and of expression, see p.85.

Inter-Faith Dialogue is Important

1) Muslims, Jews and Christians engage in inter-faith dialogue, e.g. when working for charitable causes and providing guidance on Religious Studies teaching. They hold multi-faith events, e.g. in Inter Faith Week, which is a focal point for inter-faith dialogue and offers activities for all to take part in.

- The Three Faiths Forum (3FF) is a group run by Christians, Jews and Muslims. They run various programmes to build relationships between different communities, including working in schools and in Parliament.
- The Council of Christians and Jews provides opportunities for Christians and Jews to engage with each other. It fights against prejudice, e.g. by focusing on Holocaust remembrance and on the Israel-Palestine conflict.
- Children of Abraham is a council of imams and rabbis who work for harmony between the Jewish and Muslim communities. They hold events in Parliament to discuss issues affecting the two, and other inter-faith events.

2) Inter-faith dialogue is important in Britain as it's a multi-faith society. Getting to know people of other faiths on a personal level helps people's understanding of those faiths in general.

3) Inter-faith dialogue can help religions work together to promote shared values, which makes their voices more effective — e.g. working together to campaign for peace in the world, as Religions for Peace does.

4) Working together can be particularly helpful to religions which are followed by fewer people and haven't been established as long in the UK, e.g. Islam or Judaism, as they often face prejudice and discrimination.

Many Christians Aim for Understanding between Faiths

1) Many Christians think their faith is the true path — only through Jesus's teaching can people know God. Jesus said "No one comes to the Father except through me" (John 14:6 NIV).

2) Most Christians believe people have a right to believe whatever they wish though — they're inclusivists.

3) Some are more exclusivist and believe it's their duty to convert people, following Jesus's command to "make disciples of all nations, baptising them in the name of the Father..." (Matthew 28:19 NIV).

4) Ecumenism is the aim of developing better understanding between those of different Christian traditions:

- Many Christian Churches believe in and work for ecumenism. Many British Churches are members of Churches Together — this organisation promotes understanding between denominations and helps them to communicate with each other and work together for shared causes, e.g. helping refugees.
- However, attempts at ecumenism between the Anglican and Catholic Churches have been strained by some Anglican Churches' ordination of female and homosexual clergy, and their more liberal stance on abortion.
- Ecumenism also takes place on a local level, such as different denominations holding services together.

All religions | Dialogue Between Different Groups

Harmony between Religious Traditions is Important in Islam

1) The Constitution of Madinah is a text believed to have been written by Muhammad. It formed the basis of a pluralistic community in Madinah and included protection of religious freedoms for Jews.

2) Some believe the Qur'an teaches that Jews and Christians will be recognised by Allah:

> "...those who believed and those who were Jews or Christians ... will have their reward with the Lord" Qur'an 2:62

3) Others disagree — they believe it only refers to former Jews and Christians who converted to Islam.

4) Some Muslims take a more exclusive position on other faiths. Some may feel they have a mission to convert people to Islam. It can be difficult for Muslims who leave the faith — for more, see p.85.

5) Many Muslims work to promote awareness of Islam, especially to combat the negative attitudes some have towards Muslims. 'Visit My Mosque' day — where mosques are open to all — is an example of this.

6) Intra-faith dialogue is important for Muslims, as Sunni, Shi'a and Sufi traditions have differing views on some religious matters. However, the concept of the ummah — the worldwide community of all Muslims — is significant in intra-faith relations. It stresses the idea that all Muslims are equal in the eyes of Allah.

7) The concepts of shahadah, salah, zakah, sawm and hajj (known in Sunni Islam as the Five Pillars — see p.21-23) encourage unity and equality as all Muslims should follow them.

Jews Respect Other Faiths

> "The foreigner residing among you must be treated as your native-born." Leviticus 19:34 NIV

1) Jewish identity is believed by most Jews to be passed on through mothers, so Jews don't proselytise (though it's possible to convert). Jews usually consider people who follow any faith to be righteous if they follow the Noahide Laws — a set of moral guidelines delivered to Noah and shared by many faiths.

2) Intra-faith relations can sometimes be more difficult in Judaism, though Progressive Jews tend to be pluralist — they believe there are multiple different ways to follow Judaism.

3) Orthodox Jews are often more inclusivist — they recognise Progressive Judaism and work with other Jews, but don't accept some aspects, e.g. they don't recognise Progressive Jewish converts as Jews.

4) Some Ultra-Orthodox (Haredi) Jews are more exclusivist and don't engage much in intra-faith dialogue.

5) Chabad-Lubavitch is an Orthodox Jewish movement. They focus on reaching out to as many Jewish people as possible regardless of how observant they are or if they're even religious, as they believe that if a Jew does even just one mitzvah (p.28), that will help bring the Messiah (p.29).

There are Different Groups of Non-Religious People

1) Religious groups and non-religious or secularist groups may also engage in dialogue with one another. People can be non-religious or secularist in different ways.

See p.92 for more on secularism and p.94 for more on humanism.

2) Atheists believe there is no god.

3) Agnostics believe it's impossible to know for certain if there is or isn't a god.

4) Humanists are usually atheists. They focus on a concern for humanity and on science to explain things.

5) Secularists can be religious or non-religious — they believe religion should be separate from the state.

6) These views don't require people to belong to a group, but there are organisations which represent them, e.g. the National Secular Society and Humanists UK. They campaign on various issues, often to make sure non-religious people don't face discrimination and their voices are heard, e.g.:

> Some think the census question 'What is your religion?' assumes religious belief and ignores non-religious people. Humanists UK says it gives an overly high figure for religious belief as it could cover anyone from a 'culturally religious' but atheist person, to a regular worshipper. They campaigned for people who don't practise a religion to tick 'no religion'. Some objected to this.

7) Secularists may also help other faiths have more of a voice, e.g. by disputing the C of E's role in the state.

8) Some people object to the campaigning as they see it as weakening the voice of religion, which they may see as the source of moral values in society. Others see it more specifically as undermining Christianity's influence, and object because they believe Christianity is an integral part of British culture.

Dialogue Between Different Groups All religions

Believers and non-believers may disagree on some issues, but they share many values.

Shared Values Bring Religious and Non-Religious People Together

1) Most religious and non-religious people get along well and have respect for each other.

2) However, in modern society, there can sometimes be tension between religious and non-religious people. Some religious people may try to convert non-religious people if they think theirs is the best way of life, while some non-religious people may try to convince believers that there's no evidence God exists.

3) Many religious and non-religious people share values, which makes dialogue between them easier.

4) Belief in basic freedom (broadly, people should be free to live their lives as they wish) is shared by many religious and non-religious people. This is linked to belief in equality — giving all the chance of freedom.

5) Many religious and non-religious people also share beliefs in the importance of more concrete concepts such as social justice (p.86), human rights (p.84) or environmental issues. They may work together to promote these, e.g. through initiatives organised jointly by different groups or through charities:

- An example of this is The Climate Coalition, which campaigns for action on climate change. Many different groups are members, including Christian Aid, Humanists UK, Islamic Relief UK and the Jewish Social Action Forum.
- Religious and non-religious organisations, including Humanists UK, the National Secular Society and Liberal Judaism, were members of the Coalition for Equal Marriage, which campaigned for same-sex marriage to be legal.

6) Many people value things such as compassion, kindness, loyalty and honesty, regardless of their beliefs.

7) Different perspectives can overlap, e.g. being religious and secularist. Some humanists are religious.

Religious and secular values are sometimes different, and sometimes the same. E.g. murder is seen as wrong from both viewpoints — for religious people, it's prohibited by sacred texts, and for non-religious people it's a matter of human empathy and reason.

There are also Areas of Disagreement

Some are covered on p.92-93, including issues such as marriage, abortion and education.

1) Atheist and religious people disagree on the existence of a god. This can affect their views on some topics.

2) Some religious people may feel worried by the rise in people with no religious belief and try to take action, while non-religious people may feel that religion is too influential and non-religious beliefs are ignored.

3) People disagree over the place of religion in society. Some advocate secularism (p.92), as they think it would protect the right to individual self-determination — choosing your beliefs and actions. Some think it could lead to secular values taking precedence at the expense of religious ones, which they see as unfair.

Christian Views

1. Some may want to promote Christianity as they believe Jesus is "the way and the truth and the life" (John 14:6 NIV), but most Christians believe people have a right to choose not to be religious — Jesus let people decide for themselves.
2. Calls for the secularisation of UK society are often justified by falling numbers of religious people, especially Christians, so some Christians feel they need to work to promote their religion.
3. Some may think the increasingly non-religious society threatens their beliefs, e.g. a Christian nurse was suspended for offering to pray for a patient. Some think this undermined the nurse's freedom of belief, but others argue it was wrong to mention her religion in that context.

Muslim Views

1. Qur'an 2:256 says "There shall be no compulsion in [acceptance of] the religion" — people are free to choose whether to believe or not.
2. Some Muslims may welcome secularism as a way of helping religious harmony and equality. Others see it more negatively if it's used as a way of suppressing their beliefs, e.g. the ban on the niqab in French schools.

Jewish Views

1. Jews are both a people and a religious group, so they don't try to convert non-believers. This also means some people consider themselves to be both Jewish and atheist or humanist — some Jews don't believe in God, but still perform Jewish religious rituals and are members of a synagogue.
2. Some Jews, e.g. the Society for Humanistic Judaism, support society being secular, as it would give everyone self-determination. Others may disagree — Ultra-Orthodox Jews celebrate tradition and reject secular influences.

Remember that some perspectives may overlap...

... e.g. Jews could be secularist. Now, try noting down some views on secularism so you remember them.

Revision Summary

Right, that section covered an awful lot, so it's now time to find out how much of it you remember...
These questions are similar to those in the exams — they should get you used to how much you need to write.

If there's a question you can't answer, read back through the section and try again when you've re-read it.
Remember you might need to look at p.37 and p.39-41 for attitudes towards marriage and homosexuality,
p.51-53 for views on abortion and euthanasia and p.44-45 and p.81-83 for opinions on equality.

Answer each of these questions in the context of the religion you've studied.

Let's start off with some 3 mark questions.

1) Give three features a secular society may have.

2) Describe one area of debate surrounding faith schools.

3) Name three different types of marriage.

4) Give three worldviews non-religious people may have, other than secularism.

5) State three values shared by many religious and non-religious people.

These questions are worth 6 marks. They are fairly straightforward questions,
in which you need to show your knowledge and understanding of the religion.

6) Describe how religious people may engage in dialogue with non-religious groups.

7) Outline different religious views on equality.

For these questions, your answer should refer to the diversity of religious belief in the UK, and the
position of Christianity as the main religious tradition. These questions are worth 6 marks too.

8) Describe how religious people take part in dialogue with those of other religious traditions.

9) Outline the ways in which Christianity has an influence on British society.

These are also 6 mark questions, but you'll need to give more analysis
and evaluation in your answers than you did for the questions above.
Your answers should include examples from sources of wisdom and authority.

10) Explain why sex education in schools may be a challenge for some religious people.

11) Compare religious and secular views about same-sex marriage.

12) Compare religious and secular views about abortion.

13) Explain attitudes within the religion you are studying towards those of other religions.

This is the biggy — worth 15 marks. You'll always get bullet points like this saying what you should include
— use them to plan your answer before you start writing. It's worth making a list of arguments for and
against the statement before you start, so you don't miss any out when writing your answer.

14) 'The UK should be a secular society.'

Discuss this statement. You should:

•   Apply knowledge from your whole Religious Studies course, including the beliefs,
    teachings and practices of the religion you're studying.

•   Describe different points of view and evaluate their importance
    in the context of the religion you're studying.

Have a look at the 'Do Well in Your
Exam' section for help with writing essays.

The Start of Jesus's Ministry

In this section, the <u>numbers</u> in the <u>subheadings</u> give the <u>reference</u> for the Gospel extract you need to study.

John the Baptist *Baptised People in the River Jordan (1:1-8)*

1) Mark <u>doesn't</u> have any stories about <u>Jesus's birth</u> — he starts with the story of <u>John the Baptist</u>.

2) Mark quotes from the Old Testament, where God says he will send a messenger to "Prepare the way for the Lord" (Mark 1:3 NIV). Mark says that <u>John</u> was this messenger, preparing for the coming Messiah.

3) John baptised people in the <u>River Jordan</u> by <u>total immersion</u>. The water symbolises being <u>cleansed</u> of their sins — they had <u>repented</u> and now wanted to live <u>good</u> lives. The River Jordan was also <u>symbolic</u> to these people — in the Old Testament, the <u>Israelites</u> crossed the River Jordan to enter the <u>Promised Land</u>. The people baptised in the river by John entered the new 'Promised Land' of <u>God's kingdom</u>.

4) John predicted someone <u>greater</u> would come to <u>baptise</u> people, this time with the Holy Spirit.

> "After me comes the one more powerful than I, the straps of whose sandals I am not worthy to stoop down and untie. I baptise you with water, but he will baptise you with the Holy Spirit." Mark 1:7-8 NIV

5) The Old Testament prophet <u>Joel</u> had predicted the <u>Holy Spirit</u> would be present on <u>Earth</u> when the <u>Messiah</u> came (Joel 2). So John was saying the <u>Messiah</u> was coming — this Messiah was <u>Jesus</u>.

Jesus *was Baptised by John and Tempted by Satan (1:9-13)*

1) <u>Jesus</u> was <u>baptised</u> in the River Jordan by John — this marked the <u>beginning</u> of Jesus's <u>ministry</u>. The <u>Holy Spirit</u> appeared as Jesus was being baptised.

> "...he saw heaven being torn open and the Spirit descending on him like a dove." Mark 1:10 NIV

2) He heard a <u>voice</u> from <u>heaven</u> saying "You are my Son, whom I love; with you I am well pleased" (Mark 1:11 NIV). God's words show how <u>important</u> Jesus is to him — this was God giving Jesus his <u>mission</u>.

3) Baptism is still <u>important</u> to Christians <u>today</u> — it's how people are <u>welcomed</u> into the <u>Church</u> (see p.9).

4) Then the Holy Spirit made Jesus go out into the <u>desert</u>:

> "...he was in the wilderness for forty days, being tempted by Satan... angels attended him." Mark 1:13 NIV

5) Jesus was being <u>tested</u> — Satan, God's <u>archenemy</u>, was trying to make Jesus <u>sin</u> and <u>go against</u> God. But Jesus didn't <u>give in</u> to Satan, which shows his <u>power</u>. God's love for Jesus is demonstrated by the way he sent his <u>messengers</u>, the <u>angels</u>, to <u>care</u> for him.

6) Christians believe they also will be <u>tested</u> and <u>tempted</u>. But with <u>God's help</u>, they can <u>get through</u> it just like Jesus did. Christians remember Jesus's struggle during <u>Lent</u> (see p.12) — a period which tests their ability to <u>overcome temptation</u>.

Jesus's *Titles Show How Important He Is*

1) Mark calls Jesus "the Messiah, the Son of God" (Mark 1:1 NIV). Titles such as these explain his <u>role</u>.

2) By calling Jesus the '<u>Son of God</u>', Mark means Jesus is God's <u>special one</u> — he has a unique <u>relationship</u> to God, and God gave him a unique <u>mission</u>. The title would have stressed Jesus's importance to 1st century Jews — it was used in the Old Testament for <u>kings</u>, and also for the whole <u>nation</u> of <u>Israel</u>.

3) <u>Messiah</u> means '<u>anointed one</u>' in Hebrew (Mark also uses '<u>Christ</u>', which is the <u>Greek</u> translation). It also used to be given to the <u>kings</u> of Israel. It later came to mean a <u>heavenly figure</u> who would come to <u>save</u> the <u>Jews</u> from their enemies — Mark believed <u>Jesus</u> was this saviour. The Messiah was often expected as a <u>military figure</u>, but since Jesus wasn't, he didn't <u>specifically</u> use it for <u>himself</u> (see p.102).

Don't mix up John the Baptist and John the disciple...

This section covers the Gospel of Mark in depth, and for the exam you'll need to know the key passages like the back of your hand. So get a cup of tea and a biscuit, sit down and have a read through them all.

Jesus's Miracles

At the start of Jesus's ministry, he performed many miracles as he travelled around teaching.

Jesus Forgave and Healed a Paralysed Man (2:1-12)

1) When Jesus was teaching in a crowded house, some men carried a paralysed man to him. Because there were so many people, there was no way in, so they had to find an alternative:

> "...they made an opening in the roof above Jesus... and then lowered the mat the man was lying on. When Jesus saw their faith, he said to the paralysed man, 'Son, your sins are forgiven'. " Mark 2:4-5 NIV

2) Jesus was impressed by their strong faith, but didn't immediately heal the man — he first forgave his sins.

3) There were people there who were shocked by what Jesus did: "Why does this fellow talk like that? He's blaspheming! Who can forgive sins but God alone?" (Mark 2:7 NIV).

4) They believed that only God could forgive sins — Jesus was falsely claiming God's authority.

5) Jesus then healed the man, who was able to walk out of the room. By demonstrating his power through healing, Jesus showed he also must be powerful enough to forgive sins. But to him, forgiving sins was more important.

> "But I want you to know that the Son of Man has authority on earth to forgive sins." Mark 2:10 NIV

6) The people "praised God, saying, 'We have never seen anything like this!' " (Mark 2:12 NIV). They realised that Jesus's power must have come from God. The story shows modern Christians that they must put their faith in Jesus's power.

7) Some people see this story as something that really happened, whereas others interpret it as a metaphor that shows how Jesus is powerful enough to heal people spiritually, freeing them from their sins. Some believe that modern faith healers can sometimes cure people who have a strong enough faith.

Jesus Uses the Title 'Son of Man' in this Passage

1) The 'Son of Man' is a title that Jesus often uses when referring to himself.

2) There are various interpretations of what the title means:

- Some people believed it shows Jesus's humanity.
- Some believe that in Jesus's language, Aramaic, it was the normal way of talking about yourself, like using 'I'.
- Daniel 7:13-14 talks about the Son of Man as a powerful, heavenly figure.

Jesus Brought a Girl Back to Life (5:21-24 and 5:35-43)

1) Jairus, a synagogue leader, begged Jesus to help his dying daughter: "My little daughter is dying. Please come and put your hands on her so that she will be healed and live" (Mark 5:23 NIV).

2) But the girl died while Jesus was on his way. However, Jesus told Jairus to have faith. He'd already shown his faith by going to Jesus, but Jesus encouraged even greater faith.

3) When he saw the girl, "He took her by the hand and said to her... 'Little girl, I say to you, get up!' " (Mark 5:41 NIV). The girl was brought back to life, and began to move around. The words 'little girl' are translated from a phrase in Aramaic which literally means 'little lamb', showing Jesus's care for the child.

4) Jesus tells them not to mention what had happened.

Jesus was Rejected in his Hometown (6:1-6)

1) After being away from his hometown of Nazareth, Jesus returned in his new role and started teaching in the synagogue.

> "He could not do any miracles there, except lay his hands on a few people who were ill and heal them. He was amazed at their lack of faith." Mark 6:5-6 NIV

2) But the people there knew him as their carpenter, the son of Mary. They didn't believe he could be God's chosen one.

3) Jesus said "A prophet is not without honour except in his own town, among his relatives and in his own home" (Mark 6:4 NIV).

4) Jesus previously said the disciples were his true relatives. Many Christians were (and sometimes still are) misunderstood and rejected by their families. They can take heart from the fact it happened to Jesus too.

Jesus's Miracles

Jesus Miraculously Fed 5000 People (6:30-44)

1) A large crowd followed Jesus to an isolated place, so he decided to teach them. As it got late, Jesus instructed his disciples to feed the people, but they only had five loaves of bread and two fish.

2) Jesus manages to make the little food they have feed everyone — there were at least 5000 people there but there was still lots left over.

> "Taking the five loaves and the two fish and looking up to heaven, he gave thanks and broke the loaves. Then he gave them to his disciples to distribute to the people. He also divided the two fish among them all." Mark 6:41 NIV

3) This miracle is important for many reasons:

- It would have reminded 1st century Jews of the Old Testament story where God fed the Israelites on miraculous manna (bread) while they were with Moses in the wilderness.
- For Christians today, it's a reminder of how Jesus also broke bread at the Last Supper — Christians are fed spiritually by Jesus when they remember this at the Eucharist (see p.104).
- It also reminds them to have faith that God will look after them. He can deal with big problems and do great things with the small offerings that they make in their lives.
- The story appears in all four Gospels — Christians think this makes it likely that it's true.

Jesus Restored Sight to a Blind Man (10:46-52)

1) Jesus and his followers came across Bartimaeus, a blind man, begging at the side of the road.

2) He called out "Jesus, Son of David, have mercy on me!" (Mark 10:47 NIV) and told Jesus he wanted to be able to see. Jesus healed him:

> " 'Go... your faith has healed you.' Immediately he received his sight and followed Jesus along the road" Mark 10:52 NIV

3) Bartimaeus threw away his cloak before going to Jesus. He would have used it to catch coins that people tossed to him, so he abandoned his means of livelihood to follow Jesus, just like the other disciples. This reminds Christians today that they should focus more on their faith than on worldly goods.

4) Many Christians interpret this story as meaning that they're spiritually blind without Jesus, but if they have faith and follow him, their eyes will be opened to how they should live their lives.

This is the last miracle in Mark's Gospel before Jesus's crucifixion in Jerusalem.

The title 'Son of David' was used in this story. David was the greatest of the kings of Israel in the Old Testament, so people who used this title saw Jesus as a new king who would rule justly, like David did. Also, the Messiah was prophesied to be David's descendant, so by using this title, people acknowledge Jesus as the Messiah.

The Miracle Stories Tell Us a Lot About Jesus

1) The miracles in Mark's Gospel show how Jesus had God's power. They also show his compassion for people who were suffering or in need.

2) Although Mark focuses on Jesus's actions in these stories, they also show Jesus as a popular teacher. Mark portrays how Jesus travelled around teaching, usually attracting huge crowds.

3) The miracle stories can be interpreted in different ways:

- Some Christians believe Jesus's miracles actually happened. Others think they're metaphors that symbolise a spiritual truth. Some Christians accept both meanings.
- Non-religious people would say they just didn't happen, or that there are ways to explain the events rationally using science.

Learn this and you won't need a miracle to pass the exam...

These stories show Christians how they should follow Jesus and have faith in their everyday lives. See if you can jot down a quick summary of each miracle, and why they're important for modern-day Christians.

The Later Ministry of Jesus

It's not until the <u>second half</u> of Mark's Gospel that Jesus is recognised as the <u>Messiah</u>.

Jesus was Declared the Messiah and Predicted his Death (8:27-33)

1) This is an important <u>turning point</u> in Mark's Gospel. Jesus's <u>ministry</u> in Galilee had <u>finished</u>, and he was starting to move towards <u>Jerusalem</u>, where he knew he would <u>die</u>.

2) Jesus and his disciples were travelling near the town Caesarea Philippi when he asked them, "Who do people say I am?". They told him: "Some say John the Baptist; others say Elijah; and still others, one of the prophets" (Mark 8:27-28 NIV). <u>John the Baptist</u> had been <u>executed</u>, so some people thought he'd <u>come back</u> from the dead in <u>Jesus</u>.

3) So far, <u>no-one</u> had said that Jesus was the <u>Messiah</u>. But when Jesus asked his disciples who he was, <u>Peter</u> replied: "You are the Messiah" (Mark 8:29 NIV).

4) But Peter had <u>misunderstood</u> Jesus's real mission — he may have thought the Messiah would be a <u>political</u> or <u>military</u> figure (see p.99).

5) Jesus then tells them about how he would <u>suffer</u> and <u>die</u> — but would come back to <u>life</u>.

> "...the Son of Man must suffer many things and be rejected by the elders, the chief priests and the teachers of the law... he must be killed and after three days rise again." Mark 8:31 NIV

6) Peter <u>told him off</u>. He thought it was <u>impossible</u> for the Messiah to <u>die</u>, so Jesus must be <u>wrong</u>.

7) Jesus replied: " 'Get behind me, Satan! ... You do not have in mind the concerns of God, but merely human concerns' " (Mark 8:33 NIV). Jesus was <u>criticising</u> Peter for trying to <u>tempt</u> him <u>away</u> from his <u>true mission</u> from God, just as <u>Satan</u> had tempted Jesus in the <u>wilderness</u>. However, God's plan for <u>salvation</u> involved Jesus being <u>crucified</u>.

Jesus's True Nature was Shown to the Disciples (9:2-9)

1) Jesus went up a <u>mountain</u> with Peter, James and John — the three disciples he was <u>closest</u> to. Then, his <u>appearance</u> changed:

> "His clothes became dazzling white... And there appeared before them Elijah and Moses, who were talking with Jesus." Mark 9:3-4 NIV

2) This is called 'the <u>transfiguration</u>'. The disciples were shown the true <u>divine nature</u> behind Jesus's <u>normal appearance</u>.

3) <u>Elijah</u> and <u>Moses</u> were two of the greatest figures of the Old Testament. Moses gave Jews the <u>Law</u> and Elijah was the greatest of the <u>Prophets</u>. The way that they appeared with Jesus showed he was the <u>Messiah</u> in the Old Testament <u>prophecies</u>.

4) <u>God</u> spoke: "...a cloud appeared and covered them, and a voice came from the cloud: 'This is my son, whom I love. Listen to him!' " (Mark 9:7 NIV). This demonstrates how <u>important</u> Jesus's words were.

5) On the way down, Jesus <u>forbade</u> them to speak about it until he had <u>come back</u> from the <u>dead</u>.

6) The story reveals just how <u>important</u> Jesus was, and the <u>power</u> that God had given him.

The Messianic Secret is a Big Part of Mark's Gospel

1) Jesus told his disciples <u>not</u> to <u>tell</u> anyone that he was the <u>Messiah</u>. The real <u>nature</u> of Jesus's <u>messiahship</u> is only truly <u>understood</u> after the resurrection — this is the <u>Messianic Secret</u> in Mark.

2) This has many parts. For example, Jesus told people <u>not</u> to talk about the <u>miracles</u> he performed, and his teachings in the form of parables could be <u>difficult</u> to <u>understand</u> (see p.107-108).

3) He may have wanted to keep his messiahship a <u>secret</u> in case it was <u>misunderstood</u>.

It's no secret that Jesus's ministry could be in the exam...

Give two reasons why Peter was angry when Jesus told the disciples he would die. [2]

The Later Ministry of Jesus

Although Jesus tried to keep it a <u>secret</u>, by the time he got to <u>Jerusalem</u>, people were calling him the <u>Messiah</u>.

Jesus Predicted his Death and Resurrection Again (10:32-34)

1) While going to <u>Jerusalem</u>, Jesus <u>again</u> told the disciples he would be <u>killed</u>, but would <u>rise</u> from the <u>grave</u>.

> "...the Son of Man will be delivered over to the chief priests and the teachers of the law. They will condemn him to death and will hand him over to the Gentiles, who will mock him and spit on him, flog him and kill him. Three days later he will rise." Mark 10:33-34 NIV

This was one of his 'passion predictions' — Jesus's suffering and death are called the 'passion'.

2) This was the <u>third time</u> he predicted his death — he gave <u>more detail</u> than before.

3) The Gentiles were the <u>Romans</u> — the Jews couldn't <u>execute</u> people because the Romans <u>ruled</u> over them, so they would have to <u>give</u> Jesus to the Romans.

4) The things Jesus predicted later <u>happened</u> (see p.104-105). Mark presents the events as the <u>fulfilment</u> of Jesus's <u>prophecy</u>, and as part of the <u>divine plan</u>.

5) The <u>crucifixion</u> came as a devastating <u>shock</u> to the disciples. But eventually they came to understand that it was an <u>essential</u> part of <u>God's plan</u>, not a defeat. Mark shows that Jesus <u>understood</u> this <u>in advance</u> and continued to Jerusalem despite <u>knowing</u> what awaited him.

Jesus Told his Disciples about Serving Others (10:35-45)

1) <u>James</u> and <u>John</u> asked to sit on Jesus's <u>right</u> and <u>left sides</u> when he returned to <u>heaven</u> in <u>glory</u>. They wanted to be the <u>closest</u> to Jesus, and the <u>most important</u>.

2) Jesus asked if they would to go through the <u>trials</u> he'd suffer: "Can you drink the cup I drink..." (Mark 10:38 NIV). They said yes. Jesus said they'd <u>suffer</u>, but the <u>places</u> by his side were <u>decided by God</u>.

3) The <u>other disciples</u> were <u>angry</u> that James and John wanted to be more important than them. Jesus said:

> "...whoever wants to become great among you must be your servant, and whoever wants to be first must be slave of all. For even the Son of Man did not come to be served, but to serve, and to give his life as a ransom for many." Mark 10:43-45 NIV

Only people who were <u>humble</u> and <u>served others</u> on Earth would be <u>rewarded</u> in <u>heaven</u>. Jesus would later serve <u>humanity</u> by dying so that they would be <u>reconciled</u> with God (see p.5).

4) Many Christians try to <u>serve</u> others, e.g. through their <u>job</u> or by <u>dedicating</u> themselves to the <u>Church</u>.

Jesus Entered Jerusalem as a New King (11:1-11)

1) Jesus and his disciples were getting <u>near</u> to <u>Jerusalem</u> — the <u>holy city</u> where <u>David</u> and the other kings had reigned. Jesus told two disciples to bring him a young <u>donkey</u> (a colt), which Jesus rode.

2) In the Old Testament, the <u>Messiah</u> was predicted to enter Jerusalem on a <u>donkey</u> (Zechariah 9:9). Riding in on a donkey showed Jesus's <u>humility</u> and <u>peaceful</u> nature, something Christians should try to <u>follow</u>.

3) Some people laid <u>cloaks</u> and <u>branches</u> across Jesus's path, which showed how <u>respected</u> he was. As he rode into Jerusalem, they cried "Hosanna! Blessed is he who comes in the name of the Lord! Blessed is the coming kingdom of our father David!" (Mark 11:9-10 NIV). Hosanna means '<u>save now</u>' — the people of Jerusalem believed that Jesus was the <u>Messiah</u>, and was there to <u>help</u> them.

4) Jesus is celebrated as David's successor — the new <u>messianic king</u>. This follows straight after Bartimaeus called him 'Son of David' (see p.101).

5) Christians remember this event on <u>Palm Sunday</u>, named after the branches people used. They're reminded of how Jesus was <u>proclaimed</u> as the <u>saviour</u>, and also of his <u>humility</u>. But Christians today <u>know</u> how the crowd soon <u>turned against</u> Jesus. They must be <u>careful</u> to keep their <u>faith</u> in him.

Serving others is important, so here's something for you...

See if you can summarise the events that took place in the later stages of Jesus's ministry. Extra points if you can back them up with specific references to Mark's Gospel.

REVISION TASK

The Final Days in Jerusalem

Jesus had arrived in Jerusalem, and he knew that this was where he would be betrayed by one of his disciples.

Jesus Ate with his Disciples at the Last Supper (14:12-26)

1) Jesus and the disciples ate the Passover meal (see p.35) together — this is known as the Last Supper. Passover is the Jewish festival that remembers the Jews' escape from slavery in Egypt. Christians believe that the death of Jesus also rescues people from sin and death.

2) At the meal, Jesus predicted that one of the disciples would betray him: "Truly I tell you, one of you will betray me — one who is eating with me" (Mark 14:18 NIV). They all denied it.

3) He divided up some bread and passed it to everyone, saying, "Take it; this is my body" (Mark 14:22 NIV). Then he passed around a cup of wine, saying "This is my blood of the covenant, which is poured out for many" (Mark 14:24 NIV). It reflected how Jesus's body would be broken, like the bread, and his blood shed at the crucifixion. 'Covenant' referred to the agreement God made with the Jews in the Old Testament (see p.27). Jesus was saying that his life and death created a new relationship with God.

4) Jesus's actions are still very important to Christians today — they re-enact them in the Eucharist. But there are different beliefs about what Jesus's words meant. Some believe the bread and wine had literally become his body and blood, whereas others think he meant that they just represented them. This is why the Eucharist is celebrated in different ways — read the third section of p.9 for more about this.

5) Jesus also said, "...I will not drink again from the fruit of the vine until that day when I drink it new in the kingdom of God" (Mark 14:25 NIV). He knew that his death was near.

Jesus was Arrested in the Garden of Gethsemane (14:32-52)

1) Jesus told the disciples to keep watch as he prayed in the Garden of Gethsemane, but they fell asleep.

2) Jesus asked God if he could avoid what was coming, but then he submitted to God's will.

"Abba, Father... everything is possible for you. Take this cup from me. Yet not what I will, but what you will." Mark 14:36 NIV

3) Jesus was afraid to go through with the suffering ahead — this shows that he was a real human being. But his obedience to God is an example for Christians. Early Christians followed his example in trusting God, even when persecuted.

4) Then Judas (one of the disciples) arrived with the chief priests' armed men. He betrayed Jesus with a kiss: "The one I kiss is the man; arrest him and lead him away under guard" (Mark 14:44 NIV). Jesus was placed under arrest by the men.

5) One of the disciples "drew his sword and struck the servant of the high priest, cutting off his ear" (Mark 14:47 NIV). Then, the disciples all ran away.

6) Jesus questioned why he was being captured — he asked if they thought he was leading a rebellion, which he wasn't. But he said, "the Scriptures must be fulfilled" (Mark 14:49 NIV).

Jesus was Tried by the Jewish Authorities (14:53, 57-65)

1) Jesus was tried before the Jewish high priest. The high priest asked him: "Are you the Messiah, the Son of the Blessed One?" (Mark 14:61 NIV). Jesus replied "I am... And you will see the Son of Man sitting at the right hand of the Mighty One and coming on the clouds of heaven" (Mark 14:62 NIV).

2) Witnesses gave false evidence against him, and their stories didn't agree. But Jesus was found guilty of blasphemy (because they believed he was falsely claiming to be divine) — a crime carrying the death penalty. He had to be handed to the Romans for his punishment.

This was just the beginning of Jesus's suffering...

Give two reasons why Jesus's words and actions in the Garden of Gethsemane are important. [2]

The Final Days in Jerusalem

Jesus was Sentenced to Death by the Roman Governor (15:1-15)

1) Jesus was tried before the Roman governor, Pilate, the next day. Blasphemy wasn't a crime to the Romans, but he could have been a political threat. Pilate asked Jesus if he was the king of the Jews. He answered "You have said so" (Mark 15:2 NIV). He didn't defend himself — he submitted to God's plan.

2) Pilate realised Jesus wasn't really a threat — the priests had handed him over because they didn't like him. Since a prisoner was released every Passover, Pilate offered to release Jesus.

3) But the chief priests got the people to ask for Barabbas, a murderer, instead. When Pilate asked about Jesus they said "Crucify him!" (Mark 15:13 NIV). So Jesus was flogged and sent to be crucified.

Jesus was Crucified, Died and was Buried (15:21-47)

1) Simon of Cyrene was made to carry Jesus's cross to Golgotha ('the place of the skull').

Jesus was put on the cross at 9am. A sign saying why he was being crucified said "The King of the Jews" (Mark 15:26 NIV).	Jesus was mocked while on the cross: "Let this Messiah, this king of Israel, come down now from the cross, that we may see and believe" (Mark 15:32 NIV).	It became dark at midday, showing the significance of Jesus's suffering. At 3pm, Jesus shouted "My God, my God, why have you forsaken me?" (Mark 15:34 NIV) — he felt abandoned by God. He then died.

2) As Jesus died, the temple curtain ripped in two. This curtain hid the Holy of Holies — a special room inside the temple where God was believed to be present, and only the high priest could enter. This showed that everyone now had access to God.

3) The Roman soldier who saw Jesus die said "Surely this man was the Son of God!" (Mark 15:39 NIV). He recognised who Jesus was, but the Jewish leaders didn't.

4) Joseph of Arimathea was given Jesus's body by Pilate. He "bought some linen cloth, took down the body, wrapped it in the linen, and placed it in a tomb cut out of rock" (Mark 15:46 NIV).

5) Many Christians believe that Jesus's death saved mankind and repaired the relationship with God. But there are various views about the crucifixion — read the middle section of p.5 for more detail.

Jesus's Tomb was Found Empty (16:1-8)

1) Three women went to Jesus's tomb on Sunday morning, but they found the stone rolled back and the tomb empty. There they saw a man in white (an angel). He told them "He has risen! He is not here" (Mark 16:6 NIV). He told them to tell the disciples that Jesus would meet them in Galilee.

2) The women left the tomb, frightened and confused by what they saw. They didn't tell anyone about it.

3) Some early Bibles finish the story here, but later copies added reports of encounters with the risen Jesus.

4) The resurrection turned despair to hope for the disciples. Everything hadn't gone wrong — the crucifixion was part of God's plan.

5) The resurrection is important to Christians for many reasons — read the box at the bottom of p.4. It shows that Jesus really is God's son. It would also have given persecuted early Christians hope that there was something else beyond their suffering.

6) However, many people believe the resurrection is scientifically impossible — they explain the empty tomb in other ways. But those who believe in the resurrection have arguments against these explanations.

Some say the women got the wrong tomb. But Mark 15:47 says Mary Magdalene saw the tomb where Joseph laid Jesus's body.	Others say Jesus wasn't really dead. But at Pilate's request, a soldier confirmed he had died (Mark 15:44-45).	Some think the disciples stole the body. But why would the terrified disciples risk their lives for a dead body?

Luckily for you, there's more Mark in the next section...

You need to know what happens in these events, but also what they mean to different Christians. Some things, like what Jesus says at the Last Supper, are interpreted in various ways, so learn the differences.

Revision Summary

That was quite a lot to take in there, so now try out these questions to see what you're comfortable with and what needs a bit more work. They're like the ones you'll be asked in the actual exam.

If there's anything you can't answer, go back through the section and have another go when you've re-read it. For some questions — you'll be told which ones — there are extra marks for spelling, punctuation and grammar, so check your writing carefully.

Nice and easy to start off with — some 1 mark multiple choice questions.

1) Which one of the following is <u>not</u> a title given to Jesus in Mark's Gospel?
   a) Son of God   b) Messiah   c) Son of Man   d) Prophet

2) Which of these men did Jesus help to see?
   a) Bartimaeus   b) Jairus   c) Elijah   d) Pilate

3) Which of the disciples said that Jesus was the Messiah at Caesarea Philippi?
   a) James   b) John   c) Peter   d) Judas

4) At which of these places was Jesus crucified?
   a) Nazareth   b) Gethsemane   c) Golgotha   d) Jericho

Let's up the ante. 2 marks available per question, 2 short points to get them.

5) Give two predictions Jesus made at the Last Supper.

6) Give two examples of healing miracles performed by Jesus.

7) Give two reasons why Christians believe they should serve others.

8) Give two ways that Jesus kept his messiahship a secret.

Now on to some 4 mark questions. For full marks, you'll need to further explain your points.

9) Explain two contrasting views about the meaning of the title 'Messiah'.

10) Explain two contrasting views about how Jesus's death saved mankind.

11) Explain two contrasting views about why Jesus's tomb was found empty.

12) Explain two contrasting views about the meaning of the title 'Son of Man'.

For the 4 and 5 mark questions, make sure your answer is well-organised so it's clear for the examiner.

5 marks for these questions. You'll have to include references to Mark's Gospel too — this could be by quoting, paraphrasing or referring to a chapter and verse.

13) Explain two ways in which the story of Jesus's baptism is important for Christians today.

14) Explain two ways in which the miracle of feeding the 5000 is important for Christians today.

15) Explain two ways in which Jesus's crucifixion is important for Christians today.

16) Explain two ways in which the resurrection is important for Christians today.

Everyone's favourite part of the exam — the 12 mark question (with extra marks for SPaG). You'll get a handy list of bullet points telling you what you must put in your answer, so use them to map out a plan. Jot down all the possible arguments for and against, that way you won't forget any.

17) 'The miracles Jesus performed didn't actually happen — they were metaphors.'
    Evaluate this statement.
    Your answer should include the following:
    • references to Mark's Gospel
    • religious arguments that support the statement
    • religious arguments that disagree with the statement
    • a conclusion
    You can also include non-religious points of view in your answer.

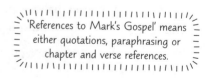
'References to Mark's Gospel' means either quotations, paraphrasing or chapter and verse references.

The Kingdom of God

This section looks at Mark's Gospel and the <u>kingdom of God</u>, 1st century <u>society</u>, <u>faith</u> and <u>discipleship</u>.

The Kingdom of God can have Different Meanings

1) The kingdom of God is the <u>time</u> and <u>place</u> where <u>God rules</u>. People will follow <u>God's will</u> and <u>live</u> according to it.

> The <u>Lord's Prayer</u> says "your kingdom come, your will be done, on earth as it is in heaven" (Matthew 6:10 NIV).

2) It was a <u>central</u> part of <u>Jesus's preaching</u>. He explained that, "The time has come... The kingdom of God has come near. Repent and believe the good news!" (Mark 1:15 NIV).

3) 'Kingdom of God' refers to <u>different times</u> and <u>places</u> in different passages of the Gospel.

4) The kingdom might exist as a <u>state of being</u> within the hearts and minds of <u>individuals</u>, or in the <u>love</u> and <u>care</u> shown within the <u>community</u> of believers. This applies both to Jesus's <u>disciples</u> and <u>Christians</u> now.

5) It can also refer to a <u>physical</u> kingdom in the <u>future</u> — God will <u>establish</u> a kingdom throughout the <u>world</u>, when Jesus returns in the <u>Second Coming</u> and the <u>Last Judgement</u> takes place (see p.6). Some think it may have already partly <u>arrived</u> in Jesus's <u>healings</u> and <u>exorcisms</u> (they show God's rule over sin and evil) but is still to arrive <u>fully</u>.

> Jesus explained what the kingdom of God is like by using <u>parables</u> — a parable is a <u>story</u> about <u>everyday life</u> which contains a <u>message</u> about <u>spiritual truth</u>.

Parable of the Sower — People React Differently (4:1-9, 14-20)

1) Jesus told a story about a <u>farmer</u> who went to <u>sow seeds</u> in his field, and the seeds <u>fell</u> in <u>different places</u>. What happens to the seeds represents how people <u>respond differently</u> to Jesus's <u>teaching</u>.

> Some of the seed "fell along the path, and the birds came and ate it up" (Mark 4:4 NIV). The birds are a metaphor for <u>Satan</u> — it's <u>easy</u> for him to make people <u>forget</u> Jesus's teaching. These people <u>hear</u> the teaching, but <u>don't act</u> on it.

> Some fell where there was <u>little soil</u>. Although they quickly <u>grew</u>, they <u>died</u> from exposure to the hot <u>sun</u>: "they withered because they had no root" (Mark 4:6 NIV). This represents people who <u>accept</u> Jesus's message, but <u>give up</u> when things get <u>difficult</u>.

> Some "fell among thorns, which grew up and choked the plants, so that they did not bear grain" (Mark 4:7 NIV). These symbolise people who <u>accept</u> Jesus's message, but get <u>distracted</u> by other things, e.g. <u>money</u> and <u>greed</u>.

> Some seed "fell on good soil. It came up, grew and produced a crop..." (Mark 4:8 NIV). This group refers to people who <u>understand</u> Jesus's teaching, and try to <u>live</u> their lives by it.

2) Jesus told the disciples that "The secret of the kingdom of God has been given to you" (Mark 4:11 NIV). The parable shows that the <u>kingdom of God</u> is present through people who <u>follow</u> Jesus's <u>teaching</u>. It encourages Christians to spread Jesus's <u>message</u>, but to <u>accept</u> that people <u>won't</u> always respond.

Parable of the Growing Seed — Symbol of the Kingdom (4:26-29)

1) Jesus told people that the <u>kingdom of God</u> was like a <u>farmer</u> who sows <u>seed</u> in a field.

> "Night and day... the seed sprouts and grows, though he does not know how. All by itself the soil produces corn — first the stalk, then the ear, then the full grain in the ear. As soon as the corn is ripe, he puts the sickle to it, because the harvest has come." Mark 4:27-29 NIV

2) The parable explains that the kingdom of God <u>grows</u> in a <u>mysterious way</u>. Christians might <u>not</u> understand <u>how</u> God is working, but they can be <u>confident</u> that he <u>is</u>.

3) The <u>harvest</u> represents <u>judgement</u> at the end of time — when the kingdom of God will be <u>fully established</u>. Those who've <u>followed</u> God's ways will be <u>harvested</u> to <u>live</u> in the kingdom of God.

Parables about farming — the cream of the crop...

For all parables in this section, make sure you understand the meaning behind each one, and what they meant for people back in the time of Jesus, and Christians in the present day.

The Kingdom of God

Jesus taught people to focus less on material things so they could be a part of the kingdom of God.

Parable of the Mustard Seed — the Kingdom would Grow (4:30-32)

1) Jesus explained that the kingdom of God "is like a mustard seed, which is the smallest of all seeds on earth. Yet when planted, it grows and become the largest of all garden plants... the birds can perch in its shade" (Mark 4:31-32 NIV).

2) Jesus was describing how the kingdom of God would grow. The parable portrays the kingdom as a community, rather than just individuals — it started with Jesus, but expanded to his first followers and then thousands of Christians.

3) Early Christians found this encouraging. Although there weren't many of them, it told them one day their movement would be great. Birds were a Jewish symbol for Gentiles (non-Jews), so it also encouraged them to look for converts in the Gentile world too.

4) Some modern Christians think the big plant refers to the Church. The Church is a large community which provides care and protection to anyone who needs it — like a large plant does to birds. Many believe it should work to create the kingdom of God on Earth.

A Rich Man is Unwilling to Give Up his Possessions (10:17-27)

1) A rich man asked Jesus what he must do to get eternal life. Jesus reminded him of the Ten Commandments, but the man explained that he already followed them.

2) Jesus told him to "sell everything you have and give to the poor, and you will have treasure in heaven. Then come, follow me" (Mark 10:21 NIV). This may mean follow his teachings — or leave his home and join Jesus, travelling around spreading God's word.

3) The man left in despair because he couldn't bear to do that.

4) Jesus said to his disciples that it's very difficult for the rich to get into the kingdom of God:

> "It is easier for a camel to go through the eye of a needle than for someone who is rich to enter the kingdom of God." Mark 10:25 NIV

5) The 'eye' of a needle is the small hole which the thread is put through when sewing, so the saying means it's almost impossible for rich people to be saved. But Jesus does also say "all things are possible with God" (Mark 10:27 NIV).

6) 'The eye of the needle' may have been a narrow gate in Jerusalem. Camels loaded with goods needed to be unloaded to pass through. So rich people have to shed their possessions before they can enter the kingdom of God, like a camel had to shed its load to enter Jerusalem.

Jesus's Teaching on Wealth was Very Surprising

Jesus's teaching on wealth surprised 1st century Jews. They believed that wealth was a sign of God's approval. But Jesus saw wealth as an obstacle to serving God fully — his disciples left their homes and possessions behind to follow him.

Modern Christians interpret Jesus's teaching in a variety of ways:
- Monks and nuns take the teaching quite literally — they give up all their possessions and take a vow of poverty.
- Many think it means people shouldn't be too attached to money or possessions, but should give generously to those in need.
- Some think that Jesus's words about wealth only applied to that man — other people have different problems to overcome. The key point is that God must be first in your life — not money or anything else.
- Some say it only applied to the time when Jesus lived. Giving away all your money is unrealistic now when people need money to buy even the basics. In the 1st century, people were more self-sufficient.
- Others suggest the teaching is just wrong. If everyone gave everything away, society would collapse. It also would mean neglecting your duty to your family.

The Kingdom of God

Jesus instructed his disciples to <u>love</u> other people. Not just their friends — <u>everyone</u>.

Jesus Welcomes Young Children Despite Opposition (10:13-16)

1) People took their <u>children</u> to see <u>Jesus</u> so he could <u>bless</u> them.
The <u>disciples</u> tried to <u>stop</u> it, but Jesus <u>overruled</u> them, saying:

> "Let the little children come to me, and do not hinder them, for the kingdom of God belongs to such as these. Truly I tell you, anyone who will not receive the kingdom of God like a little child will never enter it." Mark 10:14-15 NIV

2) He meant that the <u>kingdom of God</u> was for people who accepted it with <u>childlike joy</u> — people who are completely <u>open</u> to embracing <u>new things</u>.

3) The kingdom here is a <u>present reality</u> in the <u>hearts</u> and <u>minds</u> of individuals who apply Jesus's teaching.

4) This encourages modern Christians to <u>accept</u> Jesus's <u>message</u> in this way, and to treat children with <u>love</u>.

Love God and Love Other People (12:28-34)

1) The <u>Torah</u> (Jewish sacred text) contains hundreds of <u>commandments</u> (including the Ten Commandments).

2) A teacher of religion asked Jesus which was the <u>greatest commandment</u>. He chose <u>two</u>:

> "the Lord our God, the Lord is one. Love the Lord your God with all your heart and with all your soul and with all your mind and with all your strength." Mark 12:29-30 NIV

> "Love your neighbour as yourself." Mark 12:31 NIV

3) The teacher <u>approved</u> of Jesus's answer. So Jesus said he was <u>close</u> to the <u>kingdom of God</u>, as he had <u>accepted</u> the key messages of the kingdom.

4) The first rule Jesus chose was adapted from Deuteronomy 6:4-5. Jesus meant that <u>God</u> should be the thing you <u>love</u> most in life — <u>nothing</u> should be more <u>important</u>. This rule forms part of an important Jewish prayer (see p.31).

5) The second rule is from Leviticus 19:18. Although Jesus used the <u>same</u> words, in Leviticus the rule <u>only</u> meant love your <u>own people</u> — fellow Jews. Non-Jews <u>weren't</u> included. Jesus <u>expanded</u> this rule to cover <u>all human beings</u>.

6) It is sometimes called the <u>Golden Rule</u>, and this part of the Gospel is still regarded as an <u>important</u> rule today. It is <u>accepted</u> by most <u>secular</u> (non-religious) people.

7) Many <u>non-Christians</u> regard Jesus as an <u>important teacher</u>, and a <u>good man</u>. Lots of modern people are <u>inspired</u> by his example of <u>selfless love</u> and <u>forgiveness</u> of <u>enemies</u>.

8) Many modern Christians agree that <u>loving God</u> and loving <u>other people</u> is the <u>essence</u> of Christianity. Many Christians have <u>devoted</u> their lives to the <u>service</u> of <u>others</u> as a consequence, e.g. <u>Mother Teresa</u> of Calcutta.

What if Jesus's Teaching Contradicts the Law or Government?

1) Christians believe that Jesus's <u>character</u> and <u>life</u> show what <u>God</u> is like.
They try to <u>obey</u> his teachings and to <u>live</u> in the <u>same way</u> that he did.

2) Most Christians believe they should keep the <u>laws</u> and <u>obey</u> the <u>government</u> of the country they live in. But they believe it is <u>right</u> to <u>disobey</u> these if the laws or government are <u>wrong</u>.

3) For example, lots of Christians <u>refused</u> to obey the government in <u>Nazi Germany</u> — many <u>hid</u> Jews from the <u>government</u> so that they wouldn't be <u>killed</u>.

You must(ard) learn all this — it could pop up in the exam...

Create a spider diagram all about the kingdom of God. Include things like when and where people think it might happen, what it will be like and how to get to it. Bonus points for specific Gospel references.

People Disregarded by Society

Jesus made a point of <u>welcoming</u> and <u>helping</u> those who were <u>excluded</u> from normal society.

Outcasts were Excluded from Society for Different Reasons

Many people were <u>outcasts</u> in 1st century Jewish society. Other people <u>didn't interact</u> with them, and they were <u>excluded</u> from <u>worship</u> — so they were <u>cut off</u> from <u>God</u> as well as from other people.

1) **SINNERS** — People who deliberately <u>broke</u> the <u>laws</u> which good Jews kept were outcasts. Jews considered these laws to be <u>God-given</u>, and obeying them was <u>essential</u> to remain part of <u>God's people</u>.

2) The **ILL** and **DISABLED** — These people were sometimes seen as being <u>punished</u> by God for their <u>sins</u>. Some diseases were thought to be <u>spread</u> by <u>physical contact</u>, so sufferers were <u>isolated</u> to stop others from getting <u>infected</u>. Some were thought to make the sufferer ritually <u>unclean</u>, so they couldn't join in worship. Other people couldn't <u>touch</u> them, because that made them <u>unclean</u> too.

3) **GENTILES** — Parts of the <u>Old Testament</u> told Jews <u>not</u> to have any <u>contact</u> with non-Jews, and this was taught by some <u>rabbis</u> at the time of Jesus. They weren't considered to be God's people.

4) The **POOR** — Very poor people <u>couldn't</u> afford to buy the <u>sacrifices</u> needed for worship at the Temple in Jerusalem. These sacrifices were <u>needed</u> to <u>cleanse</u> their sins, so they remained <u>sinful</u>.

5) **TAX COLLECTORS** — They worked for the occupying <u>Romans</u>, so they were considered <u>traitors</u>. They often collected <u>more</u> than <u>necessary</u> and kept the rest for <u>themselves</u>.

Jesus Welcomed Outcasts — So Christians Must Too

1) Jesus showed that <u>outcasts</u> were welcome in the kingdom of God. He also welcomed <u>women</u> and <u>children</u> — they were considered <u>less important</u> than <u>men</u> at the time.

2) Modern Christians are inspired by his <u>compassion</u> for outcasts, and so they welcome <u>all</u> types of people. They're encouraged to <u>accept</u> and <u>love everyone</u>, whatever their gender, race, religion or past behaviour.

3) This <u>attitude</u> has gradually been <u>built</u> into the <u>laws</u> of our society. <u>Discrimination</u> (treating people badly) because of their gender or race is now <u>illegal</u>.

Jesus Healed a Leper and Helped Him Back into Society (1:40-45)

1) A <u>leper</u> (a person suffering from <u>leprosy</u>) asked Jesus for help. He said "If you are willing, you can make me clean" (Mark 1:40 NIV).

2) Jesus <u>touched</u> him (making himself 'unclean') and the leper was <u>healed</u> instantly. Jesus then told him to visit a <u>priest</u> and make the <u>sacrifices</u> needed to <u>cleanse</u> a leper and <u>remove</u> his <u>impurity</u> (only a priest could declare someone free of leprosy).

3) Jesus told the man to keep it a <u>secret</u> — but he told <u>everyone</u>.

> Leprosy is a <u>skin</u> disease that can <u>seriously harm</u> or even <u>kill</u> people. People believed it was <u>spread</u> by <u>touching</u>, so lepers were <u>driven out</u> of their homes.

4) Christians believe that they should <u>follow</u> Jesus's <u>teachings</u> and <u>example</u>. <u>Early Christians</u> cared for the sick during <u>epidemics</u>, and <u>founded</u> many of the first <u>hospitals</u> in Europe.

5) Many <u>modern Christians</u> also care for the <u>sick</u>, despite the risks. They believe <u>compassion</u> matters more than their <u>own lives</u>, and the <u>best</u> thing they can do is <u>follow</u> Jesus's teaching.

Jesus Chooses an Outcast to be a Disciple (2:13-17)

1) <u>Levi</u> was a <u>tax collector</u> who became one of Jesus's <u>disciples</u>.

> "...he saw Levi... sitting at the tax collector's booth. 'Follow me,' Jesus told him, and Levi got up and followed him." Mark 2:14 NIV

2) Jesus later went to <u>Levi's house</u> to eat — other <u>outcasts</u> were also there. <u>Visiting</u> Levi's house and <u>eating</u> with him was a sign of <u>acceptance</u> of these outcasts.

3) Some people <u>criticised</u> Jesus for it, but he replied: "It is not the healthy who need a doctor, but those who are ill. I have not come to call the righteous, but sinners" (Mark 2:17 NIV).

4) Jesus showed that God values <u>compassion</u> and <u>helping</u> those in trouble <u>above</u> punishment for wrongdoing.

People Disregarded by Society

Jesus Healed the Daughter of a Gentile Woman (7:24-30)

1) A Greek (sometimes called Syro-Phoenician) woman had a daughter who was possessed by a demon. The woman asked Jesus to heal her.

2) Jesus refused. He compared Jews and non-Jews to the children and dogs in a family: "...it is not right to take the children's bread and toss it to the dogs" (Mark 7:27 NIV). He was telling her that his mission was to help the Jews before any non-Jews.

3) The woman replied: "Lord... even the dogs under the table eat the children's crumbs" (Mark 7:28 NIV). Because of her humility and faith, Jesus healed her daughter.

4) Most Jews in Jesus's time had little to do with Gentiles, but there were several stories about Jesus helping Gentiles who approached him. Some Gentiles started becoming Christians soon after Jesus's death.

5) Jesus showed that people shouldn't be discriminated against because of their race or religion.

Jesus Drove a Demon from a Boy (9:14-29)

1) A man's son was possessed by a spirit. It affected him physically: "...it throws him to the ground. He foams at the mouth, gnashes his teeth and becomes rigid" (Mark 9:18 NIV).

2) Jesus spoke harshly to everyone, calling them an "unbelieving generation" (Mark 9:19 NIV).

3) The man asked Jesus for help. Jesus said, "Everything is possible for one who believes" (Mark 9:23 NIV). But the man admitted his faith was weak: "I do believe; help me overcome my unbelief!" (Mark 9:24 NIV).

4) Jesus told the spirit to leave the boy and never return. It screamed, caused the boy to shake and then left. The boy lay still, as if he were dead. But Jesus held his hand and helped him up — he was cured.

5) Now people would recognise that the boy had epilepsy. But 1st century Jews — including Mark when he was reporting these events — didn't know the scientific explanation for epilepsy. Illnesses were often blamed on demon possession and sufferers were shunned.

A Poor Widow Gave All She Had to the Temple (12:41-44)

1) People were giving money to the Temple. Some gave lots of money, but there was a poor widow who gave the little she had.

> Widows were very vulnerable in Jesus's society. They had no-one to protect them or provide for them — there was no help from the government.

2) The rich donated only spare money, so Jesus said the widow's gift was more valuable: "They all gave out of their wealth; but she, out of her poverty, put in everything — all she had to live on" (Mark 12:44 NIV).

3) The widow had faith that God would provide for her. This story helped early Christians believe that God would provide for them too if they had complete faith in him. It also shows that the poor are important to God — Christians should help them.

A Woman Anoints Jesus with Expensive Perfume (14:1-9)

1) Jesus was with Simon the Leper when a woman tipped a jar of expensive perfume over Jesus's head.

2) People were angry with her — it was valuable perfume that could have been used to help the poor. But Jesus defended her. He said she had prepared his body for burial — this was just before his death.

3) He said, "The poor you will always have with you, and you can help them any time you want. But you will not always have me" (Mark 14:7 NIV).

4) As well as Jesus's appreciation of this woman's actions, the story also shows Jesus's respect for lepers.

Don't disregard these stories — they're important...

Explain two ways in which St Mark's account of Jesus and the outcasts is important for Christians today. You should include references from Mark's Gospel.   [5]

Faith and Discipleship

The disciples were Jesus's devoted followers during his lifetime. The Twelve were the most important.

Jesus First Called Four Disciples to Follow Him (1:16-20)

1) Simon (later called Peter) and Andrew were brothers who were fishermen on the Sea of Galilee. Jesus said to them, "Come, follow me... and I will send you out to fish for people" (Mark 1:17 NIV). Jesus meant that they would tell people God's message. They immediately left their work behind and went with him.

2) Jesus also called James and John, two more fishermen, to go with him. They "left their father Zebedee in the boat" (Mark 1:20 NIV) — their faith was so strong that they left both work and family behind.

Discipleship Means Learning and Following

1) The number of disciples grew — there were twelve who were especially important to Jesus. Twelve was symbolic of the twelve tribes of Israel in the Old Testament. By choosing twelve, Jesus suggested they were the new chosen people of God.

2) 'Disciple' meant the pupil of a teacher, or the apprentice of a master craftsman, so the disciples learned from Jesus. It also meant following his life and his example.

3) The first disciples show modern Christians the level of faith expected of them. They sacrificed their livelihoods and followed Jesus without asking any questions. People nowadays might be a disciple by following a vocation to work for God, for example being a priest. Others might carry out what Jesus taught people, for example by being kind and helping those in need.

Jesus Told the Twelve to Preach and Heal (6:7-13)

1) Jesus told his disciples to go out in pairs to preach, heal the sick and drive out demons.

2) They took no food, money or luggage — they were to rely on the hospitality of others. If they weren't made welcome somewhere, Jesus said to leave and "shake the dust off your feet as a testimony against them" (Mark 6:11 NIV). These people had had their chance to hear the message — the disciples should spend no more time there.

3) Jesus spent most of his ministry like this, so the disciples were sharing his mission, showing their faith that God would provide for them.

4) Early Christians were encouraged by this during their missionary journeys throughout the Roman Empire.

5) Mission in the 21st century is similar — it usually involves practical help as well as preaching. Christian Aid and CAFOD are Christian organisations which give practical help where needed in foreign countries.

Discipleship has Costs as well as Rewards (8:34-38 and 10:28-31)

1) Jesus said his disciples must "take up their cross and follow me" (Mark 8:34 NIV). He was saying they might suffer and die, as he was going to.

2) But anyone who showed faith and gave things up for Jesus would be rewarded both on Earth and in heaven. Although they'd given up family, they'd have a huge new family of Jesus's followers. They may have been treated badly on Earth, but in heaven it'd be them, rather than their persecutors, who were respected. Early Christians would have been comforted by this.

> "...no one who has left home... for me and the gospel will fail to receive a hundred times as much in this present age... and in the age to come eternal life. But many who are first will be last, and the last first" Mark 10:29-31 NIV

3) Those who opted for an easy life instead would lose their future life in the kingdom of God. Anyone who disowned him would later be disowned by Jesus on the Day of Judgement.

4) Modern Christians are less likely to face the same suffering as Jesus's early followers, but they must still be prepared to give up their own wishes and be ready for hardship rather than an easy life when they "take up their cross".

Faith and Discipleship

Jesus Heals a Woman who is Bleeding Heavily (5:24-34)

1) A woman who had been suffering from a haemorrhage (excessive bleeding) for 12 years approached Jesus in a crowd and secretly touched his cloak. She believed it would heal her and it did.

2) Jesus felt power leave him. He asked who had touched him and the woman owned up.

3) The bleeding meant the woman would have been seen as unclean, and by touching Jesus she would have made him unclean too, but that didn't concern him. Jesus said to her: "Daughter, your faith has healed you. Go in peace and be freed from your suffering" (Mark 5:34 NIV).

4) The woman in the story was healed because she had faith. Jesus often said this when he healed people. Faith in Mark's Gospel means trusting God — and acting on that trust. The woman acted by seeking out Jesus and touching him. This story shows the importance of faith for Christians.

Peter Denies He is One of Jesus's Disciples (14:27-31, 66-72)

1) Just before his arrest, Jesus predicted that all of the disciples would desert him. Peter insisted he wouldn't, even if everyone else did. But Jesus said "today... before the cock crows twice you yourself will disown me three times" (Mark 14:30 NIV). Each disciple swore he would rather die than desert Jesus.

2) After Jesus was arrested, Peter was challenged three times in the courtyard outside where Jesus was being held. Each time, he denied being one of Jesus's disciples. → "I don't know this man you're talking about." Mark 14:71 NIV

3) Then he heard the cock crow twice, and recalled what Jesus had said. He was very upset: "he broke down and wept" (Mark 14:72 NIV).

> Mark considered Peter to be the unofficial leader of the disciples — he was the first to declare Jesus as the Messiah. But out of fear, even Peter deserted Jesus in his hour of need. This is a warning for Christians of the need for God's help to remain faithful. It reassures them that even the best Christians fail sometimes.

Jesus Sent his Disciples Out and Ascended to Heaven (16:14-20)

1) Jesus appeared to the disciples after his resurrection. There were only eleven of them — Judas (who had betrayed him) had gone.

2) Jesus told them off for not believing the people who had seen him alive. → "he rebuked them for their lack of faith" Mark 16:14 NIV

3) He commissioned them to tell everyone about the gospel and to baptise converts. He said, "Whoever believes and is baptised will be saved, but whoever does not believe will be condemned" (Mark 16:16 NIV). He predicted many miraculous signs would accompany their preaching.

4) Then Jesus ascended to heaven to be with God. The disciples did as he had commanded and miraculous things did happen — e.g. St Paul was bitten by a poisonous snake, but survived.

5) This encourages modern Christians to continue the disciples' work — God will protect them while they do so. Some Pentecostal Churches handle poisonous snakes in worship as a test of faith.

Mark's Gospel Suggests Only Christians will be Saved

1) Jesus's commission to his disciples could be understood to mean that only Christians will be saved. However, verses 9-20 weren't included in some original versions of the Gospel.

2) Many modern Christians reject this idea. They think that other religions can also be paths to God. They also respect good people who have no religion.

3) Excluding some people could encourage prejudice and discrimination. The rest of Mark's Gospel is against both of these, and there are laws in the UK making discrimination illegal (see p.110).

And that's the end of Mark's Gospel...

Give two examples of how people in the 21st century might carry out their discipleship. [2]

Revision Summary

That's that section done and dusted, so let's see what you've learnt. The questions below are like the ones you'll have to answer in the exam, so this is a good chance to practise.

If there's anything you can't answer, go back through the section and have another go when you've re-read it. For some questions — you'll be told which ones — there are extra marks for spelling, punctuation and grammar, so check your writing carefully.

Nice and easy to start off with — some 1 mark multiple choice questions.

1) What was the name of the disciple who disowned Jesus when he was arrested?
   a) Levi   b) Peter   c) Judas   d) John

2) What was the occupation of Jesus's first four disciples?
   a) Tax collector   b) Soldier   c) Fisherman   d) Farmer

3) Who did Jesus see giving all they had to the Temple?
   a) A disciple   b) A Gentile   c) A widow   d) A rich man

4) Who touched Jesus's cloak so that they would be healed?
   a) A leper   b) An epileptic boy c) A young child   d) A bleeding woman

Doubling up to two marks now. All you need to do is make two short points.

5) Give two examples of parables which Jesus told about the kingdom of God.

6) Give two types of people considered outcasts in Jesus's society.

7) Give two examples of what was expected of Jesus's disciples.

8) Give two examples of how Jesus's attitude towards outcasts is reflected in modern society.

Rising to 4 marks per question. You have to develop your points to get them all.

9) Explain two contrasting beliefs about Jesus's instruction to "sell everything you have and give to the poor" (Mark 10:21 NIV).

10) Explain two contrasting beliefs held by modern Christians about what discipleship means.

11) Explain two contrasting 1st century beliefs about people with illnesses.

12) Explain two contrasting interpretations of Jesus's commission to his disciples.

And some more questions — this time for 5 marks. You'll need to give references from St Mark's Gospel.

13) Explain two ways in which St Mark's account of the greatest commandments is important for Christians today.

14) Explain two ways in which St Mark's account of Jesus's treatment of children is important for Christians today.

15) Explain two ways in which St Mark's account of Peter's denial is important for Christians today.

16) Explain two ways in which St Mark's account of the parable of the sower is important for Christians today.

Drumroll please... it's time for the 12 mark question (with extra marks for SPaG). The exam question will have a list of points you need to make in your answer, so use it to plan things out first. Write down arguments for and against the statement so you don't forget any while writing your answer.

17) 'The kingdom of God has already come.'
    Evaluate this statement.
    Your answer should include the following:
    • references to Mark's Gospel
    • arguments that support the statement
    • arguments that disagree with the statement
    • a conclusion

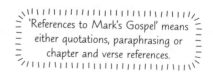
'References to Mark's Gospel' means either quotations, paraphrasing or chapter and verse references.

Section 12 — St Mark's Gospel as a Source of Religious, Moral and Spiritual Truths

Do Well in Your Exam

You've learnt all the <u>facts</u> — now it's time to get those <u>grades</u>.

The Basics — Read the Questions

1) <u>Read</u> the questions <u>carefully</u>. Remember to answer <u>all the parts</u> of the questions.

2) Be aware of how much <u>time</u> you're using. Leave plenty of time for the long-answer questions. The more <u>marks</u> a question's worth, the <u>longer</u> you should be spending on it. Try to leave yourself 5 minutes at the end to <u>check your work</u>.

3) Some questions will have extra marks available for <u>Spelling, Punctuation and Grammar</u> (SPaG). The exam paper will tell you which questions offer SPaG marks — so make your writing for these the <u>best</u> it can be (see p.117-119 for more).

4) Don't use any fancy colours — write <u>only</u> in <u>black</u> ink.

If the exam paper refers to the '<u>main religious tradition</u>' in the UK, it just means <u>Christianity</u>.

You Get Marks for What You Know and How You Express It

In GCSE Religious Studies there are two <u>Assessment Objectives</u> — these are the skills you'll need to show to get marks in the exams. You get <u>half</u> your marks for each.

> 1) <u>Describing</u> and <u>explaining</u> what you know.
> 2) <u>Analysing</u> different elements of a topic, or viewpoints on an issue, and <u>evaluating</u> their importance.

The <u>exact</u> format of your questions will depend on your exam board, but many questions are <u>quite similar</u>...

There Could be Easy Marks for Knowing What Things Mean...

You might get questions asking you about what <u>important terms mean</u>. They'll be worth <u>1</u>, <u>2</u> or <u>3 marks</u>. 1 mark questions will be <u>multiple choice</u>. For 2 and 3 mark questions, keep your answers <u>short</u> and <u>to the point</u> — but make sure you <u>define</u> the term <u>properly</u>. Don't skip over <u>tricky words</u> when you're revising.

> What does the term 'pikuach nefesh' mean?

> Pikuach nefesh means 'saving a life' and is one of the most important principles in Judaism. Jews are expected to do all that they can to protect human life, even if that means breaking mitzvot.

...or Being Able to Name or State Things

Some questions may ask you to write down some brief facts, e.g. the <u>names</u> of different <u>religions</u> or <u>festivals</u>. Pay <u>attention</u> to the <u>number</u> of things asked for — it could be <u>two</u> or <u>three</u>, depending on the exam board.

> Name three characteristics that Christians believe God has.

> God is transcendent, personal and benevolent.

This sentence has <u>three points</u> in it, so it would get <u>three marks</u>.

'Twas the night before the exam...

...and some people were up late, studying RS. Make sure you get a good night's rest before your exam — you won't be able to do your best if you're half asleep.

Do Well in Your Exam

Look closely at the number of marks for each question — it'll give you an idea of how much to write.

2 or 3 Mark Questions Might Ask You to Describe, Give or Outline

For some questions you'll have to write down beliefs, teachings, reasons, examples etc.
These questions are usually worth 2 or 3 marks, so they need a bit of detail,
but don't get carried away — they're not expecting you to write an essay.

> Make sure you read the question fully. For example, some might ask you to write down three things for 3 marks, but others could ask for just one thing for 3 marks.

> Outline three Muslim beliefs about contraception.

> Some Muslims believe that contraception is allowed in the hadith.
> Both partners should agree to use contraception.
> Others think preventing conception is against Allah's will.

> Don't be tempted to write lots — this answer would be enough to get you three marks.

Some Explain, Describe or Outline Questions Need More Detail

1) For some questions you'll need to explain, describe or outline something in detail — e.g. religious teachings or attitudes, how something influences religious people, or reasons why something is important.

2) Read the question carefully — it might specify the number of points you have to make.

3) Depending on your exam board, these questions will usually be worth 4-6 marks.
   You'll have to develop your points in order to get full marks.

> Explain two Jewish beliefs about forgiveness.

> Jews believe that God is prepared to forgive sins, and so they should accept his forgiveness and follow his example by forgiving others.
> They also believe that seeking forgiveness from others is very important. God can only forgive a sin against God, not a sin committed against another person.

> The first half of the sentence here introduces a point, and the second half develops it further.

For some Questions You Must Include Sources of Wisdom

1) Some questions will ask you to refer to sacred texts or religious teachings in your answer.
   The type of question varies depending on your exam board, so read the exam paper carefully.

2) You can add a reference by including a quotation, or by paraphrasing (explaining what's said in your own words). You'll need to say which text or teaching the information comes from.

> Explain two Muslim teachings on jihad. Your answer should refer to religious texts.

> You could also write something like 'The Qur'an gives Muslims permission to defend themselves if they're being fought'.

> Greater jihad is the struggle to live life according to Allah's teachings. It's a personal struggle, and individuals must work to be the best Muslims they can be. Lesser jihad can involve defending Islam. This could be in a peaceful way, or by fighting a threat to Islam in self-defence. The Qur'an says: "Permission [to fight] has been given to those who are being fought".

Don't let exam nerves get the better of you...

A large chunk of how well you do in the exam will come down to, well... how good you are at exams. Make sure you spend enough time practising doing exam-style questions under timed conditions. It'll pay off in the end.

Do Well in Your Exam and SPaG

And now... the final question. Pay close attention to what you write — you can get marks for SPaG.

For Long Answer Questions You Need Both Sides of the Argument

1) You'll need to write a longer answer for the questions worth 12 or 15 marks. You'll be given a statement and often a list of bullet points — these tell you what to put in your answer.

2) You need to give arguments for and against the statement, so read it carefully, then make a rough list of all the views on each side that you can think of.

3) Plan out your answer before you start writing — it needs to be clear and organised for the examiner.

> 'Animal experimentation should be allowed if it benefits humanity.'
> Evaluate this statement. Your answer should include the following:
> * examples from Christian teachings
> * different Christian opinions
> * appropriate ethical arguments
> * a conclusion.

What you need to put in your answer varies depending on the question. For some topics, you might be asked about non-religious opinions or philosophical ideas. You might need to include examples from sources of wisdom and authority.

Some Christians share this point of view. They believe that animal testing is acceptable if it is for valid reasons, such as producing life-saving medicines. But many Christians see themselves as stewards of the Earth, and believe they must care for animals — the Bible says that righteous people look after their animals. They think that the animals must be treated humanely, and no unnecessary pain caused.

This answer starts by giving some views along with some Christian teachings.

This view is reflected in the Catechism of the Catholic Church. It says that animal testing is allowed if it brings about scientific or medical advances, but the animals shouldn't be allowed to suffer.

Some Christians might look at animal testing from a utilitarian point of view, and look for the best balance of outcomes overall. If a few animals suffer, but lots of people could be helped, they might decide it's acceptable.

This paragraph explains how ethical arguments could be used.

However, not all Christian denominations tolerate animal experimentation. The Society of Friends (Quakers) are against causing any kind of suffering to animals. They would think it's wrong to inflict pain on animals just to further our knowledge of science and medicine.

This paragraph discusses arguments against the statement.

I think that, although allowing animals to suffer is wrong, if the experiments benefit humanity then they should be allowed. But only essential advances should be considered beneficial — testing out non-essentials such as cosmetics isn't a good enough reason.

Finish with a conclusion — say what you think, and back it up with ideas you've discussed.

Some Long Answer Questions Have Extra Marks for SPaG

1) Some questions have extra marks for spelling, punctuation, grammar and specialist terminology. The number of marks on offer varies between exam boards, but you could be looking at between 10 and 12 marks just for SPaG across the exams.

2) The examiner will look at your spelling, punctuation and grammar in general, but they'll also look at how many technical terms you use and how accurately you use them.

3) Leave 5 minutes at the end of the exam to check your work. That isn't long, so there won't be time to check everything thoroughly. Look for the most obvious mistakes.

4) Start by checking the long answer questions since they're the only ones that award SPaG marks. Only check the rest of your answers if you've got time.

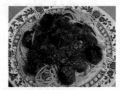

My favourite kind of SPaG...

Thou shalt use correct punctuation...

Between spelling, punctuation and grammar, there's a lot of stuff to check. This is why it's really important to practise before the exam. That way you'll start to do it automatically, and make fewer errors in the first place.

Spelling, Punctuation and Grammar

Making a mistake in your exam is <u>not</u> the end of the world. Just correct it and you won't lose any marks.

Make Your Corrections Neatly

1) If the mistake is just <u>one word</u> or a <u>short phrase</u>, cross it out <u>neatly</u> and write the correction <u>above</u> it.

> A stable family can give a child a sense of identity and a feeling of security, teaching
> him or her how to behave in different social situations and how to give and ~~recieve~~ love.
> *(receive)*

2) If you've <u>forgotten</u> to start a <u>new paragraph</u>, use a <u>double strike</u> (like this '//') to show where the new paragraph should <u>begin</u>:

> The Third Pillar of Islam commands that Muslims give 2.5% of their wealth to charity. The money is often collected and distributed by the mosque. // How money is earned is also important in Islam. Muslims shouldn't make money from anything seen as immoral, such as alcohol. They also shouldn't earn money from charging interest.

Use an Asterisk to Add Extra Information

1) If you've <u>missed something out</u>, think about whether you have space to write the missing bit <u>above</u> the line you've already written. If you <u>can</u>, use a ' ∧ ' to show <u>exactly where</u> it should go.

> Jews greet each other by saying 'shalom', which means 'peace'. Generally, they believe that war ∧ bad thing, *(is a)* but may be necessary in some circumstances, for example in self-defence or to help neighbouring countries.

2) If the bit you've missed out <u>won't</u> fit above the line, use an <u>asterisk</u> (like this '*') to show the examiner <u>where</u> the missing bit should go.

3) Write the <u>missing words</u> at the <u>end</u> of your answer with another asterisk next to them.

> Christianity teaches that animals should be treated kindly.* Some Christians believe that animal testing is wrong because they think it is unhelpful.
>   *and shouldn't be made to suffer unnecessarily.

Cross Out Anything You Don't Want to be Marked

1) If you've written something that you <u>don't</u> want the examiner to mark, <u>cross it out neatly</u>.

2) Cross out any <u>notes</u>. But — if you don't <u>finish</u> your answer <u>in time</u>, don't cross out your <u>plan</u> — the examiner might look at it to see what you were <u>going to write</u>.

3) Don't <u>scribble things out</u> without thinking — it'll make your answers look <u>messy</u>.

Spell Technical Words Correctly

1) There are a lot of <u>technical words</u> in **RS**. You need to be able to <u>spell</u> them <u>correctly</u>.

2) Here are some examples to start you off. The <u>coloured letters</u> are the tricky bits to watch out for.

reconciliation	euthanasia	deterrence
omniscient	pacifism	justice
procreation	sanctity	contraception
revelation	environment	transcendent

> Make sure you know the specific technical words for your topics. For example, if you're studying views on marriage, you would need to know words like 'kiddushin' (part of a Jewish wedding ceremony) and 'nikah' (a Muslim wedding ceremony). There's a list of technical terms in the glossary on p.120-122.

Do Well in Your Exam and SPaG

Spelling, Punctuation and Grammar

This page is full of tips for good <u>punctuation</u> and <u>grammar</u> to help you keep silly mistakes at bay.

You Need to Punctuate Properly...

1) Always use a <u>capital letter</u> at the start of a <u>sentence</u>.
    Use capital letters for <u>names</u> of <u>particular people</u>, <u>places</u> and <u>things</u>. For example:

    <u>M</u>any <u>J</u>ews live in <u>I</u>srael, where the official language is <u>H</u>ebrew.

    All sentences start with capital letters.

    The name of a group of religious believers.

    A country.

    The name of a language.

2) <u>Full stops</u> go at the end of <u>sentences</u>, e.g. 'Muslims worship Allah<u>.</u>'
    <u>Question marks</u> go at the end of <u>questions</u>, e.g. 'What is divorce<u>?</u>'

3) Use <u>commas</u> when you use <u>more than one adjective</u> to describe something or to separate items in a <u>list</u>:

    > Christians believe in a <u>benevolent, compassionate</u> God. They believe <u>the Father</u>, <u>the Son</u> and <u>the Holy Spirit</u> make up the Trinity.

4) <u>Commas</u> can also <u>join two points</u> into one sentence with a joining word (such as '<u>and</u>', '<u>or</u>', '<u>so</u>' or '<u>but</u>'):

    > Salah ideally takes place in a mosque, <u>but</u> it can be done anywhere.

    > The Earth is seen as being a product of the love of Allah, <u>so</u> we should treat it with love.

5) <u>Commas</u> can also be used to separate <u>extra information</u> in a sentence:

    > The Big Bang theory, <u>the idea that the universe began in an explosion of matter and energy</u>, was first put forward by a priest.

    When you use commas like this, the sentence should still make sense when the extra bit is taken out.

...and Use Grammar Correctly

1) <u>Don't change tenses</u> in your writing by mistake:

    > Muslims only <u>allow</u> animal testing if there <u>is</u> a good reason for it.

    This sentence is correct because <u>both</u> verbs are in the <u>present tense</u>. Writing '<u>was</u>' instead of '<u>is</u>' would be wrong.

    Past, present... they all made Brian tense.

2) <u>Don't</u> use <u>double negatives</u>. You should only use a negative <u>once</u> in a sentence:

    > Creatures with fins and scales are kosher, but Jews keeping kosher shouldn't eat <u>any</u> other seafood.

    Don't put 'no' here.

3) Write longer answers in <u>paragraphs</u>. A paragraph is a <u>group of sentences</u> which talk about the <u>same thing</u> or <u>follow on</u> from each other. You need to start a <u>new paragraph</u> when you start making a <u>new point</u>. You show a <u>new paragraph</u> by starting a <u>new line</u> and leaving a <u>gap</u> (an <u>indent</u>) before you start writing:

    This gap shows a new paragraph.

    > Weapons of Mass Destruction (WMDs) are weapons that can destroy large areas of land or lots of people at once. They harm anyone in their path, both soldiers and civilians.
    >   Nuclear weapons are one type of WMD. All Christian denominations are against the indiscriminate killing they cause, but some people think that possessing them keeps the peace.

    When <u>planning</u> long answers, remember that you should write a <u>new paragraph</u> for each main point.

Now you're fully SPaG-ed and ready to go...

Having good SPaG is a great way to get marks in the RS exams, and it might even make a difference to your grade. That's why it's really important that you learn all the stuff on this page — and all the other pages too.

120

Glossary

The purple definitions are relevant to Christianity and Catholic Christianity. The red ones are terms in Judaism. The green ones are terms in Islam. The blue ones are general terms.

abortion	Removing a foetus from the womb before it is able to survive, ending the pregnancy.
adultery	A married person having sex with someone who isn't their husband or wife.
agnosticism	The belief that it is impossible to prove either way if a god does or does not exist.
al-Adab al-Mufrad	A collection of hadith.
al-Akhirah	The concept of life after death. This is a key Islamic belief.
al-Qadr	Predestination — the idea that Allah has already decided everything that will happen.
the ascension	When Jesus rose up to heaven to be with God again.
atheism	A complete denial of the existence of a god.
atonement	Making amends for wrongdoing — often refers to people repairing their relationship with God.
bar/bat mitzvah	The coming of age ceremony — bar mitzvah for boys, bat mitzvah for girls.
benevolent	Being kind and loving.
brit milah	The circumcision of baby boys when they're 8 days old.
capital punishment	The death penalty as punishment for a crime.
catechism	A series of statements laying down the official teachings of the Roman Catholic Church.
celibacy	Not taking part in any sexual activities.
cohabitation	Living together in a sexual relationship without being married.
confession	Admitting sins to God.
confirmation	The act of 'confirming' your faith, often at an age when you can decide for yourself.
conscience	An inner feeling of what's right and what's wrong.
contraception	Also known as birth control, it stops a woman from conceiving.
corporal punishment	Punishing a criminal through physical pain.
covenant	A formal agreement between two or more people.
creed	Statement of religious beliefs.
disciples	Followers of Jesus. This can refer to just his followers in the Bible or to all Christians.
discrimination	Treating different people, or groups of people, differently (usually unfairly).
dominion	The belief that people have power over God's creation and can use it as they like.
ecumenism	Cooperation and interaction between churches from different Christian denominations.
the Eucharist	When Christians remember the Last Supper with bread and wine.
euthanasia	Ending someone's life to relieve their suffering, especially from an incurable, painful illness.
evangelism	Spreading the Christian message in order to convert people.
faith school	A school supported by a faith tradition, with some religious aspects to the education it provides.
fasting	Not eating and/or drinking for a set time.
free will	The ability to choose how to behave. All three religions believe humans have free will.
Gan Eden	Garden of Eden or paradise — where good people spend the afterlife.
Gehinnom	The place where souls go before Gan Eden. The truly wicked never move on from there.
gemilut hasadim	Kind and compassionate actions towards others.
grace	God showing favour to those who haven't earned it.
hadith	Islamic scripture containing a collection of things the Prophet Muhammad said and did.
hajj	The pilgrimage to Makkah. It's a Pillar of Islam.
holy orders	Ordination to a deacon, priest or bishop.
holy war	A war where people believe that God is 'on their side'.
homophobia	Prejudice against people who are homosexual.

Glossary

Glossary

human dignity	The idea that all human life is valuable and everyone has the right to be treated with respect.
human rights	The moral, legal and political rights that every human being on Earth is entitled to.
humanism	The belief that God doesn't exist, and humans should live good lives based on their knowledge.
immanent	God/Allah is present in the human world.
incarnation	The act by which Christians believe God became human, in the form of Jesus.
inter-faith dialogue	Cooperation and interaction between people of different religions.
intra-faith dialogue	Cooperation and interaction between people from different branches of the same religion.
jahannam	The place where people who have done bad deeds will be sent in the afterlife.
jannah	The afterlife paradise — described as "gardens of pleasure" in the Qur'an.
jihad	The struggle to be a good Muslim (greater jihad) and to make the world better (lesser jihad).
just war	A war that meets certain conditions to be classed as necessary.
justice	The idea of each person getting what they deserve, and maintaining what's right.
kashrut	The food laws written in the Torah.
ketubah	The marriage contract, which sets out the couple's rights and responsibilities.
khalifah	The belief that Muslims must look after the Earth as vice-regents or trustees.
kiddushin	Betrothal — the first part of the marriage ceremony.
kosher	Food that is permitted under kashrut.
Last Judgement	The Day of Judgement when all of humanity's actions will be judged by God/Allah.
Lent	The period spent remembering Christ's 40 days of fasting in the desert.
liturgical	Worship that follows a set pattern that's been written out by the Church.
Maimonides	A Jewish scholar — he wrote the 13 principles of faith and compiled a lot of mitzvot.
Messiah	A leader who will bring peace to Earth. Christians believe that Jesus is the Messiah.
miracle	An event believed to be the work of God, that can't be explained by the laws of science.
Mishnah	The part of the Talmud that explains how the mitzvot in the Torah should be applied.
Mishneh Torah	The list of mitzvot from the Torah compiled by Maimonides.
mitzvot	Jewish laws — there are 613 mitzvot in total.
mourning	A period of deep sorrow for someone who has died.
Muwatta Malik	A collection of hadith.
nuclear family	A family made up of a mother, a father and their children living together.
omnibenevolent	Being all-good.
omnipotent	Having unlimited powers — all-powerful.
omniscient	Knowing everything — in the past, present and future.
oral Torah	Jewish teachings passed down orally and recorded in the Talmud.
original sin	The flawed nature that humans have been born with since Adam and Eve first sinned.
pacifism	The idea that war and physical violence are wrong under any circumstances.
parable	A story about daily life which has a message about spiritual truth.
pikuach nefesh	The principle of saving a life, even if it means breaking mitzvot.
pilgrimage	A journey to a place of religious significance.
Pirkei Avot	Part of the Talmud.
polygamy	Marriage to multiple people.
positive discrimination	When someone who may often be discriminated against is given an advantage.
prejudice	Judging something or someone with no good reason, or without full knowledge of a situation.
procreation	Having children.
promiscuity	Having many sexual partners.

Glossary

prophet	A person on Earth who communicated God/Allah's will.
Purgatory	A place where Catholics believe sins are paid for before going to heaven.
racism	Discrimination against people of other races — often based on unfair stereotypes.
reconciliation	Returning to harmony and friendship after conflict.
reformation	The idea that punishment should aim to change criminals so that they won't reoffend.
reincarnation	The rebirth of a soul in a new body after death.
resurrection	Being brought back to life after death.
retribution	Punishing a criminal by making them 'pay' for what they've done.
revelation	An experience that reveals God's presence.
the Rosary	A string of beads used by Catholics when praying.
sacrament	A ceremony, or outward sign, of the direct communication of God's saving grace.
Sahih al-Bukhari	A collection of hadith.
Sahih Muslim	A collection of hadith.
salah	The action of praying five times a day — it's a Pillar of Islam.
salvation	The soul being saved from death and sin so it can reach heaven.
sanctity of life	The belief that all life belongs to God/Allah, so it is holy.
sawm	The obligation to fast during daylight hours in the month of Ramadan — it's a Pillar of Islam.
Second Coming	The belief that Jesus will return to Earth.
secularism	The belief that religion shouldn't have a role in government, education or other state affairs.
sexism	Discrimination based on someone's gender (male or female).
Shabbat	Also called the Sabbath, it is the Jewish day of rest (Saturday).
shahadah	A Pillar of Islam — the Muslim declaration of faith.
shari'ah	The Islamic religious law.
Shekhinah	God's presence in a particular place on Earth.
shirk	Believing there are other gods or that anything is equal to Allah — it's considered the worst sin.
sin	An act that breaks a religious law, i.e. when God's teaching is disobeyed.
situation ethics	An ethical principle where decisions are made based on what is best in individual cases.
social justice	The idea of fairness in society and putting the principles of human rights into practice.
Stations of the Cross	Pictures in church of Jesus's suffering, used by Catholics as a focus for contemplation.
stewardship	Taking care of the Earth as God's creation, so it can be passed on to the next generation.
Sunan Abi Dawud	A collection of hadith.
Tawhid	Belief that Allah is the one and only God.
tikkun olam	The belief that Jews should 'mend the world', e.g. by caring for the environment and the poor.
transcendent	A characteristic of God/Allah — he is beyond this world.
transubstantiation	Transformation of the Eucharistic bread and wine into the flesh and blood of Christ.
the Trinity	The belief that God exists in three 'persons' — the Father, the Son and the Holy Spirit.
tzedakah	The practice of giving 10% of your wealth to charity.
usury	Charging high rates of interest on a loan.
utilitarianism	The idea that the correct course of action has the best balance of good and bad outcomes.
virtue ethics	Deciding what course of action to follow by looking at what a virtuous (good) person would do.
vision	A religious experience where a person sees something sacred.
wudu	The ritual washing of exposed body parts before prayer.
Yawm ad-Din	The day when everyone will be judged by Allah based on their actions.
zakah	A Pillar of Islam — all Muslims must donate 2.5% of their wealth to charity.

Index

Index